Andrew Edwards is a writer and the translator of two books set in Sicily by the Spanish author Alejandro Luque. **Suzanne Edwards** trained in linguistics and is a dyslexia specialist. They co-authored the acclaimed *Sicily: A Literary Guide for Travellers* (I.B.Tauris, 2014).

'Andalusia has a rare and special quality – a magic if you will – like the enchanting force of a fairy queen's spell or the anguished cry of a heartfelt prayer. Many have felt this power – even from afar – yet few have distilled it successfully into words. This superb literary guide to one of the world's most culturally rich and diverse corners sifts through many hundreds of books and texts to present us with a fine selection of the highest quality gems; small, concentrated droplets of the essence of the place, its poetry and people. It is essential reading for anyone who has ever fallen for the charms, mystique and passion of southern Spain.'

Jason Webster, author of *Andalus* and *Duende*

'As with their impeccable literary guide to Sicily – the best of its type I know – Andrew and Suzanne Edwards, in this new book, trace the lines of a double cartography. One map is real, more or less verifiable, the other is of the emotions: intimate, impossible to photograph from satellites, invisible even to the meticulous eye of Google Earth. An itinerary which – they well know, like any good Briton – has less to do with asphalt roads and steel railways than with the stuff that dreams are made of.

The Andalucía they offer us does not neglect the familiar – sun, bulls, flamenco – it recognises that these also form a reality, but at the same time it transcends them. The southern imagery of Carmens and Don Juans appears suitably updated in these pages, enriched by a multiplicity of other viewpoints and sensibilities and, most importantly of all, contrasted in the landscape province by province, from Doñana to the Cabo de Gata.'

Alejandro Luque, cultural correspondent of the
Correo de Andalucía and author of *Palabras mayores*

Andalucia

A LITERARY GUIDE FOR TRAVELLERS

Andrew and Suzanne Edwards

Best wishes
Andy

Suzanne

I.B. TAURIS

LONDON · NEW YORK

Published in 2016 by
I.B.Tauris & Co. Ltd
London • New York
www.ibtauris.com

ISBN: 978 1 78453 390 8
eISBN: 978 0 85772 865 4
ePDF: 978 0 85772 838 8

A full CIP record for this book is available from the British Library
A full CIP record is available from the Library of Congress

Library of Congress Catalog Card Number: available

Typeset by JCS Publishing Services Ltd, www.jcs-publishing.co.uk
Printed and bound in Sweden by ScandBook AB

To our dear parents, Irene and Adrian, Patricia and Alfred.
And, how could we not, Chico.

Literary Guides for Travellers
Listed in Fathom's 24 Best Indie Travel Guides

Berlin by Marcel Krueger and Paul Sullivan

Florence and Tuscany by Ted Jones

The French Riviera by Ted Jones

Scotland by Garry Mackenzie

Sicily by Andrew and Suzanne Edwards

Tangier by Josh Shoemake

Venice by Marie-José Gransard

CONTENTS

List of Illustrations   ix
Acknowledgements   xi
Map   xiv

1   Introduction   1
2   Seville Province: Oranges, Romance and Religion   6
3   Huelva Province: Birds of Paradise   41
4   Cádiz Province: Carnival, Parties and Politics   59
5   Málaga Province: Hilltowns and Hotels   96
6   Granada Province: The Moor's Last Sigh   138
7   Córdoba Province: A Twist of Faith   174
8   Jaén Province: Army of Olives   194
9   Almería Province: Heat and Dust   224

Author Profiles   245
Chronology of Events   263
Select Bibliography   269
Index   277

ILLUSTRATIONS

1 The Plaza de España, Seville   26
2 Roman statue, Itálica   35
3 The Barrio Reina Victoria, Huelva   43
4 The Plaza del Cabildo with statues of Platero and Juan
   Ramón Jiménez, Moguer   56
5 The Paseo Fernando Quiñones bordering La Caleta
   Beach, Cádiz   67
6 Statue of Manuel María González Ángel in front of the
   Cathedral of San Salvador, Jerez   91
7 Statue of Hans Christian Andersen, Plaza de la Marina,
   Málaga   99
8 The Anglican Cemetery, Avenida Príes, Málaga   104
9 The Puente Nuevo, Ronda   126
10 The Lorca family summer residence, the Huerta de San
   Vicente, Granada   143
11 The Court of the Lions, the Alhambra, Granada   152
12 Ainadamar (The Fountain of Tears), near Alfacar   163
13 The Mezquita from Calle Torrijos, Córdoba   175
14 The Gardens of the Alcázar de los Reyes Cristianos,
   Córdoba   184
15 The Cathedral of Santa María, Baeza   210
16 Statue of Antonio Machado, Calle San Pablo, Baeza   213
17 La Chanca and the Alcazaba, Almería   228
18 The Tabernas Desert between Rioja and Tabernas   237

All images by Andrew and Suzanne Edwards with editing by Nik Guyatt

ACKNOWLEDGEMENTS

It would have been impossible to write this book without the support, help and advice of certain key individuals. We are immensely grateful to Alejandro Luque for his hospitality, knowledge and friendship. He was the perfect cicerone to his home city of Cádiz, corners of which we would never have found without his practised eye. He also gave us a grand tour of Seville from the perspective of an insider. Many thanks are due to Antonio Rivero Taravillo for his personalised tour of the city in the footsteps of the poet, Luis Cernuda – a walk brought to life once more by reading his excellent biography.

Several literary foundations provided assistance above and beyond the call of duty, especially the Fundación Zenobia-Juan Ramón Jiménez, the Casa del Poeta José Ángel Valente and, in particular, the good people at the Fundación Rafael Alberti.

We also have fond memories of convivial meals laden with *salmorejo*, prawns, wine and cake, washed down by mint tea, all by the poolside in Sancti Petri – *muchísimas gracias*, Paquita and Juan Carlos. Likewise, Judith Reason on your hillside above Almuñécar. Our photographic efforts were, once again, enhanced by the editing skills of Nik Guyatt, who will be kept in coffee. Finally, our research was always facilitated by the dedicated staff at the British Library, and we have received nothing but encouragement, support and love from our families.

In addition, we would like to acknowledge the following permissions to reproduce material included in the text:

The extracts from *Sketches of Spain* (*Impresiones y Paisajes*, 1918) by Federico García Lorca, translated by Peter Bush, are reproduced by kind permission from Serif Books. All rights reserved. Copyright © translation Peter Bush 2013.

The extract from *The Face of Spain* by Gerald Brenan is reproduced by permission from Serif Books and the Estate of Gerald Brenan. All rights reserved. Copyright © Gerald Brenan 1950. The Estate of Gerald Brenan is represented by The Hanbury Agency, 53 Lambeth Walk, London SE11 6DX.

Excerpt from *Andalus* by Jason Webster with thanks to the author, published by Black Swan Books, Copyright © 2004, Jason Webster.

Excerpt from *Shadows of the Pomegranate Tree* by Tariq Ali with thanks to the author, published by Verso Books, Copyright © 1993, Tariq Ali.

Excerpt reprinted from *Devoured by the Moon* © by Rafael Perez Estrada, translated by Stephen Stewart, by permission of Hanging Loose Press.

Excerpts from *Poet in Andalucía* by Nathalie Handal with thanks to the author, published by University of Pittsburgh Press, Copyright © 2012, Nathalie Handal.

Excerpt from *Malaga Burning* by Gamel Woolsey. Courtesy of Pythia Press.

Excerpt from *Forgotten Stories From Spain: The Ambulance Man and the Spanish Civil War* by Paul Read with thanks to the author, published by Craving Distraction Ltd, Copyright © 2014, Paul Read.

Excerpt from *The Siege* by Arturo Pérez-Reverte reprinted by permission of Orion Publishing Group, London. Copyright © Arturo Pérez-Reverte 2010. Translation © Frank Wynne 2013.

Antonio Machado: Selected Poems, translated by Alan S. Trueblood, Copyright © 1982 by the President and Fellows of Harvard College.

Platero and I by Juan Ramón Jiménez, translated by Eloïse Roach, Copyright © 1957, renewed 1985. Courtesy of the University of Texas Press.

As I Walked Out One Midsummer Morning
Reproduced with permission of Curtis Brown Group Ltd, London on behalf of the Partners of the Literary Estate of Laurie Lee
Copyright © Laurie Lee, 1969

A Rose for Winter
Reproduced with permission of Curtis Brown Group Ltd, London on behalf of the Partners of the Literary Estate of Laurie Lee
Copyright © Laurie Lee, 1955

Selected Poems
Reproduced with permission of Curtis Brown Group Ltd, London on behalf of the Partners of the Literary Estate of Laurie Lee
Copyright © Laurie Lee, 1985

Excerpt from *Words of Mercury* by Patrick Leigh Fermor reproduced by permission of John Murray Press, an imprint of Hodder and Stoughton Limited, Copyright © 2010 Patrick Leigh Fermor.

'Almeria' from *The Cicadas and Other Poems* by Aldous Huxley. Copyright © 1931 by Aldous Huxley. Reprinted by permission of Georges Borchardt, Inc., on behalf of the Aldous and Laura Huxley Trust, Mark Trevenen Huxley and Teresa Huxley. All rights reserved.

Excerpt from *Fuente Ovejuna* by Lope de Vega, translated by William E. Colford is reproduced by permission of Barron's Educational Series, Inc, Copyright © 1969.

Excerpt from *Dog Days in Andalucía* is reproduced by permission of Random House, Copyright © Jackie Todd, 2010.

Cervantes: A Biography, Byron, W., Orion Publishing Group, all attempts at tracing the copyright holder were unsuccessful, but we would be happy to rectify any omissions in future editions should the copyright holder come forward.

Juan Goytisolo
Fragmento de *La Chanca*
© 1962, Juan Goytisolo
Fragmento de *Campos de Níjar*
© 1960, Juan Goytisolo

José Ángel Valente
Fragmento de 'No amanece el cantor', *Al dios del lugar*
© 1989, Herederos de José Ángel Valente

With thanks to Penguin for their permission to use extracts from *Federico García Lorca: Selected Poems*. All attempts at tracing the translators were unsuccessful, but we would be happy to rectify any omissions in future editions should the copyright holders come forward.

Extracts from pages 6 and 214, *South from Granada* by Gerald Brenan (Viking, London, 1963) Copyright © Gerald Brenan 1963. Reproduced by permission of Penguin Books Ltd.

Extract from *Cocaine Nights* by J G Ballard reprinted by permission of HarperCollins Publishers Ltd
© J G Ballard 1996

Extract from *The Blind Man of Seville* by Robert Wilson reprinted by permission of HarperCollins Publishers Ltd © Robert Wilson 2003.

Extract from *Luis de Góngora: Selected Shorter Poems*, translated by Michael Smith reprinted by permission of Carcanet Press, 1995.

Map of Andalucia

Portugal

Extremadura

Fuente Obejuna

Medina Azahara
Córdoba

Rio Guadalquivir

Écija

Itálica

Huelva Moguer
  Palos

Seville

Osuna

El Rocio

Coto Doñana

Anteque

Arcos de la Frontera

Jerez

Ronda

El Puerto de
Santa María

Cádiz

San Fernando

Vejer de la Frontera

Trafalgar

Gibraltar

Castilla-La Mancha

(Sierra Morena)

Parque Natural Sierra de Andújar

Andújar

Úbeda

Baeza

Jaén

Frailes

Fuente Vaqueros Víznar Guadix

Granada

Mojácar

Tabernas

Nijar

Alpujarras

Almería

Málaga Almuñécar

San José

Costa del Sol

Murcia

Provinces

2. Seville   6. Granada

3. Huelva   7. Córdoba

4. Cádiz   8. Jaén

5. Málaga   9. Almería

Note: Province numbers refer to book chapters

❁ 1 ❁

INTRODUCTION

Introducing Andalucia is a task that requires careful negotiation of the pitfalls created by the region's stereotypes. The second largest of Spain's autonomous communities, Andalucia encapsulates the outsider's traditional image of the country as a whole – a land laden with the sounds of flamenco guitar where the inhabitants in their wide-brimmed hats or swirling skirts are prone to the lure of the celebratory night with little thought for the day to come. These passions have spilled from many foreign pens, spawning images of the blood and dust of a bullfight, the intensity of a lover's revenge or the internecine intrigues of Moorish potentates.

It is possible to demolish a good many of these hackneyed images, but the remains provide clues to the origins of the truth behind our popular imagination: the unique sparks that ignited the artistic minds of writers such as Washington Irving, Prosper Mérimée, François-René de Chateaubriand and Lord Byron, whose embellishments have left the legacy that many modern Andalucians find so tiresome. In this story of the region's literature, it would be incredibly remiss to leave out the local voice, a voice that has become international in this most rich of literary communities. The likes of Federico García Lorca, Antonio Machado and Juan Ramón Jiménez have justifiably joined the greats of international letters.

The origins of settlement in Andalucia may be lost in the distance of prehistory, but the area has witnessed many of the great civilisations – the Phoenicians, the Greeks, the Romans, the Visigoths, the Moors and the reconquest Christians. Through them it has accumulated the traditions and cultures that have inspired the words of writers fascinated by a region that has seen the best of human tolerance and the worst of human cruelty. The invaders, conquerors and settlers profited from the area's riches, as noted by Pliny the Elder in his *Naturalis Historia*, in turn leaving their own lasting legacy. The Moor, Averroes, built his philosophy on Greek Aristotelian traditions, whilst the Jew, Maimonides, tried to enlighten the eternally perplexed. Yet these two great cultures – Arab and Jewish – would be swept aside by the all-encompassing Christian reconquest which, itself, spawned a golden age of literary endeavour, personified by the Cordoban Luis de Góngora, and the universal Miguel de Cervantes.

The first millennium BC, prior to Pliny, is shrouded in literary mystery. The great historian Herodotus wrote of Tartessos, the semi-legendary harbour and settlement at the mouth of the Guadalquivir River. He assures readers that it was beyond the Pillars of Hercules, one of which is formed by Gibraltar. The Romans were equally sure of its existence, parroting the Greek texts. Was Tartessos Atlantis? If so, where was it? In 2004, R. W. Kühne, a latter-day Heinrich Schliemann, discovered circular configurations on a satellite image of the Coto Doñana, a wildlife reserve in the Guadalquivir marshes. Tentatively, archaeologists have gone in search of these mythic origins, trying not to disturb the fragile environment.

From the marshes of the Coto, Andalucia sweeps up to the largest peaks in Spain. The Sierra Nevada is home to Mulhacén, the highest European mountain outside the Caucasus and the Alps. The name proudly immortalises the penultimate Muslim king of Granada, Muley Hacén, and if legend is to be believed, he lies buried at the summit. The villages that populate the foothills of these peaks were home to the last vestiges of Moorish Spain, acting as refuge to the Muslims fleeing the fall of Granada in that quintessentially Spanish year of 1492, when Columbus altered the history of the world.

Today, the Alpujarras, as these hills and valleys are known, play host to those in search of a Spain they can no longer find on the coast. In the twentieth century, authors and subsequent hispanophiles, notably Gerald Brenan and Chris Stewart, have written of their experiences on these slopes – one escaping the psychological consequences of war and the relative constraints of genteel English poverty; the other looking for adventure and a new way of life in the off-grid manner of the millennial Westerner, escaping the materialism of a complacent society.

Many modern Andalucians may look askance at the lifestyle of Chris Stewart, living in a way that they have spent generations trying to escape. In a bid to bolster its economy, Andalucia promoted itself as the original package tourist destination. Its rampant success was ultimately to be its downfall, evident in the massive property bubble that eventually burst, leaving the hollow shells of many unfinished *urbanizaciones*. However, the region will survive the chaos, as it always has, finding its way through upheaval and tumultuous change.

As a generalisation, Andalucian writers possess a sense of fatalism, some of them inextricably bound to preoccupations with death. Death may be the ultimate conclusion or simply a metaphor for new beginnings and the shift of one world passing to another. For the poet Lorca, death was ever present, a constant premonition of his ultimate fate at the hands of a Falangist firing squad during the Spanish Civil War. The conflict was fought with particular severity in parts of the region, especially the great coastal city of Málaga. In many respects, democratic Spain is only just starting to come to terms with this war that set family against family, a conflict tacitly buried in a pact of forgetting.

If the region is one of extensive geographical contrasts, then it is also one of renowned cities possessing their own distinctive characters. The melancholy of a somnambulant Córdoba, quietly lamenting its lost caliphal past, contrasts markedly with the demanding vibrancy of the capital, Seville. The city is a product of its sixteenth-century experience, a time written of so evocatively by Cervantes, when the riverside docks saw the unloading of unimaginable riches from the

Indies. It became a centre of publishing and was called the 'great Babylon of Spain' by Góngora, who describes its widespread appeal, saying it was a 'map of all the nations, where the Fleming finds his Ghent and the Englishman his London'. The riches flowed into the arts, into palaces and the Baroque – a style of architecture that found its way to Spanish colonies in South America and the rest of Europe, especially Sicily. Seville is a city where the Spanish love of noise and vitality is personified.

Granada, by contrast, has a certain gentility, perhaps redolent of the bourgeoisie that Lorca found so distasteful. It carries the weight of the Alhambra, the red fort that dominates the hill overlooking the city and the minds of all who see it. Nowhere in Europe has a Moorish palace been so well preserved, and it was under the romantic spell of these magical environs that the pens of Irving and Théophile Gautier became animated. The soft shoes of slippered Arab poets also once glided through these marbled courtyards, writing verses to laud the virtues of a ruler or the beauties of a concubine.

The history of Andalucia can also be read in the land and the produce it has given a grateful population. It was the Phoenicians who first introduced wine-making to the region, a skill continued by the Romans and refined by the Moors, who introduced the practice of distillation, a fortification process that is used in the production of brandy and fortified wines. Sherry is, of course, the prime example, a wine once beloved by the English, who have added their own stamp to the town of Jerez.

Olives, also brought by the Phoenicians, with the ample aid of the Greeks, are part of the Andaluz soul and landscape. As more than one modern writer has pointed out, the massive groves of Jaén Province can be seen from space. Yet they were, and to an extent still are, examples of the *latifundia* agricultural system – whereby large tracts of land are privately owned by wealthy landlords – that favoured the few and disadvantaged the many. Such inequality is not lost on the more socially aware writers who have turned their gaze to these endlessly mesmerising horizons.

From coastal strip to high mountain, marshy deltas to arid flatland, Andalucia has many moods. The insight caught by a writer in one district or landscape may be very different to that envisaged by another whose own agenda determines an altogether different experience. Inevitably, though, the nineteenth-century trend towards romantic stereotyping owes much to the public appetite for such notions in a then-industrialising and increasingly homogenous world. Andalucia has now joined that world but has no problem in retaining an identity of its own.

Unsurprisingly, it has been impossible to include every contribution to the literary landscape of the region – one of the most heavily populated literary locations in the world. To readers with a favourite author we may have excluded, we can only apologise, but we have had to make difficult choices whilst maintaining the breadth of work and experience from multiple cultural and intellectual perspectives.

Finally, on a more prosaic note, we have used the Spanish spelling of Andalucia (without the accent) and thus 'Andalucian' rather than the more common 'Andalusian'. Occasionally, we have borrowed the Spanish adjective, 'Andaluz'. All place names reflect Spanish spellings, with the exception of the universally recognised Seville. With regard to book titles, if originally written in a language other than English, the title of the translation is given first, followed by the original. If no translation exists, we have reversed the order and provided an English title ourselves.

2

SEVILLE PROVINCE

Oranges, Romance and Religion

In Seville was he born, a pleasant city,
Famous for oranges and women – he
Who has not seen it will be much to pity.

(Byron, *Don Juan*, 1819)

Seville

Seville is the capital of Andalucia and, like many capital cities, has a long and mercurial history. At its zenith, during the dazzling years of Spanish imperial power in the sixteenth and early seventeenth centuries, Seville was the darling of Empire. The mighty Guadalquivir that flows through its heart brought wealth from the Indies. Over a thousand years earlier, it had been the demand for local precious metals that first attracted the Greeks and Phoenicians. They brought their own goods, particularly ceramics, to trade for the minerals excavated from the mountains. Seville, located on a plain, was the perfect staging point. The constant landscape with its gentle undulations was integral to the original Phoenician name, Hispalis, adopted by the Romans and meaning 'flat land'.

Georg Braun's 1565 *Civitatis Orbis Terrarum*, an idiosyncratic book of illustrated world views, visually portrays Golden Age Seville. A cuckolded husband at the forefront of the picture rides his donkey towards the distant city. Aside from this quirky insight into marital disharmony, the picture is an otherwise dramatic representation of the dominant presence of the cathedral and the adjoining Giralda tower. Braun's printed image is reflected in the words of many travellers as they approached Seville, whether on foot, by boat along the river or using Sancho Panza's favourite means of transport, the aforementioned donkey.

Edmondo De Amicis, the Italian journalist, novelist and travel writer, took the water route in the early 1870s whilst working for the Rome-based newspaper, *La Nazione*. His correspondence from Spain proved to be useful reference material in the composition of his successful travelogue, *Spain* (*Spagna*), a book which indulges his love of Andalucia. As he drifted along the Gualdaquivir, his prose evokes the seemingly mirage-like encounter with Seville:

> The ship glided with the ease of a gondola over the quiet and limpid waters which reflected like a mirror the white dresses of the ladies, and the air brought us the odor of oranges from the groves on the shore peopled with villas. Seville was hidden behind its girdle of gardens; and we could only see an immense mass of very green trees, above them the black pile, the cathedral, and the Giralda, all rose-color, surmounted by its statue flaming like a tongue of fire.

The Giralda pre-dates the cathedral and took 12 years to build, having been started in 1184. Unsurprisingly, this minaret, converted into a bell tower, is a UNESCO World Heritage monument. Its distinctive cultural position, spanning the divide between Moorish and Christian Spain, is Seville's primary testament to its Arab past. The Moors were finally driven from the city in 1248 by King Fernando III of Castile, León and Galicia, at which point the Christian conquerors adopted the mosque as their place of worship.

The shifting sands of faith were mirrored by the equally unsteady forces beneath the Andalucian soil. Few associate southern Spain with earthquakes, yet it was just such a phenomenon that put paid to the mosque's uneasy accommodation of Christian worship. In

1356, the seismic disruptions badly damaged the old mosque and provided the city fathers with the opportunity to plan for a new building, and in 1401 these plans were realised as work started on what is now Seville Cathedral. The need for a bell tower was negated by the splendid isolation of the Giralda, which had survived the earthquake. The Renaissance saw essential repairs and the irresistible temptation to embellish; however, not everyone has seen these changes as detractions. In 1775, the English travel writer Henry Swinburne visited Seville and appreciated the tower's sympathetic melange. Swinburne was the great-uncle of the more famous Victorian poet, Algernon Charles Swinburne.

Always happier on the Continent than in the isle of his birth, the Catholic Henry Swinburne had something of a rollercoaster life, his later years being dominated by financial ruin and the death of his son in a storm at sea. But at the age of 32, Henry had begun his Spanish travels, which were to last two years and result in the well-respected book, *Travels through Spain, in the Years 1775 and 1776*. The less than snappy title did not deter sales, and future editions included the author's own drawings and led to a French translation. Even Edward Gibbon, famed for his *Decline and Fall of the Roman Empire*, paid Swinburne the compliment of quoting him in his text.

As Swinburne circled the cathedral, strolling through the Patio de los Naranjos (the Court of the Orange Trees), he admired the Moorish fountain which, in the way of Andalucia, incorporates a previously Visigothic font. His attention was then drawn to the bell tower: 'At one angle stands the Giralda, or belfry, a tower three hundred and fifty feet high, and fifty square [...] the Christians have added two stories, and a prodigious weathercock, which, altogether, agree much better with the ancient building than patchwork is wont to do.' In fact, the weathervane, or *giraldillo*, was the inspiration for the structure's name. No visit to Seville is complete without ascending the tower's steps to gaze over the magnificent view of the city.

Richard Ford did just that in the process of writing his *Handbook for Travellers in Spain* – the quintessential nineteenth-century traveller's bible for all things Iberian. An Oxford-educated would-be lawyer who never actually practised, Ford had the financial opportunity and ample-enough time to pursue his peripatetic Spanish itinerary. His comments on the climb chiefly concerned the 'colony of the twittering, careering hawk, the *Falco tinunculoides*'. Many a guidebook today mentions the modern-day equivalent, a colony of kestrels. Ford's legal training may have caused him to see things in black and white, and he was certainly not shy of giving very trenchant opinions, as illustrated by the following haughty missive on the cathedral's chapter library:

> Above the book-shelves are hung portraits of Archbishops, and the pictures themselves mark the rise and decline of church power. The older, the Tello, Albornoz, Luna, Toledo, Fonseca, and Mendoza, are men of master mind, who bore their great commissions in their looks; the latter, in their blue and white ribbons and periwigs, are mere stall-fed courtiers or boudoir-frequenting Abbés. The 'cretinised' Bourbon Cardinal Luis is the climax of the imbecile.

From the above quote, it may be expected that the cathedral itself would be a rampant display of decoration; although there are some areas that gleam with an intense aura, the whole impression is one of a quiet, cohesive grandeur and colossal space. In fact, Seville Cathedral is the largest Gothic church in the world; the only traditional churches that are larger are St Paul's in London and St Peter's in Rome. It is this vastness that writers have felt compelled to express in their descriptions. Théophile Gautier, the poetic guardian of French Romanticism, who contributed much to Andalucian myth-making in his verses and prose, compared it to a seemingly Lilliputian Notre Dame:

> It is a mountain scooped out, a valley turned topsy-turvy; Notre Dame at Paris might walk about erect in the middle nave, which is of a frightful height; pillars, as large round as towers, and which

appear so slender that they make you shudder, rise out of the ground or descend from the vaulted roof, like the stalactites in a giant's grotto.

Eight years before the appearance of Gautier's *Wanderings in Spain* (*Un voyage en Espagne*), the idiosyncratic Englishman par excellence, George Borrow, found himself in Seville Cathedral. Borrow's quirky opinions will make themselves heard more than once as we progress around Andalucia. A grammar-school boy with an innate talent for languages, Borrow veered away from a legal career towards the quixotic task of bringing the Bible to Catholic Spain at a time when priests were the arbiters of holy writ. He brought to the mission a tenacity of purpose and a somewhat original character.

He had first employed his linguistic skills for the Bible Society in 1833 during a trip to Russia, where he also soaked up the local Gypsy culture to such an extent that he was able to publish a dictionary of their language. Speaking Portuguese, Castilian Spanish and Gypsy Caló, Borrow crossed the border from Portugal at Badajoz in Extremadura, heading for Madrid and then whirling south to Seville. His travels were turned into the book *The Bible in Spain* which, despite its title, does not reference his religious intentions as often as one would expect. This was not his first published work on Spanish matters – it was preceded by *The Zincali*, a reasonably successful piece on the Andalucian Gypsies. The second book, however, became a bible of an altogether secular sort for those interested in the peninsula. It brought him acclaim and a certain celebrity which his subsequent works failed to capitalise upon.

Borrow's eccentricities are apparent in his writing and, despite a deep affection for Gypsy culture, he could also be extremely cutting. His pages are peppered with anecdote, exemplified by a little aside he makes whilst climbing the Giralda, mentioning the fact that King Ferdinand VII of Spain is supposed to have ascended it on horseback. These additions make for an interesting read, although one is never quite sure whether Borrow is telling the whole truth. On the other hand, when he is inside the cathedral, there is no doubting his sincerity: 'In the chapels allotted to the various saints, are some of the most magnificent paintings which Spanish art has produced; indeed the Cathedral of Seville is at present far more rich in splendid paintings than at any former period.'

In the Sacrastía Mayor of the cathedral are displayed the seventeenth-century paintings of St Isidore and St Leander by Bartolomé Esteban Murillo, 'the pride and also the curse of Seville', according to Gautier. The Frenchman found the painter mentioned wherever he went. St Isidore is portrayed holding a book, which is clearly a reference to his writings. Isidore, the former archbishop, was not only an author but also a proto-scientist; he is most remembered for the *Etymologiae*, an early attempt at cataloguing the encyclopedic knowledge of the ancient world. As the title would suggest, rhetoric and language are included in the work, as is everything from forms of medicine to cosmological matters and warfare. Such eclectic knowledge has led the Vatican to name Isidore the patron saint of the internet. Murillo's other painting in the sacristy is of Isidore's brother, Leander, who converted the Visigothic King Reccared to Catholicism in 587. Until this date, the Visigoths had been in thrall to Arianism – a doctrine which placed the Son of God in a subordinate position to the Father.

In the seventeenth century, Catholic depictions of Christ on the Cross reached their emotional peak in the sculpture of Juan Martínez Montañés. The cathedral's Capilla de San Andrés houses just such a crucifixion, one of the building's most valuable works. Albert F. Calvert, a traveller, art critic and, rather more surprisingly, a mining engineer, who also wrote a biography of Murillo, describes Montañés's many religious figures in his 1912 work, *Sculpture in Spain*, as expressing 'perfectly the deep religious feeling which animated Spain in the seventeenth century'. The Christ figure in the chapel has a little blood spilling from his wounds but it is the strained body and emotional intensity which move the viewer in its beauty and pain. The sculptor became known as the Phidias of Seville and was the master of what was to become the Andalucian School.

A stone's throw from the cathedral, in the Plaza del Triunfo, is the Alcázar, also known as the Alcázares Reales or the Royal Palace. The complex was originally Moorish, housing the representatives of the Cordoban caliph, but little remains from the eleventh century except the Jardín de Crucero – named for its cross-shaped outline. The present structure owes its appearance to the fourteenth-century Christian monarch, Pedro the Cruel or the Just, depending on which side of the fence you sat. It is a splendid example of Mudéjar architecture, the style influenced by Moorish taste and workmanship. Pedro's building work in this style created the sensual surroundings in which he housed his mistress, María de Padilla, who supposedly used witchcraft to keep hold of her king. While Pedro, rather expensively, maintained just one concubine, his Moorish predecessors had devoted a whole section of the palace to a harem, with other rooms set aside for more political matters. Typically, Borrow preferred the Alcázar's Hall of the Ambassadors to the one in Granada's Alhambra.

The Royal Palace borders onto the Santa Cruz district. Once the Judería or Jewish quarter, the area is now a tourist honey pot with its labyrinthine network of whitewashed narrow alleyways and churches. After falling into disrepair owing to the expulsion of the Jews, the district could claim to be an early example of gentrification. In 1809, fresh from Cambridge, an English peer arrived at a guesthouse on the edge of the barrio (district) in Calle de las Cruces, now 21 Calle Fabiola. Like many wealthy young men, he was intent on a Grand Tour; unlike many, this Romantic was equally intent on doing things his way.

The loose-linen-shirted dandy, fluid of sexuality and confident in his striking looks, despite a deformed foot, was George Gordon, Lord Byron. Yet to have the epithet, 'mad, bad and dangerous to know', although undoubtedly working on it, Byron had taken the

Spanish route to avoid Napoleonic France and to indulge his lust for experience. In a letter home to his mother, the poet describes his initial impressions and the owners of his guesthouse:

> Seville is a beautiful town, though the streets are narrow they are clean, we lodged in the house of two Spanish unmarried ladies, who possess *six* houses in Seville, and gave me a curious specimen of Spanish manners. – They are women of character, and the eldest a fine woman, the youngest pretty but not so good a figure as Donna Josepha, the freedom of women which is general here astonished me not a little, and in the course of further observation I find that reserve is not the characteristic of the Spanish belles.

Byron's letters go on to enlighten us further about his stay in Seville. It seemed that the elder of the two women had formed a particular fondness for Byron and invited him to share her apartment, which, he assures us, his 'virtue' led him to decline. Undeterred, she took a lock of his hair and presented him with a swirl of her own dark flowing tresses. Byron sent this home to his mother and it is now preserved in the poet's archive held at his long-suffering publishers, John Murray, in London.

It came as a pleasant surprise to Byron that Andaluz women were not encumbered with the social constraints he had found at home, especially after they had been married, at which point he tells us that they 'throw off all restraint'. He was clearly smitten with their sultry difference: 'Long black hair, dark languishing eyes, clear olive complexions, and forms more graceful in motion than can be conceived by an Englishman used to the drowsy, listless air of his countrywomen'.

Despite the relatively short time the poet spent in Andalucia, it left an indelible mark on his two most famous works – *Childe Harold* and *Don Juan*. *Childe Harold* is the tale of a world-weary young man's travels through the Mediterranean towards the Ottoman East. It is, at heart, a reflection of Byron's own journey and, regardless of his protestations to the contrary, contains many autobiographical elements. It was this poem that made him the English-speaking world's first literary celebrity, and it led to his iconic throw-away line, 'I awoke one morning and found myself famous.'

The Andalucian segment of the Childe's wanderings is set against the backdrop of the Peninsular War, which ended in 1814. Whilst Byron was travelling across the region, the invading French troops under Napoleon were in conflict with the Spanish forces and their allies, the British and Portuguese. The British were led by Arthur Wellesley, later to become the Duke of Wellington. Byron, with his usual predilection for the plucky underdog, put his full support behind the embattled Spanish. When Childe Harold reaches Seville the hounds of war are not far behind:

> Full swiftly Harold wends his lonely way
> Where proud Sevilla triumphs unsubdued:
> Yet is she free – the spoiler's wished-for prey!
> Soon, soon shall Conquest's fiery foot intrude,
> Blackening her lovely domes with traces rude.
> Inevitable hour! 'Gainst fate to strive
> Where Desolation plants her famished brood
> Is vain, or Ilion, Tyre, might yet survive,
> And Virtue vanquish all, and Murder cease to thrive.

The following verse clearly harks back to the poet's other Sevillian passion – the city's women. In the face of imminent threat, the Childe's Seville is one of hedonistic pleasure-seeking with a penchant for living in the moment:

> But all unconscious of the coming doom,
> The feast, the song, the revel here abounds;
> Strange modes of merriment the hours consume,
> Nor bleed these patriots with their country's wounds;

> Nor here War's clarion, but Love's rebeck sounds;
> Here Folly still his votaries enthralls,
> And young-eyed Lewdness walks her midnight rounds:
> Girt with the silent crimes of capitals,
> Still to the last kind Vice clings to the tottering walls.

This is Byron at his full Byronic best, where the poem's hero broods on war and peace, love and betrayal, the human condition in defiance of oppression and the bitter hope for a better future. Yet there is undeniably more than a hint of the poseur in these verses that our poet has still to shake off. The enormous success of the poem inevitably led to some stinging criticism, not least of which came from Samuel Taylor Coleridge, who, in a letter to Wordsworth, and not without reason, called Byron a 'Picturesque Tourist' who 'must be troubled with a mental Strangury, if he could not lift up his leg six times at six different Corners, and each time piss a Canto'.

Years later, when permanently exiled on the Continent owing to his failed marriage and scandalous affair with his half-sister, Byron mentally returned to Seville for his masterwork, *Don Juan*. The more mature poet packed every facet of his literary persona into this poem, and some critics see it as the resolution of his many trains of thought. Its satire is biting, with barbs gleefully aimed at Wordsworth and his aforementioned critic, Coleridge. The content of the epic caused a scandal back in Britain.

As the name suggests, it is based on the legend of Don Juan Tenorio, the mythical seducer from Seville who may or may not, in reality, have been a Sicilian. In a playful twist, Byron turns Juan into the seduced rather than the rake. Canto I sees the hero living in the Andalucian capital with his father, José, and his mother, Inez, who was 'a learned lady' whose memory 'was a mine: she knew by heart / All Calderon and greater part of Lopé'.

It is not long before the young Juan is smitten with the older and married Donna Julia. On the discovery of this affair, Inez sends her son away to travel, fearful of the wrath of Julia's husband, Alfonso:

The pleasant scandal which arose next day,
The nine days' wonder which was brought to light,
And how Alfonso sued for a divorce,
Were in the English newspapers, of course.

Byron never managed to finish his version of the story, the final cantos remaining unwritten as he died amongst the malarial swamps of Missolonghi during the Greek War of Independence. Other versions of the story did not suffer this fate and, in addition to his conquests of the opposite sex, Don Juan has seduced many other writers. The Romantic poet from Valladolid, José Zorrilla, penned his own version which also drew on a text from Alexandre Dumas, who in turn looked towards Prosper Mérimée, a writer we will meet later in the tobacco factory. In the Plaza de los Refinadores at the heart of the Barrio Santa Cruz stands a statue dedicated to the seducer. His haughty upright stance and proud mouth convey the self-aware bravura of the character. High leather boots, gloves and carefully draped cape complete the image of an overly confident Lothario.

Life was first breathed into the legend in 1630, when a work on Don Juan, attributed to Tirso de Molina, was first published. Molina was from Madrid and – surprisingly, given the subject matter of the writing – a practising monk. Molina's playwriting was prolific and his popularity only just behind that of the now more famous Lope de Vega. The play, *El burlador de Sevilla y convidado de piedra* is variously translated into English as *The Trickster*, *The Seducer* or *The Playboy of Seville and the Stone Guest*. Juan kills Gonzalo, the father of one of his lovers, only to find himself invited to dine in a graveyard by Gonzalo's ghost. The phantom has his revenge by striking the womaniser dead and dragging him to Hell.

Some researchers see a connection between the fiction and the real-life history of Miguel de Mañara, who turned his back on a life of vice, dedicating it to the Fraternity of Sacred Mercy in 1662. He founded the Hospital de la Caridad, a beautifully ornate building decorated with Dutch tiles in Calle Temprano. The only problem with this connection is that the play was already being worked on in 1616.

Whatever the origins of the tale, this romantic band of Andaluz myth-makers have done much to imprint a stereotypical image of Seville in the popular imagination. Heat, passion, picaresque revenge and a *carpe diem* attitude with little regard for the consequences were the vivid colours of life that these stories evoked, but as we know, there are many more shades on the palette of truth.

When considering contributors to this exotic caricature, it is impossible to ignore Washington Irving, the author of *Rip Van Winkle* and *The Legend of Sleepy Hollow*. He was one of the first American writers to find a ready audience in Europe and a devoted Hispanist. The nineteenth-century polymath turned his hand to many fields: short stories, biographies, essays and histories, in addition to being a diplomat. His stay in Seville was primarily to carry out research in the archives of the cathedral, and it is perhaps indicative of his romantic vision that the city reminded him of *A Thousand and One Nights*. He stayed at 2 Calle de Agua, near to the Alcázar Gardens, and a plaque on the wall of the house commemorates his love for the country.

Irving's most famous Spanish work, *Tales of the Alhambra*, will feature in the Granada chapter so we will leave him researching in the fusty archives for now. Undoubtedly, his books have been read by many wordsmiths who followed in his footsteps, but not all shared his picture-postcard version of Orientalised Andalucia. The English author Somerset Maugham admitted to recognising the thoughts and feelings of these writers from a more romantic era, but he clearly wanted to make Seville his own.

Staying at 2 Calle Guzmán el Bueno, a street not far from Byron's earlier lodgings, Maugham found himself comfortable in the house of the British vice-consul. The street cannot have changed very much in the intervening century; it is still a narrow thoroughfare, clearly not intended for cars. Halfway down, it opens out on to a small square lined with iconic orange trees and houses dressed with wrought-iron balconies. From the upper storeys of no. 2, the writer could almost have leaned out across the street and touched the building on the opposite side.

These congenial surroundings allowed Maugham to produce a prodigious outpouring of words. In just eight months, he managed to write his travelogue, *The Land of the Blessed Virgin*, four short stories and a novel. If not exactly ashamed of the travel account, in later years he was well aware that it was a youthful work. He was always happy to revisit Seville, and in 1934 he travelled to Andalucia with Gerald Kelly, the Cambridge-educated son of a wealthy clergyman. The upshot of his stay was another travel book that reworked themes from *The Blessed Virgin*, but with more concentration on Spanish history and literature, including the great dramatists, Calderón and Lope de Vega. This work, *Don Fernando*, was named after a bar owner whose establishment was adorned with the kind of traditional *charcuterie* found in the mountains of Andalucia, the hams and chorizo that Maugham no doubt washed down with a good local wine.

Graham Greene considered this second account of Spain to be Maugham's best work – significant praise, given Somerset was the writer of *The Moon and Sixpence*, *Of Human Bondage* and *The Painted Veil*. Without doubt, a gifted writer and trained medic, Maugham was also a complex character, often thought of as reserved, though this may have been due to his stammer. He described himself as three-quarters 'queer' but was also aware of the need for discretion. A lonely childhood, owing to his parents' early death, his speech impediment and closet bisexuality were a cocktail that led to his self-conscious and aloof demeanour.

His Andalucian travels hint at relationships with men and women, particularly Rosarito, whom he mentions explicitly in *The Land of the Blessed Virgin*. Her startling eyes clearly had a dramatic impact. There are further mentions in later writings of someone with green eyes; as Selina Hastings mentions in *The Secret Lives of*

Somerset Maugham, her carefully researched biography, the gender of the person in question remains unspecified.

Maugham loved what he perceived as the undercurrent of licentiousness in Seville. His night-time strolls were often punctuated with the casual observation of courtship rituals in action. For the first time, he felt himself to be the young man he actually was and revelled in the sexual tensions that surrounded him. On one occasion, he visited a brothel, where his passion quickly turned to compassion when the skinny young girl undressing in front of him revealed herself to be 13. On being questioned as to why she was compelled to prostitute herself, it became clear that hunger was the answer.

By this time, Maugham had found a way of negotiating his stammer that meant he could partake fully in the social life around him – whether in English or Spanish. His current beau would be thrust forward at the start of any conversation to make the necessary initial engagement that so horrified Maugham. There is a famous incident relating to his speech impediment which occurred much later in his life. It concerns another travel writer who will appear further on in these pages – Patrick (Paddy) Leigh Fermor.

The gregarious and ebullient Leigh Fermor was once invited to Maugham's house in the south of France. At dinner, Paddy, somewhat well-oiled with whisky, was recounting a story about a stammerer. Later in the evening, Maugham went to bid his guest goodnight and in so doing also bid him farewell, implying that Leigh Fermor would be gone by the time he rose in the morning. Having expected to stay for a few days, Leigh Fermor was sure he had been summarily dismissed owing to his previous gaffe. He recounted the story in a letter to Deborah Devonshire, telling her that an aged Maugham looked as if he had been rotting in the Bastille.

It is a shame that this incident occurred as it is likely that the two writers could have shared their love for Spanish Golden Age authors. At the top of the list would surely have been Miguel de Cervantes Saavedra, the author of the immortal *Don Quixote* and the *Exemplary Novels* (*Novelas ejemplares*), some of which are set in Seville. Maugham writes vividly of Calle Sierpes, now a central shopping street, praising the *manzanilla* sherry and hams on sale there. His description could well have been one that Cervantes would have recognised.

Miguel de Cervantes spent two significant periods in Seville. The first was in the author's younger days after his family had already spent time in Alcalá de Henares, near Madrid, and Córdoba. Cervantes's twentieth-century biographer, William Byron, paints a convincing portrait of the young man watching the incredible activity in what was then the capital of the world:

> Every spring and every fall, scores of ships massed in the Guadalquivir to load supplies for the colonists of the New World; every fall, scores more would arrive, pressed deep in the water by their loads of precious metals, hides, pearls, ambergris, timber, medicinal plants, spices, sugar. Around them, like bee-eaters around a hive, flitted vessels from all Europe [...] Streets swarmed with Portuguese, Bretons, Flemings, Ragusans, Moriscos, blacks. The world came to Seville.

It is not surprising that one of his *Exemplary Novels*, 'Rinconete and Cortadillo', has two young urchins hanging around this very area vying for the opportunity to act as porters whilst keeping one eye out for pockets to pick. Cervantes would have to wait a long time to draw on this inspiration, as the novels would not appear until 1613, many years after these first observations.

It was his second extended period in Seville that led to an outburst of creativity. At the time, Cervantes was carrying out the very unglamorous role of purchasing officer for the navy, with additional spells spent collecting taxes, the only government employment he could attain after years of war, struggle and captivity at the hands of Moorish pirates. His biographers mention his run of bad luck and even acknowledge a slight mystification as to how he managed to survive, given the fact he never seems to have been properly paid for his purchases.

Cervantes was fortunate enough to know a certain Tomás Gutiérrez, a friend from childhood, who had made something of himself in Seville. He owned a well-appointed establishment in Calle de Bayona, now Federico Sánchez Bedoya, near to the cathedral, where the hidalgos (gentlemen) came to drink and talk. Gutiérrez would have given him a place to stay and accompanied him on trips to the taverns along Sierpes. It is in this very street that the observant will find one of the city's 17 plaques dedicated to Spain's most famous author. It makes an entertaining day to track them all down, as each one commemorates references to the city taken from his *Exemplary Novels*.

Among these moral stories that reference the capital of Andalucia are: 'The Spanish-English Lady' ('La española inglesa'), 'The Dogs' Colloquy' ('Coloquio de Cipión y Berganza') and, most often of all, the aforementioned 'Rinconete and Cortadillo'. This last is in the long tradition of the Spanish picaresque, a fictional account of the Sevillian underworld with the two cheeky rascals in the title as the main protagonists. They are taken to Monipodio, a proto-Godfather who rules over the clandestine criminal fraternities of the city.

As an interesting aside, John Dickie, the scholarly author of several histories of Italian criminal organisations, quotes this tale when he mentions the foundation myths of the Cosa Nostra, Camorra and 'Ndrangheta. Supposedly, three Spanish knights landed on the Sicilian island of Favignana. Osso, Mastrosso and Carcagnosso had left Spain after bloodily avenging the violated honour of their sister. There are no prizes for guessing that the knights split to form the above criminal gangs. Monipodio is evoked by Dickie as an Andalucian prototype for the likes of Don Corleone.

The house where Monipodio and his cohorts met was in Calle de la Cruz, now Calle Troya, just over the Guadalquivir via the Puente San Telmo. In this Cervantine excerpt, the gang master has decided where his new recruits will be working and is portioning out their territory:

> To Rinconete and Cortadillo I assign for their district, until Sunday, from the Tower of Gold, all without the city, and to the postern of the Alcazar, where they can work with their fine flowers. I have known those who are much less clever than they appear to be, come home daily with more than twenty reales in small money, to say nothing of silver.

The 'fine flowers' in question refer to the pair's ability to card-sharp the unwary. Lest the reader should be concerned for the fate of our two unlikely heroes, the story ends with Rinconete's awakening to the realities of their trade and his determination to follow a better path. He describes Monipodio as 'nothing better than a coarse and brutal barbarian'. The boys managed to escape the clutches of the magistrates and time in a cell. Sadly, not so their unfortunate author, who found himself incarcerated in the city's gaol, then bordering Calle Sierpes and Calle Francisco Bruna. Cervantes was wrongfully imprisoned under the erroneous assumption that he had returned no monies to the governmental treasury as part of his employment. William Byron, in his biography of Cervantes, has some very detailed descriptions of what the gaol would have been like. On entering, the future author of *Don Quixote* would have seen the following: 'thousands of men milling around, prisoners, visitors, officials, lawyers. Men were shouting at each other in the stentorian bellow that passed for a normal conversational tone.'

Cervantes would have gone up a flight of steps and through two gates. There was a further staircase leading up to the so-called Silver Gate where coins of this metal were needed to avoid shackles; fortunately, it seems he avoided this higher tier reserved for the worst offenders. As Byron points out, everything in gaol could be bought, including the ability to stroll outside the walls under the auspice of an informal day pass.

Some Cervantists believe that the kernel of *Don Quixote* was conceived and possibly written down during the author's time in the Cárcel Real de Sevilla. Given the descriptions of the clamorous conditions, it is difficult to imagine how anyone could have concentrated to that extent. These days, somewhat ironically, the prison is now a bank, home to the modern world's legalised money-lenders and usurers. Keeping a weather-eye on their activities, Cervantes's bust sits on a plinth in front of the concrete-clad and terracotta-painted walls. Holding a book, wearing a doublet and splendid ruff, he meditates on the many twists of fate his life has taken.

With such a magnificent literary legacy, it is no surprise that twentieth-century Spanish writers referenced past heroes; the Sevillian Luis Cernuda was no exception, although his literary hero was Garcilaso de la Vega, the sixteenth-century Toledan poet. Cernuda himself was part of the Generation of '27, a poetic movement of influential writers who first gathered in 1927 to celebrate the three hundredth anniversary of the death of Luis de Góngora, the baroque Cordoban wordsmith. Other members of the group included García Lorca, Vicente Aleixandre, also from Seville, and Cernuda's literature professor at the university, Pedro Salinas.

Cernuda was perhaps the most unusual of this group in terms of character and temperament. Introverted and almost pathologically shy, Cernuda carried the added burden of his homosexuality in what was then a very macho society. At the age of nine, he discovered the rhymes of Gustavo Adolfo Bécquer. The stanzas of this nineteenth-century Sevillian poet were the impetus that turned him to verse. Although he studied law at university, he was drawn to the talks given by Pedro Salinas, who encouraged his literary endeavours after seeing Cernuda's work in a student magazine. Salinas was also instrumental in finding him a position as a reader in Spanish at Toulouse University.

At the outbreak of the Spanish Civil War, Cernuda was back in Spain supporting the Republican cause through his radio broadcasts. In common with so many of his artistic contemporaries, he was forced into exile as Franco's troops swept across the peninsula. He was able to remain in Britain thanks to the English poet Stanley Richardson, who had arranged for him to give some lectures at Oxford and Cambridge. Times were undoubtedly hard for the Sevillian cast from his native soil, scraping a living, grappling with a new language and inhibited socially by his innate shyness.

His British years are tainted with a melancholic nostalgia for an Andalucia that he feared he might never see again. His prose poetry and verse were riven with this sadness, particularly the works composed in a rain-soaked Glasgow during his time at the university there. In 1941, he finished his work, *Ocnos* – a mythic title borrowed from Goethe for a work that was originally to be called *Guirnalda para la juventud* (*A Wreath for Youth*). The reference to youth describes well the content of this unprecedented work of prose poetry, a form uncommon in Spanish literature. Antonio Rivero Taravillo, Cernuda's twenty-first-century biographer, describes the text as 'a shell of memory'; indeed, it is a paean to his early days in Seville.

The son of a colonel, Cernuda had been born in Calle Acetres, living a solitary, bookish childhood. The local government have ensured that Cernuda's memory is perpetuated on the walls of more than one property in Seville. Inscribed into a plaque, this time in marble and commemorating his birthplace, are the words from the segment of *Ocnos* called 'El tiempo' ('Time'): 'I remember that corner of the patio in the house where I was born, alone and seated on the first marble step' ('Recuerdo aquel rincón del patio en la casa natal, yo a solas y sentado en el primer peldaño de la escalera de mármol').

The plazas del Pan and El Salvador, in the centre of the city, also make an appearance in *Ocnos*, specifically in 'Las tiendas' ('The Shops'). Today, the pastel-coloured, balconied shopfronts mix with the graffitied metal shutters of shops closed by the twenty-first-century economic recession. Almost a century earlier, Cernuda described impoverished shops with their small windows, open to the walls of San Salvador Church, staffed by neatly dressed little men, silent as they weighed goods on their balancing scales.

Back in the Jewish quarter, specifically Calle Judería, which borders the Alcázar Gardens, there was once a magnificent magnolia tree; the purity of its snowy-white flowers made it something of a spiritual touchstone for the poet. Once more, his sentiments are immortalised on the wall, even if the tree may not be the original. Cernuda recognised that the specimen possessed something more than a 'beautiful reality'.

Other sites across the city that are referred to in *Ocnos* include the Convent of San Leandro, Calle Aire – his last residence before leaving the city – a brothel in Monsalves and the Church of the Anunciación. In particular, the Eslava Summer Theatre, on the site of what is now the glorious Hotel Alfonso XIII, is worthy of consideration as the scene of Cernuda's first crush. We can imagine the poet attending the outdoor theatre in the velvet night of a Sevillian summer, his eyes drawn across the crowds towards a young man sitting amongst his companions. Speaking in the second person about his own feelings, he describes the unavoidable, yet furtive attraction to someone he recognised as being a kindred spirit.

By now, we can see that Cernuda was painfully aware of the social inadequacies that succeeded in dogging his footsteps. In Rivero Taravillo's biography, there is a revealing vignette which describes a meeting in the United Kingdom between Cernuda and the English poet Stephen Spender, who had Spanish Civil War experience and was smitten with Seville's 'winding streets opening on to little squares'. On the surface, the two men had much in common – homosexual feelings, Republican sympathies and a flair for poetic verse. The meeting, however, was a disaster. Fortunately, a third party, Martínez Nadal, acted as something of a bulwark. Every attempt by Spender to breach Cernuda's monosyllabic wall was met with sad smiles. The following day, Spender charitably hinted that Cernuda should be left alone, saying 'he is suffering too much.'

One Sevillian location crops up in three texts from *Ocnos* – the Parque de María Luisa, which, along with the neighbouring Plaza de España, formed part of the 1929 Expo. The vast open

1   The Plaza de España, Seville

plaza, ringed by a Venetian-style canal and Renaissance-revival buildings, has more of an impact on the modern visitor than it did at the time, when the exhibition was considered a failure. Niches in the buildings are tiled with scenes from the Spanish regions. La Mancha, of course, champions Don Quixote and his faithful squire, Sancho Panza. Today, an attempt has been made to turn the whole semi-circle into an open-air library, with a local bookstore supplying second-hand classics for the passing public to peruse.

The adjacent park has many other literary echoes. In its leafy confines there is a monument to the writer who triggered Cernuda's love for poetry – the nineteenth-century romantic, Bécquer. Embracing a water cypress tree are three allegorical female figures dressed in intricately carved, tiered gowns comforting each other through the vagaries of love. Bécquer, his back to the tree, towers above them, flanked by winged bronzes pierced by love's wounds. The collective is a melancholic ensemble encapsulating the Romantic's obsession with tortured feelings.

Born Gustavo Adolfo Claudio Domínguez Bastida in 1836, Bécquer's life was a short and sad affair. Epitomising the melting pot of Golden Age Seville, Bécquer, who took the surname from his artist brother, was a descendant of Dutch nobles. When he was orphaned at an early age, his uncle and godmother gave him something of a stable upbringing, and the latter's extensive library encouraged the boy's reading. As an orphan of noble birth, he was permitted an education at the Nautical College of San Telmo for a few years. Following in his brother's footsteps, he started to paint, being assured that rich foreigners would always buy his pastoral scenes. However, his love of literature drew him to poetry. In *Legends, Tales and Poems*, Bécquer describes his early love-affair with words:

> When I was a boy of fourteen or fifteen, and my soul was overflowing with numberless longings, with pure thoughts and with that infinite hope that is the most precious jewel of youth, when I deemed myself a poet, when my imagination was full of those pleasing tales of the classical world.

Unfortunately for Bécquer, his 'infinite hope' was not to last for long. After a series of itinerant writing jobs, he was fired from a government sinecure, having been caught sketching and scribbling during office hours. He eventually landed some prestigious work as a journalist, during which time he was able to write his *Rhymes* (*Las rimas*). Little of his poetry was published during his lifetime, although some of the *Rhymes* were printed in the newspaper he worked for, *El Museo Universal*. Much of his inspiration came from the natural world and the human search for an often-unfulfilled love. In true Byronic style, Bécquer actually married disastrously after being rejected by the real love of his life, Julia Espín y Guillén.

He also wrote a sequence of folk tales known as *The Legends* (*Las leyendas*) which, despite falling in and out of fashion, are studied in schools throughout the Hispanic world, along with his verses. One of the most recognised and iconic of his stanzas comes from 'Rhyme 21' and is written in the style of a conversation between two lovers:

> What is poetry?, you say whilst fixing
> your blue eyes on mine.
> What is poetry! And you ask that of me?
> Poetry ... is you.

Bécquer's poetic life ended at the age of 34, in poverty, having succumbed to the same consumptive end as John Keats. It is thanks to his loyal friends that his extant manuscripts were collected together and prepared for publication. Fortunately for his descendants and the reading public, edition after edition followed. His artistic endeavours have also endured in musical form, owing to the renowned composers Isaac Albéniz and Joaquín Turina who set some of his verses to music.

These musical evocations of his work and the posthumous publishing of his texts allow us to visualise the drama of Bécquer's life and surroundings. When recalling his youthful walks through the city of Seville, Bécquer's love for his environment pours from his prose as he conjures up the banks of the city's mighty river:

[A]long the Guadalquivir, and close to the bank that leads to the convent of San Jerónimo, may be found a kind of lagoon, which fertilises a miniature valley formed by the natural slope of the bank [...] A willow bathes its root in the current of the stream, towards which it leans as though bowed by an invisible weight, and all about are multitudes of reeds and yellow lillies.

Hiding within this descriptive passage is an explanation for Seville's decline. As we have seen from Cervantes's *Exemplary Novels*, the quays were once the entrepôt for goods from the Indies, yet the city's fortunes waned as its river silted, forming lagoons and sluggishly flowing, reed-infested channels. The diminishing wealth did not detract from the waterway's passionate allure. The Englishman Paul Gwynne (aka Ernest Slater) – who wrote such lurid tales as *The Bandolero*, subsequently turned into a film – was drawn to follow the river's path from source to sea in his 1912 travelogue, *Along Spain's River of Romance*. He rather haughtily points out that his compatriots would have dredged the river and made the city twice as large as Liverpool, although he is gracious enough to imply that, had they lived in such a climate for 10 to 12 centuries, then things may well have been different.

If the river brought the exchange of goods, it also brought people from the Americas and the essential interchange of ideas. One South American writer who spent a youthful winter in Seville was the Argentinian, Jorge Luis Borges. The Borges family arrived in the autumn of 1919, fresh from a stay on the island of Mallorca. It was thanks to the Sevillian magazine *Grecia* that Borges had his first poem published, 'Himno al mar' ('Hymn to the Sea'). The poet remembered his time in the city as one of literary ferment, when he joined a band of like-minded writers known as the Ultraístas.

The group's self-declared aim was to revitalise the world of literature, rejecting the current trend for rhythmic modernism, whilst evoking imagery and technology. The ultraist-in-chief was another Sevillian, Rafael Cansinos-Asséns, whom Borges was later to meet in Madrid. The timid Argentinian described Cansinos-Asséns as a man totally preoccupied with literature and with little regard for money or fame. In today's world where celebrity is all, the attitude of this polyglot writer is somewhat refreshing. Although he considered Cansinos-Asséns a maestro, Borges eventually turned away from Ultraism, once he had exported it to his native country. He would eventually establish a reputation as one of the world's most innovative writers never to have won the Nobel Prize.

The riches from the Indies that came to Seville were clearly not all financial; however, the classic postcard image of the Guadalquivir river usually contains the Torre del Oro, or Golden Tower, first constructed in 1221 by the Moor Abul-Ula. It was used by King Pedro as a treasure house and went on to become a store for the gold and silver from the Americas. It is not without irony that Antonio Rivero Taravillo notes that Luis Cernuda had himself photographed against the tower's honeycomb walls, a Communist Party poster partially on display; Cernuda, a left-leaning Republican set against that bastion of Spanish imperialism.

Across the water from Pedro's warehouse is the district of Triana, the area of Seville most associated with Gypsy culture. Not part of the traditional tourist trail, it now attracts increasing numbers of visitors keen to search out good tapas and examples of the artisan tile work famous in the area. In George Borrow's day, there was no permanent bridge over the river – the only span being made up of boats roped together. This impermanent structure was due to the regular flooding, which would have swept away earlier attempts at construction. Richard Ford, our guidebook author, writes of one such inundation in a letter home during February 1831:

> We are here blockaded by the waters, and almost cut off from all communications. The country from the top of the Giralda looks like Venice, and in many of the streets people go about in boats. The state of the poor is very lamentable, and they are distributing bread, etc. Still, the suburb of Triana has risen, and a troop of soldiers has been obliged to be sent there.

Triana was, and is, a *barrio obrero* (a working-class neighbour-hood). George Borrow, in his own inimitable style, said that it was, 'inhabited by the dregs of the populace, and abounds with Gitanos or gypsies', a typically blunt statement from this contradictory character. Despite appearances, we know Borrow to be a champion of the Gypsies, befriending many during his time in Seville. In *The Zincali*, the book he wrote specifically on Spanish Gypsy culture, he gives us a portrait of life in nineteenth-century Triana:

Here they may be seen wielding the hammer; here they may be seen trimming the fetlocks of horses, or shearing the backs of mules and borricos with their cachas; and from hence they emerge to apply the same trade in the town, or to officiate as terceros, or to buy, sell, or exchange animals in the mercado.

The Gypsies were renowned for their work with horses and mules, trading in the markets and bartering for the best deals. The other common associations with the *gitano* way of life are music and dance, specifically flamenco. Triana was home to the major flamenco families of Seville, who often lived in *corrales* – those iconic courtyard properties dripping with flora. Sadly, few remain and the musical dynasties were displaced to other areas of the city during development in the twentieth century.

Triana is also home to one of the essential parts of Semana Santa, the intense Holy Week celebrations held over the Easter period. On Good Friday, a candle-lit procession brings the effigy of the Virgin, Esperanza de Triana, back over the bridge to an enthusiastic reception from the people of the barrio. Semana Santa is celebrated in a similar fashion throughout Spain, and these Spanish traditions have even reached former colonies, including Sicily. However, Seville's processions and celebrations are without equal.

Although a religious occasion, it attracts many for the pure spectacle and passion. Unsurprisingly, it makes a dramatic vehicle for the writer, and several have taken on the challenge of binding its essence into fictional narratives. An author who has done this in some style is Robert Wilson, the English creator of Javier Falcón – an outwardly cold detective grappling with demons from his family's past. Wilson, a winner of the Crime Writers' Association (CWA) Gold Dagger Award, knows this part of Andalucia well and divides his time between Spain, Portugal and the UK. There are four books in this series, the first of which is *The Blind Man of Seville*. The *Guardian* newspaper described it as the detective story that Paul Bowles never wrote.

With the action flitting between Tangiers and Easter in Seville, Falcón's life and sanity begin to unravel from the moment he looks on the tortured cadaver of the killer's first victim – the worst he has ever seen. Through the discovery of his father's diaries, the truth starts to emerge. An unsettled Falcón unwittingly finds himself caught up in the rapturous clamour of the religious processions:

> The crowd shoved forwards. The *paso* bore down on their awestruck faces, the Virgin towering above them, her whole body shuddering from right to left under the straining costaleros. Earsplitting, discordant trumpets suddenly blasted out the passion. The sound in the confines of the narrow street reverberated inside Falcón's chest and seemed to open it up. The crowd gasped at the glorious moment, at the weeping Virgin, at the height of ecstasy … and the blood drained rapidly from Falcón's head.

The key to the mystery lies in the aforementioned diaries and paintings of his famous father, many of which were painted in North Africa during the 1960s. Whether or not the novel strictly adheres to Andalucian police procedure, the adroit and delicate interweaving of past deeds with the macabre present does mirror the escalating passions of the participants in the processions. A fictionalised Seville becomes an essential point of reference, keeping the central protagonist rooted in a normality that he feels slipping from his grasp.

Like many a successful noir, the book attracted the attention of television executives. The resulting series, although evocative of location, has not managed to capture the emotional essence or portray the complexities of the novels. As a consequence, the programmes never gained the critical acclaim and popular appeal of series such as *Wallander* or *Il Commissario Montalbano*.

Indisputably, Semana Santa, with its swaying Virgins, confraternities, conical-hatted followers and pressing crowds, is a Sevillian institution. Before leaving the city, it would be remiss not to mention that other famous icon – the Royal Tobacco Factory, now part of the university. The building itself is worthy of mention. Commissioned by King Fernando VI, it was fundamentally a town in miniature and second only in size to the immense Escorial Palace near Madrid. There was even a barracks and underground waterways linking the complex to the Guadalquivir.

The entrance is a grandiose affair, with the statue of a winged female trumpeting her presence to those passing the porticoed façade. Leaving aside literary connotations, the resident workers of the factory, the *cigarreras*, already had a certain fame and notoriety in Seville, but it was thanks to a Frenchman, Prosper Mérimée, that their reputation spread to the wider world. Mérimée, of course, wrote 'Carmen', a short story that was turned into Bizet's even more famous opera. The image that both portray of jealous desires and love's ruination is not a stereotype that sits well with all Andalucians. Carmen and her Don José have been accused of caricature and melodrama.

Mérimée was much more of a Hispanist than Bizet yet, without the latter, it is distinctly possible that the story would have been nothing more than an interesting piece of early nineteenth-century literature. An archaeologist, linguist and translator, Prosper credited the tale to the gloriously titled María Manuela Enriqueta Kirkpatrick de Grivegnée, Countess of Montijo, the daughter of an expatriate Scottish businessman. Certainly the Countess cannot have been as wily as the Gypsy *cigarrera* Carmen, who entrapped the smitten José, persuading him to abandon his military post and lead an itinerant life. Bedazzled by the picador, Lucas, Carmen follows her new *amor* to the bullfight. A bitter José cannot accept his fate, killing Carmen before turning himself in to the authorities.

As can be intuited from the above, Carmen is the epitome of wild, untamed beauty. Mérimée provides us with this vision:

She was wearing a very short skirt, below which her white silk stockings – with more than one hole in them – and her dainty red morocco shoes, fastened with flame-coloured ribbons, were clearly seen. She had thrown her mantilla back, to show her shoulders, and a great bunch of acacia that was thrust into her chemise. She had another acacia blossom in the corner of her mouth, and she walked along, swaying her hips, like a filly from a Cordoba stud farm.

The reality of working in the tobacco factory was somewhat more prosaic. The women had to fight for decent working conditions as they ground, chopped and rolled the leaves of this South American plant. Unbelievably, estimates of the number of workers inside the complex during the early part of the 1800s are as high as 12,000. One perk of the job was chewing the tobacco, which did nothing for the workers' health or their teeth.

Another Frenchman, Théophile Gautier, whom we first met in the cathedral, comments on their habit of consuming the product: 'Some of them had got the end of a cigar boldly stuck in the corner of their mouth, with all the coolness of an officer of hussars, while some – O Muse, come to my assistance! – were chewing away like old sailors.' The one rule that was strictly enforced prevented the women from taking any of the product from the premises. Richard Ford implied that they found ways to smuggle it that would make a customs officer blush.

The modern denizens of what is now an academic institution are far removed from these descriptions. The students of today are studying for degrees in law, science and literature, an education undreamt of by the hardworking *cigarreras*. The undergraduates are reminded of the former occupants by paintings inside which depict the cigar makers, most notable of which is by Gonzalo Bilbao, whose images of these women also hang in the city's Museo de Bellas Artes.

Itálica

To the north-west of Seville, some ten kilometres (six and a half miles) from the centre, lies the town of Santiponce, home to the first Roman city outside Italy. It was founded by the legendary general, Scipio

2   Roman statue, Itálica

Africanus; the Roman historian, Appian, describes its foundation in the following terms: 'Scipio settled the wounded in a town which, in memory of Italy, he called Itálica.' It was also the birthplace of the emperors Trajan and Hadrian, who clearly remembered their roots. Traces of construction marked with their imperial nomenclature have been discovered, although neither was in a hurry to return: Hadrian, in particular, preferring Hispalis – Roman Seville.

The site is mainly of a rectilinear design, following the usual Roman grid pattern, interspersed with the footprints of houses varying in grandiosity and complexity. The most notable are the House of the Exedra, which encompassed a central pool, and the House of the Peacocks, including two fountains and the eponymous mosaics showing the birds in all their glory. It is worth strolling the extensive site as well-preserved tessellated flooring appears relatively unannounced in the small depressions that form the foundations of once-magnificent buildings.

Itálica underwent a comprehensive renovation just before the 1992 Expo in Seville. The beautifully presented amphitheatre gives an easily imagined impression of the gladiatorial combat that took place between man and beast, which some believe to be the forerunner to the modern bullfight. The only significant part missing from the structure is the upper ring of terracing that would have provided extra seating and the bolster to canopies shading the spectators from the blistering summer sun.

The site has not always been so well cared for. Richard Ford, in one of many excursions from Seville during his three-year stay, noted that the location was used as a quarry for local buildings and that, in the course of their excavations, the populace encountered a plethora of old Roman coins. Much against Ford's antiquarian propensities, the people from Santiponce were apt to 'polish them bright [...] They do their best to deprive antiquity of its charming old coat.' Ford had to push his way through the typical Mediterranean vegetation that still, to this day, colonises any unloved ruins, in order to find what he considered a 'sad and lonely' scene.

The last real occupiers of the site were the Moors, yet nobody really knows why they abandoned the location. Deviations in water flow have been posited as a plausible explanation. Ford's compatriot, Borrow, gives us a very evocative description of the amphitheatre when he decided to make the trek to Itálica from Seville in the 1830s:

> On all sides are to be seen the time-worn broken granite benches, from whence myriads of human beings once gazed down on the area below, where the gladiator shouted, and the lion and the leopard yelled: all around these flights of benches, are vaulted excavations, from whence the combatants, part human, part bestial, darted forth by their several doors. I spent many hours in this singular place, forcing my way through the wild fennel and brushwood.

Perhaps the most apocryphal story concerning the site and its famous emperors comes from the pen of Edmondo De Amicis, the Italian journalist whose waterborne description of Seville started this chapter. A former military officer from the Ligurian town of Oneglia, De Amicis made his name abroad through his travel writings and the novel *Heart (Cuore)*, a children's tale inspired by his two sons, Furio and Ugo – the latter of whom would tragically kill himself, making De Amicis's last years grief stricken and torturous.

In his description of Seville's Casa de Pilatos, a house constructed after the owner of the land had been on a pilgrimage to Jerusalem, De Amicis tells us the story of the urn supposedly containing Trajan's ashes. The garden of the palace was filled with remnants brought from Italy by Don Pedro Afan de Ribera, a former viceroy of Naples. De Ribera had placed the aforementioned urn in a privileged position in his garden. It seems that a rather clumsy gardener bumped into the sacred container and tipped the reluctant Trajan all over the soil and nobody was able to scoop him up in his entirety and return him to his resting place. As De Amicis says, 'Thus the august monarch, born at Italica, had returned, by a strange accident, to the neighbourhood of his native city, not quite in a condition to go and meditate upon its ruins, it is true.'

Écija

On the opposite side of Seville from Santiponce is the road that leads from the capital to Córdoba. It is now a fast-flowing motorway, but in 1829 it was one of the dusty roads that Washington Irving took on the way to his eventual destination of Granada. He travelled with a member of staff from the Russian Embassy, describing his companion as a fellow romantic with similar tastes. In his account of the journey in *Tales of the Alhambra*, Irving is keen to disabuse the reader of some of the common misconceptions about the Spanish landscape. He describes it as far from being a 'soft southern region, decked out with the luxuriant charms of voluptuous Italy' and forces home his point by mentioning the craggy mountains, endless plains and a terrain that was 'indescribably silent and lonesome'.

The highway mirroring Irving's journey through the east of Seville Province still reveals the vast somnolent agricultural plains laced with a touch of melancholy, yet the silence he found so remarkable is now a distant memory in our mechanised world. Apart from concerns over food and water, Washington's biggest preoccupation was with matters he euphemistically called 'the dangers of the road'. He sent his baggage on ahead with muleteers, carrying only enough with him for essential needs and to pay off any would-be assailants. The pair of travellers also employed a young man from the Basque country to act as guide, groom and guard. He carried a rifle and professed to be able to defend them from everything except groups of bandoleros (bandits) such as the 'Sons of Ecija'.

Fortunately for the travelling trio, they were not assailed by the infamous 'Sons', continuing their journey without significant problems. Despite the bandits, Écija was, and continues to be, a hospitable place. In a manner not dissimilar to other regions in the Mediterranean, Écija owes its baroque appearance to an earthquake which destroyed significant parts of the town in 1755. Needless to say, reconstruction took place in the dominant style of the period, leaving the town with a glorious collection of intricate colourful towers and palaces.

The town's noteworthy monuments ribbon out from the Plaza de España – known by the locals as 'El Salón', an appropriately homely name for a place to meet and chat with friends. Along the curved street, Calle Castellar, formerly known as Calle de los Caballeros, is the remarkable Palacio de los Marquéses de Peñaflor. In his *Wanderings*, first published in 1843, Théophile Gautier evokes the thoroughfare in his own enthusiastic style: 'you have some difficulty in believing that you are in a real street, between houses that are inhabited by ordinary human beings. Nothing is straight, neither the balconies, the railings, nor the friezes; everything is twisted and tortured all sorts of ways, and ornamented with a profusion of flowers and volutes.' The years have muted the colours, but the delicate curvature of the buildings and balconies gracefully deny some of Gautier's more painful allusions. He even compared some of the church spires to Sino-Japanese temples, feeling that their ornately sculptured appearance had more to do with Buddha than Christ.

If architecture preoccupied many travellers, it was the climate that dominated their complaints. Gautier felt that the area's reputation as one of the hottest places in Spain was more than merited. He compared Écija's situation in a gentle basin to that of a concentric mirror, its sandy slopes reflecting the vicious rays of the sun. Richard Ford passed through in a coach. Writing to his friend Addington, he called the journey 'very preposterous', describing 'the heat without intense, inside (six inside) infernal'. He referred to the town's nickname, commenting that it was 'another hell, and well deserves to be called La sartenilla (the frying-pan) de Andalucía'. Indeed, the best time to visit is spring or autumn.

The English poet Laurie Lee found himself in Écija in winter whilst retracing the walk he made through the peninsula in his youth before the Spanish Civil War. As we will see in the Cádiz chapter, his Spanish peregrinations led to three books, the last of which, in terms of narrative chronology, *A Rose for Winter*, was actually written during this trip in the mid-1950s and was published first. In this work, his impressions of Écija mirror much of Gautier's opinions, yet his poet's eye is not closed to the sometimes harsh realities of postwar provincial hardship. The December sun, still hotter than an English May, revealed a town in a state of decline but with an obviously resplendent past. He was soon ankle-deep in infant beggars whose chief pleasure, especially in summer, was whiling the day away by the river. The rural child in Lee was happy to join them.

Miguel de Cervantes would have encountered the same climate but a very different place. Prior to the earthquake, Écija would have had far more of its medieval heart intact. In the September of 1587, Cervantes was sent on a mission to buy up supplies of wheat from the town. He went equipped with a staff of justice and a hired mule but, as his biographer William Byron points out, the said purchases were to be made using promissory notes and no cash down. The task entailed collecting the Crown's quota of grain and fodder, signing any pertinent documentation and arranging for shipment. The reluctant Miguel also had the power to remove items forcibly and enter properties without the explicit permission of the owner.

Byron cites a town council meeting in the same month where mention was made of the royal wheat collector who was required to take everything, 'leaving only what is needed for food and planting'. One can only imagine the uproar at the meeting as the stark reality of Cervantes's task hit at the core of this farming community. Understandably, the townspeople were in no hurry to give their precious harvest to an indebted and capacious Crown. Miguel had the unenviable job of persuading them that his promises to pay were valid – in fact, he was passing notes for a debt that was probably never likely to be honoured and was undertaking an employment he was never fully compensated for. Once again, William Byron hits the nail on the head: 'The instructive nature of Cervantes' new occupation was affirmed in Écija, where he was introduced to a world of absurdity in which even a Quixote may have lost his bearings.'

3

HUELVA PROVINCE

Birds of Paradise

*The horizon glistened with the sheen of Flamingoes in thousands, and
the intervening space lay streaked and dotted with flights and flotillas of
aquatic fowl.*

(Walter J. Buck and Abel Chapman, *Wild Spain*, 1893)

Huelva

The inhabitants of Huelva are known as Onubenses, an adjective
that springs from the city's Phoenician origins. Drawn to the rich
mineral deposits, especially copper, they set up a trading post which
they named Onuba. By association with Christopher Columbus,
Huelva also takes the title 'La orilla de las tres carabelas' (The
shore of the three caravels). To be accurate, Columbus's three ships
actually sailed from La Rábida, 12 kilometres (seven miles) to the
south. The city is better known today for industry, specifically
petrochemicals, ore shipping and canneries.

This industrial heritage, together with the 1755 earthquake that
destroyed a large percentage of the historical centre, give Huelva
a functional and rather modern air. Near the sea and suspended
between the rivers Odiel and Tinto, it earned a reputation for trade
through its proximity to the second of these two rivers. The Río
Tinto (literally Stained River) is so called due to the dissolved ores
that tint the water a reddish brown. It would not have taken a

genius to discover that the waterway and surrounding countryside were rich in minerals.

We know the Phoenicians exploited this resource, closely followed and expanded on by the Romans. It was not until 1556 that the mines were rediscovered, yet it took nearly 200 years more for the Spanish to start excavating once again. Large-scale production only came about when itinerant British entrepreneurs in the nineteenth century realised the opportunity for massive exploitation of ores from this area. They set up the Rio Tinto Company which, for good or ill, was to have a considerable influence. Therefore, despite the mass tourism in other jurisdictions, this little-known province bears a bigger British imprint than just about any other in Andalucia.

One of the best documenters of the nefarious aspects of this impact is the writer Michael Jacobs, who set up home in the equally unfashionable province of Jaén, writing down his experiences in an autobiographical travelogue (*The Factory of Light*, 2004). Despite his name, Jacobs was born in Genoa to an Italian mother and an Anglo-Irish father. His education at the Courtauld Institute in London triggered his writing career as an author of art history guides for the layman. He found his real metier when he moved to Spain in 1988 in order to research a book on Andalucia.

The Spanish newspaper *ABC* in one review called him 'the George Borrow of the high-speed train era', which, although complimentary, does not really do him justice. Before his death in 2014 at the age of 61, he was a walking companion of Alpujarran adoptee Chris Stewart, and a friend of many Spanish writers. Lauded for his ability to capture the literary essence of both Spain and Latin America as well as the world beyond these ivory towers, the modest and ever-curious Jacobs managed to combine erudition with an eye for the quirky or gritty side of life in rural Andalucia. His book, *Between Hopes and Memories: A Spanish Journey*, lives up to such praise, particularly when talking about Huelva.

Jacobs introduces his segment on Rio Tinto by musing on the British presence in the region as a whole, specifically the aristocratic and merchant exchange in towns such as Jerez, concluding that this residual impact was never as strong as the engineering upheaval in Huelva. Jacobs compares the average English mining engineer to a member of the colonial service in India posted to a remote hill station. The job of these overseers was to organise the extraction of copper and sulphur through the employment of Spanish labourers. Sadly, it will come as no surprise to the twenty-first-century reader that the Onubenses were mercilessly exploited.

The British colony, as described by Jacobs, was eccentric and amusing but also rather shameful, especially when one reads that the locals were called 'natives' and the 'colonials' lived in separate guarded communities, one of which can still be seen in Huelva today. Located at the eastern end of the Alameda Sundheim and indicated by the positioning of a quintessential red telephone box, is the Barrio Reina Victoria. The streets are organised in a grid pattern, unimaginatively sporting the names Calle A, B, C and so on. When

3   *The Barrio Reina Victoria, Huelva*

they were constructed, there was no concession whatsoever to Spanish design, and when one enters the barrio, it is almost as if suburban Surrey has been parachuted into the 40-degree heat of an Andalucian summer.

The houses and bungalows are now owned by the 'natives' whom Rio Tinto so eagerly spurned, and they have had the good taste to try and brighten the mock-Tudor gable ends and picket fences with vibrant colours more fitting to the environment. The lawn ringed by a series of bungalows has now gone to seed, Huelvans being less interested in the cricket, croquet and cream teas that no doubt took place in these hallowed environs. One sport, however, handed down by the British incumbents, managed to bury its roots deeply into Iberian soil – football. Approaching central Huelva along the Avenida Andalucía, you will see the statue of a player caught in the act of kicking a ball, celebrating the city's role as the initiator of Spanish soccer. Although the city's football history runs deep, the local team has seldom matched its origins and currently languishes towards the foot of the second division.

Although maybe grateful for this new sport, the inhabitants had little else to thank the British for, apart from their initial employment. Jacobs cites the story of Henry Clay, who discovered a book in Mexico written by a former miner who had been forced into exile owing to his union activities. The Englishman Clay was shocked by his compatriots' treatment of the workers, whose fight for rights were often cruelly crushed in a manner analogous to the treatment of the indigenous peoples of Latin America. A similar British settlement known as Bella Vista, located in the actual village of Rio Tinto, used to refuse entry to the locals, whilst any Englishman who had the gall to marry a Spanish woman was summarily banished from the community. It was not until the 1920s that these strictures were lifted, with the proviso that the spouse become anglicised.

The history of mineral extraction is documented in the Museo de Huelva, which is also in the Alameda Sundheim, the thoroughfare that carves into the centre of town. The exhausted mines of Rio

Tinto bear further and more significant witness to the practices of extraction and the social order these created. Visitors to the Parque Minero de Riotinto, over an hour's drive distant from the city, can ride the mineral railway, explore an opencast dig, look round the museum and even see the lifestyle of the Victorian engineers by entering the bleakly titled House 21.

Back in the Alameda where the street joins the Avenida Martín Alonso Pinzón, the bar-lined avenue named after one of Columbus's captains, there stands a group of clamouring men in their rolled-up shirt sleeves struggling to support Nuestra Señora del Rocío, which rather lyrically translates as Our Lady of the Dew. This dark bronze sculpture celebrates the annual pilgrimage to the village of El Rocío on the edge of the Coto Doñana. Confraternities travel from Huelva, Seville, Cádiz and even further afield to their properties in the village, from where they present their own copies of the Virgin's statue, before the original icon makes its appearance.

El Rocío and the Coto Doñana

The pilgrimage to El Rocío is the region's biggest religious festival and an excuse for a colossal party. The settlement is located on the northern fringes of the Coto Doñana, the delta of the river Guadalquivir, a national park and nature reserve famed for its birdlife. In many ways, the village has grown just to service the annual celebration that takes place on Whitsunday, the seventh Sunday after Easter. It is a festival whose origins date back to the Muslim conquest in 711. Fearful of the new religion, Christians in the area removed their precious statues from the churches and buried them. When the people realised that they would be allowed to continue worshipping, many statues were retrieved, and those that were not, were uncovered in subsequent centuries.

It seems that the Virgin of El Rocío was discovered when a hunting dog came across the statue in the hollow of a tree, some

100 years after the Christians had retaken control. (Scholars think the wooden sculpture is a thirteenth-century image.) The owner of the dog took the statue back to his village. After drifting off to sleep during the siesta, he awoke to discover the icon missing. Returning to the tree, he found the image in its original location. When the hunter went back to his village, Almonte, he reported the story and persuaded a group of his fellow citizens to accompany him back to the hollow. They tried to rescue her once more, only to find that she preferred her original hiding place. The village priest interpreted this as her divine will, inferring that she should be worshipped in that very spot.

The Pulitzer Prize-winning James A. Michener visited El Rocío in the 1960s whilst researching his epic travelogue, *Iberia: Spanish Travels and Reflections*. The bestselling American, known for his meticulous research, had already encountered eight other stories of miraculous appearances of the Virgin, but it was this one that appealed to him the most. He was fortunate enough to meet John Culverwell, an Englishman resident in the area who was given the privilege of carrying his community's flag in the pilgrimage, and recounted his experiences to a fascinated Michener.

Culverwell describes a gathering of thousands with drums, guitars, carts, clapping and the impossibility of sleep. It seems that the order of the day was also to provoke other confraternities by stealing wine or by trying to kiss their rivals' girlfriends – fisticuffs were not uncommon, but usually prevented by the cry '¡Viva la Paloma Blanca!': the nickname of the Virgin – which evoked a degree of humility, the sharing of a drink and the shaking of hands. The only way to escape the constant hubbub was, and still is, to wander out into the surrounding marshland and sleep under a tree.

The real mayhem starts when the original icon is brought out and men clamour to have the honour of trying to lift her aloft, as depicted by the statue in Huelva. When the Virgin returns home on the Monday, the festival finally begins to wind down after a frenetic weekend. Michener was too early to see the finished hermitage that was constructed to house the image and inaugurated in 1969, although not completely finished until over a decade later. Its gleaming white façade has a rather faux-baroque appearance, with a scalloped arch sheltering the main entrance. Inside, the Virgin is housed in a shimmering golden altar, recalling the rococo excesses of a world once in thrall to the gold of the Indies.

The hermitage is fronted by a flat sandy plaza providing ample parking and the opportunity for horse and carriage rides. As you face the church, a glance to the right confirms how close the building is to the surrounding marshland. Pilgrims of a different kind come to El Rocío, using it as a base for worshipping the natural beauty of the Doñana.

The road south to Matalascañas passes the turning to the Acebuche Visitors' Centre which strictly controls access to the Coto. The hacienda-style centre offers the usual visitor attractions of shop and café, in addition to providing all-terrain-buggy tours to the heart of the reserve. Alternatively, there is a network of raised wooden walkways that snake into the surrounding countryside, punctuated at regular intervals by hides that overlook expanses of water that attract the migratory birdlife for which the national park is so well known. Needless to say, the intense summer temperatures dry both water and grassland to parched extremes; spring is the most appropriate time to visit.

The area has always been a favourite haunt for aristocrats keen on the hunt, and it derived its name from Doña Ana de Silva y Mendoza, a duchess of Medina Sidonia who lived in the palace built by her husband. The residence, often referred to as the Palacio de Doñana, is located a 40-minute walk, for those allowed to do so, from the Lagoon of Santa Olalla and a further two hours from the beach resort of Matalascañas – the only coastal development of significance within the confines of the Coto. In 1797, the palacio played host to the artist Francisco de Goya, who spent his time there creating his 'Álbum de Sanlúcar', a series of vignettes of everyday life and female portraits. Many say that this was also the scene of two other works, his *Maja Desnuda* (*The Nude Maja*) and *Maja Vestida* (*The Clothed Maja*) – the famous naked and clothed portraits of the same woman who, it is speculated, may have been Goya's hostess, the Duchess of Alba, although it is more likely to have been Pepita Tudó, the mistress of Prime Minister Manuel de Godoy.

At the southern end of the park, a few kilometres across the Guadalquivir from Sanlúcar de Barrameda, is the other building of significance, the Palacio de las Marismillas, which was a country estate also owned by the Medina Sidonia family. Guillermo Garvey of sherry fame purchased the whole wetland from the family in 1900 and decided to completely reconstruct this *finca* in a pseudo-English style. Today, it is often used by the Spanish prime minister as a summer escape and has played host to other political figures, including Helmut Kohl and Tony Blair.

In the late nineteenth century, the Coto became an area to hunt wild boar, which inevitably attracted northern Europeans and North Americans, who were not always completely obsessed with the killing of animals, but occasionally in their preservation. One such pair were the hunters-*cum*-naturalists Walter J. Buck and Abel Chapman. Buck had established himself in Jerez as an exporter of wines; Chapman had also found his way to the area as part of the wine trade. The English pair struck up a friendship based on their love of hunting, leading to early notions of conservation. They became the managers of a 64-kilometre-long (40-mile) segment of Doñana which they turned into a proto nature reserve. Their two books, *Wild Spain*, first published in 1893, and the subsequent *Undiscovered Spain*, brought the area to an international audience for the first time.

Despite the fact that they still clung to their hunting traditions, the two men's love of the wildlife shines through in this passage from *Wild Spain*:

> The spring-months abound in interest to the naturalist. Imagination can hardly picture, nor Nature provide, a region

more congenial to the tastes of wild aquatic birds than these huge *marismas*, with their silent stretches of marsh-land and savannahs, cane-brake and stagnant waters, and their profusion of plant and insect life. Here, in spring, in an ornithological Eden, one sees almost daily new bird-forms.

Of the two men, Buck became more embedded in the Anglo-Spanish aristocratic society of Jerez, whereas Chapman became the more recognised of the two as an early environmentalist. Yet both were willing to surmount the considerable difficulties involved in an expedition to the wetland via a craft resembling a punt. Sunstroke affected more than one of their local crew members.

Their ordeals were rewarded with the spectacle of flamingos 'in herds of 300 to 500, several of which are often in sight at once, they stand like regiments, feeding in the open water, all heads under, greedily tearing up the grasses and water-plants that grow beneath the surface'. At one point, they were confronted with the even stranger vision of two distant creatures that 'stood too high on their legs for deer, and had a much greater lateral width ... their contour, in fact, somewhat resembled a couple of long-stemmed, conical-topped, stone-pines, which are so characteristic of the adjoining woodlands'. The apparitions proved to be wild camels, let loose after an early nineteenth-century experiment in using them as pack animals. By the 1950s only eight remained; they have now died out.

Serious scientific expeditions to the Coto started in the 1950s. The naturalists ranged over the dunes, *marismas* (marshes) and the forests, covering all the habitats. One of the key figures on the treks was the field guide author Guy Mountfort, who was driven to visit the area after reading his predecessors' *Wild Spain*. Jorge Molina, in his 2011 history of the national park, *Doñana*, gives us an insight into those who made up the expedition parties in the 1950s. As well as Mountfort, there was Julian Huxley, brother of the writer Aldous, and previously the first director general of UNESCO. Added to this list of well-intentioned Britons was Max Nicholson, director of his country's Nature Conservancy Council. Recommended as a guide by Mauricio González-Gordon was a certain José Antonio Valverde, known to all as Tono, and later referred to as the 'Padre de Doñana'.

Mountfort wrote up his experiences in the travelogue, *Portrait of a Wilderness: The Story of the Coto Doñana Expeditions.* In the book, he praises Valverde for his extensive knowledge and tireless application. The Spaniard was an opponent of the then wide-ranging plan to dry out the marshes and use them for agriculture. Both Mountfort and Valverde knew the ecological disaster that this would entail. The pair were involved with the World Wildlife Fund for Nature, now the World-Wide Fund for Nature, and it was the intervention of international organisations like this, prompted by Valverde's campaigning, that helped halt development and resulted in the opening of the national park in 1969 under Tono's directorship.

There are still pressures, notably from the tourist hub of Matalascañas and disasters such as the 1998 pollution from toxic mining waste; however, it is thanks to these campaigning naturalists that the area still has rare species, the most endangered of which is the Iberian lynx. Around the edges of the protected zone, urban development and agricultural clearing encroach. Moving westwards towards Huelva, the amount of concrete increases. Past the tourist town of Mazagón the silence and serenity of the Coto are completely left behind, especially as the road skirts the Nuevo Puerto Industrial Park, beyond which the rivers Odiel and Tinto meet at La Rábida.

La Rábida and Palos de la Frontera

La Rábida has a place in the history books as the point from which Christopher Columbus set sail on the first of his voyages to what he thought would be the Far East and his ultimate destination of Cipangu, the name recorded by Marco Polo for Japan. As we now know, the American continent got in the way and Columbus triggered the colonisation of the Indies by the Spanish. Over the centuries, a whole ocean of print has been dedicated to the subject of Columbus; indeed, the admiral himself wrote up accounts of his travels which later found their way into book format.

One of the best late twentieth-century biographies of the explorer comes from the pen of the Anglo-Spanish academic, Felipe Fernández-Armesto. His 1992 text, simply entitled *Columbus*, starts with the interesting assertion that the sailor could be considered a crank from certain points of view. Fernández-Armesto lists Columbus's eccentricities, which include hearing celestial voices, occasionally dressing in chains or a monk's habit when appearing at court, and using cumbersome navigational aids. The historian notes that such behaviour often accompanies genius, yet it has had the detrimental effect of attracting wild theories about his life.

Fernández-Armesto considers the evidence for the explorer's Genoese birth to be 'rationally unchallengeable', although the more maverick have posited Jewish, Portuguese, Galician or even Majorcan origins. What is certain is that the stars of history aligned in 1492, when Columbus's search for patronage to support his idea for a short route to Asia finally bore fruit. Despite toting notions of new discovery, the Catholic Monarchs (the term for the joint rulers of Spain, Ferdinand II of Aragon and Isabella I of Castile) were more interested in the spices and gold of the Orient, which was the temptation that finally sold Columbus's plan.

He was not without support in his endeavours to find backing, especially in La Rábida, where the Franciscan monastery was key to his plans. The settlement by the Río Tinto is still a small collection of houses leading from the monastery, with the modern addition of a university campus. Lying opposite a small forest of umbrella pines, the monastery is a short walk from the Muelle de la Reina (Queen's Dock). It dates back to the thirteenth century, but the buildings visible today were built in the following two centuries and would have been well known to Columbus. He obtained the support of two important friars: the court astronomer, Fray Antonio de Marchena, and the Queen's confessor, Fray Juan Pérez.

It was the 1491 visit Coumbus made to the monastery that put him in touch with Martín Alonso Pinzón, the captain and shipowner who would sail with him. As Fernández-Armesto tells us, it was also to La Rábida that a disconsolate Columbus was heading, only to be overtaken by a messenger from court with the spectacular news that the Catholic Monarchs had agreed to his expedition.

The room in the monastery where the soon-to-be admiral used to converse with the monks has, appropriately enough, been renamed the Columbus Conference Room, and a small patio displays a collection of 1930s frescos by Daniel Vázquez Diaz detailing the voyages. The library holds the first ever map to show the coast of America. Outside the inner confines, the gardens are home to a column which was erected to commemorate the passing of 400 years since the first journey.

The Queen's Dock now hosts the Muelle de las Carabelas, the caravels in question being the replicas of the *Niña*, the *Pinta* and the *Santa María*, the three ships that set sail from La Rábida. Although the dock sports a somewhat kitsch reconstruction of a late fifteenth-century harbour, complete with wheels of plastic salted sardines, the ships themselves have undergone the same rigours as the originals, crossing the Atlantic for the quincentenary celebrations.

The visitor centre contains some original accoutrements from the period and a series of reproduction maps and documents. Apart from a small display of pre-Columbian art and the account of how Padre Bartolomé de las Casas came to write his denunciation of mistreatment of the indigenous peoples, there is little to tell the story of the devastating impact colonisation had on the original inhabitants of the Americas. There is more than a hint, however, of the cramped conditions and the leap of faith that these brave mariners must have taken in sailing uncharted waters. To set the scene, we turn to Washington Irving, who is never short of a romantic evocation of times past. In *The Life and Voyages of Christopher Columbus*, published in 1834, he gives us this image of trepidation felt by the locals involved in the project:

Nothing could equal the astonishment and horror of the community, when they learnt the nature of the expedition, in which they were ordered to engage. All the frightful tales and fables with which ignorance and superstition are prone to people obscure and distant regions were conjured up concerning the unknown parts of the deep, and the boldest seamen shrunk from such a wild and chimerical cruise into the wilderness of the ocean.

Nearby Palos de la Frontera supplied many of the sailors, by no means least of whom were the Pinzón brothers. The aforementioned Martín Alonso commanded the *Pinta* and Vicente Yañez Pinzón, the *Niña*. It seems that the captain of the *Pinta*, a seasoned navigator, found it difficult to take orders: Irving relates that Martín Alonso, 'having furnished two of the vessels, and part of the funds for the expedition, seemed to think himself entitled to as much authority and importance as the admiral'.

The Pinzón family are much venerated in Palos, where their home in the conflictingly named Calle Colón is now a museum (Columbus is known as Colón in Spanish). The street of low white houses leads to the Plaza Comandante Ramón Franco, where the oldest of the Pinzóns stands on a plinth, one foot on a rope, one hand around a cross and the other resting on the hilt of his sword. It is with these three items that the Spanish conquered the Americas, leaving a complex legacy of conflict, discovery and settlement.

Moguer

Ten kilometres (six and a half miles) from Palos, Moguer also supplied crew members for Columbus's voyages and was once a vibrant port, long since fallen into disuse. Many visitors come to the town in search of a favourite book from their childhood or to follow in the footsteps of its author, the poet and Nobel Laureate, Juan Ramón Jiménez. The book in question is his 1914 *Platero and I*

(*Platero y yo*), the story of a soft, silver-coloured donkey, a companion to the writer. Although the lyrical language of the book appeals greatly to the young, Jiménez stated that he never intended it to be a children's book, believing that children could read the same level of appropriate material as adults, something the precocious Jiménez had obviously done.

Platero and I is set in Moguer, and the local council have celebrated this fact by placing ceramic-tiled quotes from the volume on the walls of certain buildings. One of the most entertaining ways to spend an afternoon is to stroll its narrow streets, text in hand, searching for the plaques to give an immediate visual stimulus to the printed page. In so doing, you will inevitably find yourself in front of the Casa-Museo de Zenobia y Juan Ramón. This building in Calle Nueva, the street now re-baptised with the name of the poet, was the house in which Jiménez spent his adolescence. The Zenobia in question is Zenobia Camprubí, his wife and muse, but also a writer and translator in her own right. She lived much of her childhood in the United States and had connections with Puerto Rico.

Juan Ramón was the son of a wealthy wine merchant who, owing to his social status, would not have found it seemly to allow his son to play with the children from the local barrio. Consequently, the poet's childhood was full of bookish and solitary pursuits where he could find an outlet for his poetic imagination. Another writer who studied law but turned his back on the profession to follow his true vocation, Jiménez published his first works at the age of 18. This auspicious event was dwarfed by the death of his father, a personal tragedy that caused the nascent writer to fall into a tailspin of depression that led to spells in sanatoriums in Bordeaux and Madrid.

It was during this inauspicious period that he embarked on a series of casual affairs, including one with his doctor's wife. His poetry in *Libros de amor* (*Books of Love*) reflects a sexual awakening that documents these liaisons, including romps with the novitiates who attended him at the Madrid sanatorium. However, these verses should perhaps be treated with healthy suspicion as they may emanate from his febrile imagination. It was two years later, in 1914, that he returned to his hometown in the paragraphs of *Platero*.

The book starts with a dedication, and it would be as well to start any tour of Moguer in the spot it references, Calle del Sol. This street is no longer found on maps, having been renamed Calle Rábida, although occasionally the town subtitles its signs with the old nomenclature. Jiménez dedicated *Platero and I* 'To the memory of Aguedilla, the poor demented girl of del Sol Street who used to send me mulberries and carnations'. Calle Rábida leads directly to the central square, Plaza del Cabildo, which has the impressive façade of the eighteenth-century town hall.

However, your gaze is stolen by the far more humble bronze donkey standing on the cobbles, ears pricked forward, with half an eye on the statue of his master in the centre of the square. The seated figure of Jiménez was inaugurated in 1981 on the centenary of his birth. Today, a series of pavement-level fountain jets spring forth around the poet at regular intervals to relieve the heat of a Moguer summer. The pretty plaza is a meeting place for the locals to sit and chat or take an evening *paseo* (stroll).

Some of the streets radiating from the square are pedestrianised; one such is the Calle Reyes Católicos, which connects to the Plaza de Nuestra Señora de Montemayor, a spot once favoured by the local children for high-spirited ball games that would have caused the poet's mother to admonish the most noisy, as the family home was only a stone's throw away. The church that gives the square its name has a Mudéjar tower crowned in a similar manner to the Giralda of Seville, which 'from close up looks like Seville's from far away', as Jiménez once famously wrote. It remains a focal point and is immortalised in these beautiful lines from *Platero*: 'Night falls, hazy and purple. Vague green and mauve luminosities persist behind the tower of the church. The road ascends full of shadows, of bells, of the fragrance of grass, of songs, of weariness, of desire.'

The Zenobia and Juan Ramón Museum in the writer's old family home was once run by Juan Cobos Wilkins, an Anglo-Spanish

4 *The Plaza del Cabildo with statues of Platero and Juan Ramón
Jiménez, Moguer*

writer from Minas de Riotinto. The building was constructed
towards the end of the eighteenth century and is described as a
casa solariega, a noble residence of some antiquity. Its wrought-iron

balconied frontage stands out from the others in the long terrace that forms the street.

Inside, the open marble lobby is coloured by the stained-glass skylight that spreads its luminescence over the entrance and the upper floor. The museum, which holds the writer and his wife's library, together with many personal items including clothing, documents, keepsakes and his accomplished paintings, was inspired by Jiménez's receipt of the Nobel Prize. One of the most evocative rooms is the study furnished with the poet's desk, upon which sits the old-fashioned ribbon typewriter used to create his works.

Much of the furniture was brought back here from Madrid, having been removed from his house in the capital and placed for safekeeping in the Museo Romántico. The couple had to vacate their property quickly in order to escape the potential wrath of advancing Nationalist troops. Jiménez, like so many of his literary generation, was a supporter of the Republic. After spells in Cuba and the United States, the writer and his wife ended up in Zenobia's mother's island of Puerto Rico, never to return to Moguer in life.

Jiménez was hypersensitive and could be rather cantankerous, especially in relation to other writers. He had an ongoing antagonism towards the Chilean Pablo Neruda, who was his complete antithesis, although he did finally apologise to his rival. He was also plagued with a persecution complex and was not above ranting at his numerous doctors, using the most cutting sarcasm. His irascible personality meant he had to receive as many barbs as he issued, notably from the always-provocative Luis Buñuel and Salvador Dalí, who sent him a telegram describing Platero as 'the least donkey-like donkey, the most hateful donkey we have ever come across'; the missive ended with the word 'SHIT'.

Jiménez was of a former generation with a different artistic philosophy that was always going to irritate these surrealists from northern Spain. As Ian Gibson tells us in *Cuatro poetas en Guerra* (2007), the man from Moguer, still hurting years later, would refer to Dalí as 'the terrible little Catalan'. In his own way, Jiménez suffered the shyness and pain in dealing with the real world that Dalí masked with his overblown personality and eccentricities. It was Zenobia who managed to anchor him, and losing her to ovarian cancer two days after receiving the Nobel Prize was the ultimate blow. He struggled on for another two years before also dying in Puerto Rico. His nephew managed to repatriate the couple in death to be buried in Moguer's de Jesús cemetery. The man who carried a stone from the town in his pocket had finally made it home.

4

CÁDIZ PROVINCE

Carnival, Parties and Politics

*There is a public walk or alameda on the northern ramparts which
is generally thronged in summer evenings: the green of its trees, when
viewed from the bay, affords an agreeable relief to the eye, dazzled with
the glare of the white buildings, for Cadiz is also a bright city.*
(George Borrow, *The Bible in Spain*, 1843)

Cádiz

Cádiz is almost an island linked to the rest of Spain by a sandy strip
which meets the mainland at San Fernando. The only other means
of connecting to the interior is via a road bridge, recently joined by a
second construction of twenty-first-century design. The city and its
hinterland form a superb natural harbour and it was inevitable that
nature should demand its use as a port. In fact, so perfect has the geography been that Cádiz is Spain's oldest continuously inhabited city.

Gadir to the Phoenicians who founded the settlement, the city
shifted name, becoming Gades to the Romans and Qādis to the
Arabs, from which derives the Spanish pronunciation. To an Anglo-
Saxon mind, it conjures one obvious connotation drummed into
adolescent ears during school history lessons – the sack of Cádiz
by Sir Francis Drake, *el gran pirata* to the Spanish. The odour of
Philip II's burning facial hair still lingers in the modern era for
those with no first-hand knowledge of the city.

One Englishman, Laurie Lee, briefly mentioned in Écija, who did know Spain and the city more intimately, now deserves a fuller introduction. Lee found particularly fertile ground for his work in Andalucia. Born in the English county of Gloucestershire in 1914, he had a rural childhood epitomised in the autobiographical work *Cider with Rosie*. Already keen to explore life outside his pastoral milieu, Lee admitted he was prompted to choose Spain as his destination by a friendship with a sultry, glamorous expat girl from Buenos Aires who taught him a few words of Spanish. This twist of fate led him to strike out for Spain, on foot, in the summer of 1935.

His eventual destination was Almuñécar on the Costa Tropical – the location with which he would become most associated. On the way, he visited much of Spain, which later in his life would produce the text for three books: *As I Walked Out One Midsummer Morning*, *A Moment of War* and *A Rose for Winter*. They detail his involvement in Spanish matters, with the middle of the three being the pivotal point of the Spanish Civil War although, as already mentioned, the last was written first. Some critics have questioned the veracity of his accounts, particularly the timelines.

Whatever the truth and the tricks that time plays on memory, it is undeniable that Lee's prose, reflecting his other vocation as a poet, is very rarely bettered by his fellow countrymen. This fine example evokes his first glimpse of Cádiz: the location, 'from a distance, was a city of sharp incandescence, a scribble of white on a sheet of blue glass, lying curved on the bay like a scimitar and sparkling with African light'. Once inside the labyrinth of streets, Lee's tone darkens as he compares the dwellings to a 'Levantine ghetto' enveloped by the sea. He took up residence in a guesthouse he called an 'evil old posada' – an abode full of the Spanish picaresque, the kind of ne'er-do-wells Cervantes would have recognised: mariners, mendicants and hustlers.

Lee joined the colourful throng trying to prise a few coins from those with disposable income. He took to the streets, playing his violin, but was warned off by the local police, who informed him such activity was illegal if the intention was to earn money. This did not stop him enlisting the help of a blind brother and sister who accompanied him on drums. He met many people with disabilities, struggling to survive, creating ingenuity born of desperation. One story, which may be apocryphal, concerns a ghostly figure who haunted a tenement roof near to the neo-classical cathedral. It seems he was very much of flesh and blood but his howling ghostly antics were intended to so terrify his landlord that the rent would be reduced.

It is clear from Lee's descriptions that Cádiz was not experiencing its most prosperous times. Some of the areas described in *As I Walked Out One Midsummer Morning* have now been gentrified, and even the outer-lying tenement blocks have recovered slightly from their deep issues with drugs in the 1980s. The centre of the city has recaptured much of its old splendour but that is not to say that Cádiz is free from its long-standing socio-economic problems. The unemployment rate, at the time of writing, is one of the highest in Europe.

The city's glory days were firmly rooted in its past as a trade hub for the Indies, replacing Seville with its silted river, and as the location for Europe's first liberal constitution set up by the Cádiz Cortes in 1812. The constitution sounds remarkably modern, attempting to enshrine a constitutional monarchy with a free press, equitable land distribution, free trade and universal male suffrage, although votes for females appear to have been a step too far.

Unsurprisingly, the Cortes has provided the canvas for writers to paint their own impressions. Two notable Spanish men of letters have taken this opportunity to create narratives around the momentous event – Arturo Pérez-Reverte and Benito Pérez Galdós. Just over a century separates these two very different authors.

Pérez-Reverte is a character who often divides opinion in Spain, some seeing his personality as deliberately brusque and his pronouncements provocative. He was born in 1951 and made his name as a war correspondent. Many have pigeon-holed him as a writer of historical fiction, or a latter-day Alexandre Dumas, chiefly through his series of works based around the fictional seventeenth-century Captain Alatriste.

For a long time, he went untranslated in English, possibly owing to his own reluctance to see his works translated into anything other than French. His historical novels were the first to appear in English, notably *The Fencing Master* (*El maestro de esgrima*) in 1998, soon to be followed by more of his material, including books dealing with modern issues, such as drug-smuggling across the Straits of Gibraltar in *The Queen of the South* (*La Reina del Sur*). His work focusing on Cádiz in 1812 is *The Siege* (*El asedio*). Winner of the 2014 CWA International Dagger Award, the book pitches us into the desperate defence of the city as the inhabitants and their English allies confront the besieging Napoleonic troops, who start their attack by hurling projectiles from their ships anchored in the bay.

There is a pretence of normality as the citizens – the *gaditanos* – claustrophobically huddle in their encircled town, denying the fact that a cannon round could kill them at any moment. If this were not sufficient danger, Pérez-Reverte spices the mix with the added complication of a serial killer. The political ferment in 1811, leading to the establishment of the constitution, opened up the freedom of the press, a freedom that is amply demonstrated in the book during a discussion between the police commissioner, Tizon, and an agitated town governor who fears that these new liberties will mean that journalists could divulge the existence of the psychotic murderer stalking the streets.

Every level of society is represented, from tavern dwellers to the upper echelons; each central character imbued with a particular agenda and nuance of temperament. The city is yet another personality atypically turning inwards from a sea it has embraced for centuries, although the waves remain a constant presence:

> Less than two hundred paces away the unfinished cupola and half-built spires of the new cathedral, still ringed with scaffolding,

are framed against the skyline, the expanse of sea, the sandbar, white and shimmering in the sunlight, that extends beyond the reef, curving towards Sancti Petri and the heights of Chiclana like a dyke whose banks are about to be burst by the deep blue of the Atlantic.

Pérez-Reverte's canvas is, indeed, a broad one; readers are not only given a murder to solve, but are also taken on a journey through the war of Spanish Independence, in a suffocating city under threat, toying with liberal ideas for a better future.

If the creator of Captain Alatriste is another Dumas, then by way of connection, Benito Pérez Galdós could be considered a Dickens, or for that matter, Dickens could be a Galdós. In fact, Galdós was Charles Dickens's Spanish translator and one of the nineteenth-century Hispanic world's most respected authors. Like Pérez-Reverte today, he was a member of the Royal Spanish Academy of Letters; a prolific writer, his best-known work throughout the world is the monumental *Fortunata and Jacinta*, which follows four characters throughout their lifetimes.

Although not an Andaluz – he was born in the Canary Islands – Galdós set several works in the region. One of his major projects was to chart, in fiction, some of the most significant events in Spanish history. These 'National Episodes' ('Episodios Nacionales') constitute 46 novels, divided into five series, written in the relatively short period of 40 years, from 1872. The first book deals with the Battle of Trafalgar, and included in the first series is also the text entitled *Cádiz*.

Undeniably a political figure, Galdós would have been naturally drawn to the events surrounding the Cortes. In his lecture 'Galdós and 1812', Stephen G. H. Roberts of the University of Nottingham acknowledges, along with the above book, another Galdosian reference to these political ramifications. In 1865, Galdós wrote a piece for *La Nación* newspaper in Madrid giving voice to his opinions and lamenting 'the sad and so different situation today'.

He was fervent in his respect for what had been achieved in Cádiz, so prodigiously epitomised by the marble-white monument in the Plaza España. As quoted by Roberts, the writer felt that the Constitution was the wisest and most venerable of political codes.

The boy who appears in Galdós's novel *Trafalgar*, Gabriel de Araceli, becomes the narrator and protagonist at the heart of *Cádiz*. Galdós built on the personal opinions he had expressed in the *Nación* article and, similar to Pérez Reverte, set the entire book in the city between 1810 and 1812 during the siege. De Araceli has fallen in love with Inés, who is kept under the thumb of the conservative Countess de Rumblar and her priestly advisers. The anti-clerical Galdós is clearly depicting the forces lining up against the liberalism in which he believed. Into this stew of war and oppression lands an English milord who cuts a swathe through the city, picking up admiring glances from noble women left and right. Given Britain's status as ally in the fight against Napoleon, Gabriel and this Lord Gray become embroiled in moves to halt the French. The Oratorio de San Felipe Neri makes an appearance in the novel, being the location for parliamentary meetings during that period. Today, the pastel building in the square of the same name is encrusted with plaques and escutcheons commemorating its moment in the sun.

De Araceli's life also crosses amatory paths with Lord Gray as he mistakenly believes that Inés has designs on the rakish Englishman. If Gray is beginning to sound familiar – dashing, an adventurer, an ambivalent, hedonistic outsider – it is because he is, in essence, Byronic; perhaps even Galdós's interpretation of Lord Byron himself. However, Galdós informs us that Gray arrived with the English poet some six months before the narrator picks up his story. Roberts, in his piece on the novel, believes the aristocrat is looking for a mythical Spain, not the country that is trying to forge a radical political future. This is an accurate depiction of Gray's lust for sentiment over clear thinking, especially when he calls the Cortes a *canalla* – a rabble.

To be fair to Gray, we also find out that he hates English hypocrisy – a freedom-loving nation that trades in slaves. In this respect, he is more akin to the real Byron, who was well portrayed by Emilio Castelar in his biography of the poet written in 1873. Castelar was born in the city, spending his life as a novelist, journalist and political activist. In fact, he went on to become the fourth president of the Spanish Republic. It is apparent that Byron cast a shadow over Cádiz, despite only spending a few days in the city.

From Seville, Byron reached Cádiz in the August of 1809. It seems that the city soon replaced the Andalucian capital in his affections; writing to his mother, he describes his first impressions: 'Cadiz, sweet Cadiz! is the most delightful town I ever beheld, very different from our English cities in every respect except cleanliness (and it is as clean as London) but still beautiful and full of the finest women in Spain, the Cadiz belles being the Lancashire witches of their land.'

It is a cliché to say that wherever Byron went, a certain loose morality followed but, in truth, his first Grand Tour was doubtless a foray into the sybaritic experience he craved. He was happy to accept invitations from the local grandees, including Admiral Cordova whom he accompanied to the opera. He was much taken with Cordova's daughter and her ilk. Comparing their charms to English women, he declared them to be by 'no means inferior' and, as mentioned above, possessing a fire that was lacking in his 'drowsy listless' female compatriots. The misogynistic tones of his insight reflect his era and personality – a vision he compounds further by describing the local marital behaviour:

I beg leave to observe that Intrigue here is the business of life, when a woman marries she throws off all constraint, but I believe their conduct is chaste enough before. – If you make a proposal which in England would bring a box on the ear from the meekest of virgins, to a Spanish girl, she thanks you for the honour you intend her, and replies 'wait till I am married, & I shall be too happy.'

Byron assures us this is 'literally & strictly true', but his *gaditano* biographer, Castelar, in an otherwise favourable portrait of the poet, took exception to Byron's assertions. He questioned why George Gordon had been able to understand the qualities of the Spanish male, but had misunderstood the virtues of the Spanish female. He attributed this one-sided view to the brevity and superficiality of his visit. Yet there is enough in Byron's writing to suggest his experiences were more than second-hand gossip. He remembered Cádiz in the first canto of *Childe Harold*, written shortly afterwards, his youthful enthusiasm shining through:

> But Cadiz, rising on the distant coast,
> Calls forth a sweeter, though ignoble praise.
> Ah, Vice! how soft are thy voluptuous ways!
> While boyish blood is mantling, who can 'scape
> The fascination of thy magic gaze?

The opera house our poet visited, with its boxes resembling those he knew from English theatre, 'large and finely decorated', was probably the Teatro Principal in the Plaza Palillero. It was one of Spain's finest in its day but was pulled down in 1929. On the derelict site a cinema was constructed, which now sits next to the town hall's Cultural Centre. Today's theatre occupies the Plaza Fragela and is named after the composer Manuel de Falla, born in the city in 1876. He was one of twentieth-century Spain's most important composers and a good friend of the poet Federico García Lorca.

The Gran Teatro Falla is constructed in faux-Mudéjar style, with pink and cream Moorish arched doorways that lead into the atrium. Stairways spiral up to the tiered galleries that form a U-shape around the stage. The ceiling is painted with a romantic vision of Paradise completed by the artist Felipe Abarzuza y Rodríguez de Arias. The Falla hosts a variety of concerts and plays, including the contests of the *chirigotas* singers during the famous Cádiz carnival.

The *chirigotas* are groups, dressed in costume, who perform satirical songs on the topics of the day.

One writer who took inspiration from the carnival was Fernando Quiñones. Quiñones was from nearby Chiclana de la Frontera but is most associated with Cádiz, having spent his adolescence and much of his adult life there. His successful literary career started at the magazine *El Parnaso*. Travel and journalism followed, allowing him to dedicate his life to literature completely in the early 1970s. The recent anthology *Relatos de Don Carnal: 12 historias de carnival* (*Stories of Don Carnal: 12 Stories of Carnival*) includes a piece by Quiñones. The text is a fragment from his last and unpublished novel, *Los ojos del tiempo*, rendered into English as *The Eyes of Time*, or perhaps, less prosaically, *The Weather Eye*. It concerns Nono, an illiterate self-obsessed madman who inhabits La Caleta Beach. From the age of 14, Nono has had visions that recreate history, so he

5 *The Paseo Fernando Quiñones bordering La Caleta Beach, Cádiz*

literally sees events as they unfold. When the sand from the beach blinds him, Nono slips into one of his yesterdays. The encounter Quiñones recounts in *Don Carnal*, via a journalist who takes an interest in Nono, is between a younger version of this hare-brained mystic and a group of masked carnival revellers, particularly a grande dame in her fifties. It seems the lady in question took a 'carnal' shine to the rough and ready younger man and had her wicked way with him right there on the beach – the same beach along which Quiñones would take his daily walk.

Another contributor to the above book is the journalist, author and native of the city, Alejandro Luque. Luque, born in 1974, started his career with a literary review and the local paper. He now writes for *El Correo de Andalucía* based in Seville. In his biography of Quiñones, he focused on one of the more interesting aspects of Quiñones's life – his friendship with the Argentinian, Jorge Luis Borges. In the book *Palabras mayores: Borges–Quiñones, 25 años de amistad*, Luque details the 25 years the pair of authors spent in friendly communication. Quiñones was one of the first in Andalucia to discover and promote the genius of Borges after leafing through a book of his he found on a street stall in the city.

Quiñones is most well known for his love of flamenco, notably recounted in the work he dedicated to Cádiz's style of singing – *De Cádiz y sus cantes* (*Cádiz and its Songs*). He also contributed a wonderful introduction to José Luis Ortiz Nuevo's text on Pericón, a revered *gaditano* flamenco artist. The work, entitled *A Thousand and One Stories of Pericón de Cádiz*, reflects the singer's capacity for storytelling. Quiñones's overview recalls the man and his own burgeoning interest in the genre:

In that Cádiz of the early 40s – shining but ailing, shivering in the destitute post-war sun – Pericón, still young, but with a touch of grey at his temples and with a ducal or cardinal air, always went well-dressed and clean shaven against the elements. He paused in an almost ritual manner, but without abandoning the *ángel*, which accompanied him always, and thus impressed my childish imagination. He was a boulder, a first and legendary guidepost to a world of the popular art of Andalucía that was awakening in me a sensibility, still waiting to gel, but already intuited and loved to some degree.

As Quiñones tells us, Pericón knew that opera and flamenco were not as different as many supposed, the key variance being the pitch of the voice – opera going up and flamenco, appropriately enough in its role as the Andalucian Blues, heading downwards. Fernando extends this concept to the disparity in social class between the two genres and the latter's picaresque elements.

Cádiz remembers one of its favourite sons with a statue and a walkway out into the bay of La Caleta – the Paseo Fernando Quiñones. He was also a habitué of several cafés in the town, notably the literary venue of the Café de Levante, in Calle Rosario. The café's website, true to its roots, dedicates a section to poetry written in homage to the locale. Quiñones's offering compares the Levante to a gathering of ships from days past whose sails guard their memory.

Alejandro Luque's poem, 'Los que quedamos' ('Those of Us Left Behind') captures the bohemian spirit of the café, with its walls clad in photos and posters, and its dark furniture down-lit in yellow light:

> What secret route drives us
> through the nocturnal hustle, to this Café
> de Levante, when the hands
> turn against the clock,
> and the phones are seized
> by bad news.
> – I'll get the next one. Do you want to go?
> Those of us left behind, the urban restless,
> drink petrol from the puddles
> we've lost every battle
> and there's nothing we can do

> when the refuse cart
> takes away our soul.
> You know what? I know your face ...

It is a place where the writer Gerald Howson would have felt at home. He is one of the best foreign documenters of the Cádiz flamenco scene. In his book *The Flamencos of Cadiz Bay*, Howson admits he was drawn to the city in order to learn the flamenco guitar. His 'cover' was as an English teacher – a rarer status in the 1960s when the book was written than in the Spain of today, now dotted with private language schools. His search started in the Galician city of Vigo, a place that he acknowledges had less flamenco than London – but he had arrived. Fortunately, Howson secured a transfer to the Andalucian coast and his desired *gaditano* location. Arriving by train, his spirit lifts and he describes the city as 'a string of domes and towers floating on the skyline of the sea'.

After settling in and making the acquaintances of his fellow employees, Howson finally found himself a guitar teacher who happened to live near to the birthplace of Manuel de Falla. Sadly, the man did not turn out to be the guru Howson wanted, but it was his introduction to the world he sought. Howson admits that the surrounding arches, fountains and scents are a cliché, especially when joined by the sound of a guitar, but they can still be genuine, even if accompanied by the untrained hands of an artisan guitarist. In fact, he feels that some of the more accomplished professionals living in northern cities lack the intrinsic 'very flamenco' ability. Perhaps this is the infamous *duende* spirit that so concerned the poet Lorca. *Duende* almost defies definition. Traditionally a sprite or goblin, it is now a concept closely associated with the otherwordly power that takes over a flamenco performer.

After two years of practice, Howson's first encounter with a flamenco great was a meeting with Aurelio Sellés Nomdedeu, otherwise known as Aurelio de Cádiz. Howson eventually tracked him down in the Bar Europeo facing the Plaza San Juan de Díos.

Moving to the Arco de la Rosa and a bar next to the eponymous arch by the cathedral square, Howson finally got to play for the great man. The inevitable nerves settled enough for him to acquit himself respectably, although it was clear he had much to learn. His words echo his fears: 'Any amateur who has suddenly found himself in the midst of professionals will recall, I imagine with horror, the sensation. Aurelio's ear was accustomed to the support, as a matter of daily business, of the greatest guitarists of Spain.'

Howson felt the need to change some names in the text of his account in order to protect identities during the Franco dictatorship, but the reissued 1994 edition reveals some individuals behind the pseudonyms. This updated version also notes the changes in the flamenco tradition since the 1960s. Perhaps the most important aspect of the book for an English-speaking reader is its ability to capture a unique moment in time and an era that, although past, haunts the present. These characteristics have been most responsible for the critical acclaim that his book received, especially from the famous travel writer and journalist Jan Morris.

One facet of the *gaditano* music scene has been the so-called *canciones de ida y vuelta*, those songs with a return ticket to the Americas. Indeed, they reflect Cádiz's long-lasting connection with the Latin American world. This link has also extended to literature. The Alameda de Apodaca, along the northernmost seafront of Cádiz, contains busts of the Cuban writer José Martí and the Nicaraguan Rubén Darío. The local poet Eduardo de Ory, whose former house fronts the Alameda, exemplified that relationship. He acted as the consul for Costa Rica and Nicaragua, also founding three magazines, in particular *España y América*, which naturally referred to the Hispano-American link. It is very easy for the Anglo-Saxon world to forget that Costa Ricans, Ecuadoreans or Argentinians are also Americans.

The pages of de Ory's literary journals were full of collaboration with poetic voices from the Americas. He was also instrumental in the creation of the city's Academia Hispanoamericana. As a poet, he was a modernist, moving away from the previous tendency towards Realism. Amongst other things, modernists of the late nineteenth and early twentieth centuries were characterised by their inclination for escapism and a rejection of bourgeois society – something which can be seen in de Ory's poem 'Bohemia':

> Love! The cup full
> With wine, so that sorrow
> Turns to joy.
> Pleasure! Red lips
> Kisses in the eyes …
> Laughter and enjoyment!
>
> Artists and grisettes,
> Painters and poets:
> Let's raise up to love
> A tune full of mirth …
> Songs and smiles
> From lips made flowers.

One of de Ory's greatest influences was the aforementioned Rubén Darío, a key figure in Modernism. When the maestro's boat anchored in Cádiz harbour, de Ory was desperate to have an audience with the Nicaraguan. By this time a prodigious drinker, Darío was in no condition to receive an acolyte and remained somewhat hungover in his cabin.

Like the greats of flamenco, de Ory passed the poetic gene to his son, Carlos Edmundo. A poet of an altogether different stripe, the son reflected the avant-garde, creating the movement known as Postismo (Postism) – a poetry full of intricate language play. It is unsurprising that Carlos found himself on the receiving end of Fascist censorship. Some critics find his role in Spanish letters to be analogous with that of the Beat poets in the United States. Indeed, Allen Ginsburg dedicated one of his poems to him.

These movements are a far cry from the traditionalist works of Cecilia Francisca Josefa Böhl de Faber. A quick perusal of any text documenting the history of Spanish literature would be unlikely to contain a reference to this writer as she assumed a male pseudonym, taken in its entirety from the municipality of Fernán Caballero, in the quiet backwaters of Castile-La Mancha. In fact, as her real name suggests, Böhl de Faber was born in Morges, Switzerland, to a German father and an Andalucian mother who hailed from Cádiz. Cecilia's childhood was chiefly spent in Germany, but at the age of 17 she returned to the city by the bay, where her parents were already well known in literary circles.

Her father, Johann Nikolaus (Juan Nicolás to the locals) was a respected Hispanist who, aside from carrying out business and consular duties, maintained a significant library. He was a devotee of the Schlegel brothers and the Golden Age playwright Calderón de la Barca. His tastes were conservative and he supported a traditionalist Spanish nationalism. In such a milieu, Cecilia took up similar bookish pursuits. Her writing, very centred on local custom and tradition, was originally intended for the eyes of a select few.

Her first marriage ended abruptly with the death of her infantry captain husband in Puerto Rico. Back in Puerto de Santa María near Cádiz, she met and married the Marquis of Arco Hermoso. It was during this time that she made the acquaintance of Washington Irving on his first trip to Spain. His diary on New Year's Eve 1828 records the following: 'Call this morning [...] on the Marchioness of Arco Hermoso, make a long visit, the Marchioness relates many village anecdotes of the village of Dos Hermanas. Return home & make a note of two of them.'

Dos Hermanas was an estate belonging to Cecilia's husband. It is now a satellite town, some 14 kilometres (nine miles) from Seville. E. Herman Hespelt and Stanley T. Williams, in their article on Irving's notes relating to Cecilia, are sure that her intimate knowledge of local manners and patterns of behaviour enriched Irving's works, introducing him to the *costumbrista* style we can see in his *Tales of the Alhambra*. It would seem that, as early as the 1820s, Cecilia was regaling her family and friends with stories gleaned from the local inhabitants.

Outliving the Marquis and a third husband, there came a time during and after her last marriage when financial difficulties dictated the need to find a larger audience for her works. With the help of friends such as the dramatist Juan Eugenio Hartzenbusch, her stories were published and Fernán Caballero was born.

Her most well-known story, *The Seagull* (*La gaviota*) was actually written in French and translated by José Joaquín de Mora. It tells of a German military surgeon lost in the Andalucian countryside. Cursed with an infection, he makes his way to the village of Villamar. Here, he falls in love with the daughter of a fisherman and is taken into the hearts of the villagers, who greatly appreciate his medical skills. Marriage to the eponymous *gaviota* soon follows but she is not the faithful wife he was expecting. In the big cities of Seville and Madrid, her head is turned by the matador Pepe Vara. The world around her disintegrates as the deceived German flees, losing his life to a fever in Havana. Pepe also meets his end in the bullring, leaving our seagull to fly back home to her father.

Caballero has been criticised for a lack of depth in her work, especially those shorter stories told with a comic touch. The charge of stereotyping is also one that hovers in the background, but the works' true worth lies in the author's ability to capture the real nature of village and country life. Few would put her in the same league as the verist from Sicily, Giovanni Verga, but she did document nineteenth-century Andalucia in such a way that it prompted multiple translations and somewhat lofty comparisons to Walter Scott.

In *The Last Consolation*, one of her more serious pieces, Caballero returned to the Cádiz of her youth, capturing the magnificent location of the city jutting out into the sea, and its marsh hinterland:

A narrow estuary runs up between it and the strong *presidio*, or fort of Trocadero, up to the small port of Puerto Real. The northern shore of the isthmus consists of salt-marshes which are intersected by numerous dykes and trenches, which let the sea overflow it at high water. It forms a soft muddy surface, called *albinas* and *rabizas*, on which large quantities of sea-salt are collected on the ebbing of the tide, and are formed into high pyramids of a dazzling white, which are most striking and picturesque.

Picturesque they may have been, but life on these shores was far from easy. The story focuses on the aged couple Antonio and Maria Parra, whose wayward son ends up in the *presidio* after a knife-fight with his cousin's betrothed. The son, Bernardo, decides to escape on the very night that, unbeknownst to him, he was to be released. In the middle of the *albinas*, the fleeing prisoner sinks to his death in the marshy land.

The Trocadero district and its island still exist, forming the upright of the inverted T of Cádiz bay. Across the sweep of water from the Isla del Trocadero is the town of San Fernando.

San Fernando

San Fernando is popularly known as La Isla, although it is no longer an island and is now connected to the mainland by development. Like Cádiz, the town had a key role in resisting the Napoleonic French. The liberal parliament at the core of Cádiz's fame also met in San Fernando, specifically at the Comedy Theatre, now known as the Real Teatro de las Cortes in honour of its illustrious past.

The location is rather flat, giving free rein to some fierce winds from the sea. Two beaches of very distinct natures characterise the town. The first, the Playa de Camposoto, faces the Atlantic to the south of the district, its pale virgin sands receiving the tides from the Americas. The other beach, the Playa de la Casería, faces inland towards the bay, with homespun muddy shores. Throughout its history, San Fernando has had links to both the sea and the neighbouring settlements that ring the bay of Cádiz.

Mention the town to any Andalucian, and one of the instant connections will be to the flamenco singer known as Camarón de la Isla (the Shrimp of the Island). Christened José Monje Cruz, but soon universally recognised as the 'Shrimp' owing to his fair complexion, slim build and light hair, Camarón soon graduated from singing in the town's inns to a residency in one of Madrid's famous *tablaos* or flamenco venues. Sadly, his life was a short one, ending at the age of 41 from lung cancer caused by his prodigious nicotine habit and exacerbated by heavy drug use. He was widely mourned and the Spanish daily newspaper *El País* commented, 'Camarón revolutionised flamenco from a state of absolute purity.'

From a literary perspective, San Fernando was the adopted home of Luis Berenguer. The town has honoured his memory by renaming the municipal library in Calle Real the Biblioteca Pública Municipal Luis Berenguer. Originally from Franco's hometown of Ferrol in the Celtic north of Galicia, Berenguer moved to the Andalucian town because of his career as a navy engineer. He rose to be a frigate captain whilst continuing to follow his literary life. Perhaps owing to his time-consuming occupation, he was somewhat late in publishing his first work, which did not appear until 1966, when he was 43. *El mundo de Juan Lobón* (*The World of Juan Lobón*) was a success and Berenguer was a finalist for the prestigious Alfaguara Literary Prize.

The book centres on the life of Juan Lobón, a poacher in the area of the Almoraima, an estate of 15,000 hectares (37,000 acres) situated 120 kilometres (75 miles) east of Cádiz, around Castellar de la Frontera. In fact, Berenguer based his tale on a character he knew in Alcalá de los Gazules, almost equidistant between Castellar and San Fernando. The text captures a world on the point of disappearing, as Lobón and the owners of the land in question fight for control in a post-Civil War world.

The novel was serialised on Spanish television in the late 1980s. Despite this media popularity and his other novels obtaining prizes,

Berenguer is something of a forgotten author in Spain. In 1998, the University of Cádiz produced a text, *La narrativa de Luis Berenguer* (*The Fiction of Luis Berenguer*) in order to return him to the literary stage. San Fernando has even created a prize in his honour. His house is also in Calle Real, an elegant façade of greyish-blue punctuated with arched windows underlined by wrought-iron balconies. A plaque recognises the location and its respected inhabitant.

El Puerto de Santa María

Mirroring the position of San Fernando on the northern side of Cádiz is the town of Puerto de Santa María, commonly shortened to El Puerto. El Puerto is dissected by the Guadalete River once sailed by the Arabs and the site of the Visigoths' last stand against these Moorish invaders. The local houses are of a simple yet graceful design, many of them bathed in the traditional whitewash that mesmerises against an azure sky. They sit amongst the splendid baroque buildings constructed from the wealth of Indies trade.

Synonymous with the town is the poet Rafael Alberti. As his name suggests, both his grandfathers were Italian, not an uncommon occurrence in the Bay of Cádiz, where maritime trade was the lifeblood of many. Born in 1902, Alberti experienced almost the whole twentieth century – he died in 1999 – living through some of the century's most dramatic and personally tumultuous events. He was part of the aforementioned Generation of '27 and was friends with many of its alumni, including Dámaso Alonso and Vicente Aleixandre. He met Lorca, Luis Buñuel, the filmmaker, and Salvador Dalí at the famous Students' Residence in Madrid.

With the advent of the Civil War in 1936, Alberti honoured his Communist Party credentials and was active in broadcasting from the capital. With little choice but to flee after the Republic was defeated at the hands of Franco and his troops, Alberti – along with his wife, María Teresa León – relocated to Paris, where they shared an apartment with the Chilean poet Pablo Neruda.

Paris became an unsafe haven when the Germans invaded in 1940, forcing Alberti to Argentina, where he spent the majority of his years in exile. He returned to Europe and the Italy of his ancestors in 1963, settling in Rome. It was only the death of Franco and the transition to democracy that allowed him to return home in 1977. It is significant that Alberti's ashes were scattered over the beloved water of his Cádiz Bay. The sea was in his very soul and fundamental to his poetry.

In his introduction to Alberti's poetry collection, *Concerning the Angels* (*Sobre los ángeles*), the Hispanist Ian Gibson remarks that Alberti's early poetic tone is 'predominantly light-hearted, buoyant, sparkling, his Andalusia an emblem of grace and sunny elegance'. Rafael's first collection was titled *Marinero en tierra*, variously translated as *A Sailor on Land*, or *Sailor Ashore*. The first poem is 'The Sailor's Dream', the first verse of which alludes to the grey sweet river whose arm stretches to the sea of Andalucia – no doubt an inspiration from the Guadalete of his childhood.

In addition to being an accomplished poet, Alberti was also an artist of some note, often combining the two media. This ethos is comprehensively illustrated in the exhibition of his works at the Museo Fundación Rafael Alberti, instituted after his death and located in Calle Santo Domingo, a short distance from the river. On entering the adapted interior of his old family home, the visitor is greeted by walls displaying some of the verses he brought to life with colour and design, the two elements of poetry and painting intrinsically interwoven in a fascinating and personal style.

Some biographers have claimed that the two developed together, which is partly the case, but Alberti's first love was art. In his Madrid years, he enjoyed nothing better than to while away hours in the corridors of the Prado Museum, soaking up the paintings of Velázquez and Goya. When we contemplate Alberti's output, it is easy to understand some critics' accusations of levity, as his art is aesthetically pleasing – consider his pictorially poetic treatment of the four seasons. Yet, as Gibson notes, books such as *Concerning the Angels*, even written before the war, have a more tormented and unsettled side. Especially after the conflict, it would be unusual if all the years of exile had had no impact on his writing or art.

The foundation also houses a collection of correspondence between Alberti and notable literary figures. One letter sent by Luis Cernuda, also an exile in the United States, illustrates the fight that dissident Spaniards had to go through to publish their work. At the time, Alberti was working for the Losada publishing house in Buenos Aires and Cernuda was interested in having his translation of Shakespeare's *Troilus and Cressida* published.

In 1953, Alberti published *Ora Maritima* (*Maritime Prayer*), a collection of poetry dedicated to the legends and history of the Bay of Cádiz, laced with nostalgia for his childhood home. The foundation has produced a marvellous audio tour of El Puerto in the poet's footsteps, in which Alberti tells us of his return, of the river, the San Alejandro Bridge, his primary school and the Bay of 'rhythm and grace'.

The lyrical legends of San Marcos Castle, which is a slingshot from Alberti's home, are also captured by the poet, who refers to the mythical appearance of the Virgin to the thirteenth-century King Alfonso the Wise as a spur to victory before he embarked on the capture of El Puerto. The King dedicated some of his poetic songs to this vision.

In the Plaza del Polvorista, so-named after a firework manufacturer, there is the magnificent Casa de las Cadenas, a royal retreat for King Philip V during his stay in the town in the eighteenth century. The main doorway is flanked by Tuscan columns, reflecting the eclectic tastes and background of those who made their money from America. In the square's gardens is a bust of 'the eternal sailor on land', Rafael Alberti.

Trafalgar

Before we move inland from the coast there are two more destinations that draw the literary traveller, both inextricably linked to key conflicts of the eighteenth and nineteenth centuries: Gibraltar and Trafalgar. Mention Trafalgar to someone from Britain and the image that readily comes to mind is a stone column in the eponymous central London square that supports Lord Nelson's statue. In fact, Trafalgar is a cape some 60 kilometres (37 miles) south-east from Cádiz.

The southernmost extension of Cabo Trafalgar is a sand spit gesturing towards the Atlantic and North Africa, its lighthouse guiding ships more fortunate than those involved in the famous battle. The area, known as the Tómbolo de Trafalgar, is now part of a network of natural spaces protected by the Andalucian regional government. Next to the lighthouse are the remains of a ninth-century tower constructed by the Arabs as a lookout post in another era of conflict.

Various information boards around the site explain the geological formation of the spit and the battle that took place off the point. In 1805, the combined forces of the French and Spanish navies engaged the British fleet led by Admiral Lord Nelson. The result of the conflict was a resounding victory for the British, yet they suffered the famous loss of the Admiral himself. He died in the presence of HMS *Victory*'s captain, Thomas Hardy, who may have heard Nelson utter the celebrated words: 'Kiss me, Hardy' or, as some would claim, 'Kismet, Hardy'. Eyewitnesses did report that Hardy knelt to kiss Nelson on the cheek and then the forehead. The battle was immortalised by J. M. W. Turner in two canvases, especially the painting imagined from *The Mizen Starboard Shrouds of the Victory*, now hanging in the Tate Gallery, London.

It would not be long before the invasion of the peninsula in 1808 prompted the Spanish to take arms against Napoleon and ally with the British. They seized the remnants of the French fleet located in Cádiz harbour and used them to attack their former allies. Returning to Trafalgar, such dramatic events with the cannon, rifle and sword have invited the attentions of many pens. We have already seen that Benito Pérez Galdós wrote the first of his National Episodes about the encounter off this sandy cape. Following the adventures of Gabriel de Araceli, Benito pitches us into the heart of the action as the young Gabriel's ship, the *Trinidad*, begins to sink:

> Up through the hatchways came a hideous shriek which I think I can hear as I write, freezing the blood in my veins and setting my hair on end. It came from the poor wretches on the lowest deck who already felt the waters rising to drown them and vainly cried for help – to God or men – who can tell! Vainly indeed to men, for they had enough to do to save themselves.

De Araceli's actions are realistically portrayed as his impending fate fades his stoicism and the instinct for survival takes over: 'I thought only of saving my life, and to stay on board a floundering vessel was clearly not the best means to that laudable end.' The launch that saved him was full of Spaniards and Englishmen; rather touchingly, Galdós describes the 'common danger' faced by these foes. In Galdós's words, de Araceli 'saw the same tokens of fear or of hope, and above all the same expression, sacred to humanity, of kindness and fellowship which was the common motive of all'. The young de Araceli is left wondering why there are wars and why men cannot live as brothers.

The writer Arturo Pérez-Reverte once again followed his illustrious colleague's lead and penned his own version of the combat, *Cabo Trafalgar*. On the eve of the bicentenary of the battle, the Spanish publishing house Alfaguara asked Pérez-Reverte for his own take on events. As is customary with Pérez-Reverte, he brought to bear his extensive historical research and his own inimitable style. One of the most striking features of the book is the use of Frenchified Spanish and dialect to conjure a sense of atmosphere – a taxing combination for any prospective translator. The book's jacket précis describes the text as 'a thrilling key to understanding the tragic day that changed the history of Europe and the world'.

Richard Sharpe would not necessarily have agreed with the above statement in terms of its tragic content. Sharpe is the creation of Bernard Cornwell and is a soldier of the 95th Rifles who climbed his way through the ranks using a mixture of cunning, courage and astuteness. To see Trafalgar from the other side, we turn to *Sharpe's Trafalgar*, the fourth in Cornwell's series of novels. Now an ensign on his way back from India, Richard finds himself caught up in the battle as a French ship, *Revenant*, engages Sharpe's vessel, *Calliope*. Among the intense descriptions of the brutality of war, there is even an encounter between the hero and Nelson. The cauldron of conflict is laced with Sharpe's dangerous longing for the beautiful Lady Grace.

A Cape Cod resident, Cornwell is prolific, leading Sharpe into further battles on *terra firma* in the peninsula itself, where he takes up arms in defence of Spanish independence and against the invading armies of Napoleon. Cornwell was born in England and grew up reading the C. S. Forester novels about Horatio Hornblower, a fictional officer in the Royal Navy during the Napoleonic Wars. Both Forester's output and Sharpe's campaigns have been turned into successful television serials, with the latter being set in Spain and featuring many Spanish characters.

Gibraltar

Gibraltar is 93 kilometres (58 miles) east from Trafalgar. Opposite the mainland town of Algeciras, it has always been something of an anomaly. The name derives from Jabal Tariq – Tariq's Rock – after Tariq Ibn Ziryab, the Moorish governor who occupied the area in

711, and the Rock remained in Moorish hands until 1309 when it was assaulted by the Spanish nobleman, Guzmán el Bueno. Having swapped back to Moorish rule, it was finally and definitively taken by the Duke of Medina Sidonia in 1462. It was the War of the Spanish Succession that saw Britain seize the Rock in 1704 under the command of Sir George Rooke.

In the aftermath, at the Treaty of Utrecht, Philip, Duke of Anjou, acceded to the Spanish throne as Philip V, thus fulfilling the will of the last Spanish Habsburg monarch, Charles II. The price paid for the crown was a high one, and Spanish territories such as Sicily, Milan and the Spanish Netherlands were portioned out to other rulers. Britain contrived to keep Gibraltar 'in perpetuity': a crafty manoeuvre which was surely based upon the strategic importance of having a base on one side of the Pillars of Hercules.

In a world of fewer borders, Gibraltar maintains its anomalous status. We can only imagine what would be felt in the United Kingdom if the Isle of Wight belonged to Spain. Given this backdrop, the locals in mainland La Línea and San Roque have often had good relations with the Gibraltarians – indeed, some still have familial connections there. Over the years, Gibraltar has attracted people from the length and breadth of the Mediterranean, often coming to take advantage of its trading position and tax benefits. The average inhabitant of the Rock is an amalgam of its history, speaking both English and Yanito, a dialect of Andalucian Spanish peppered with words adopted, magpie-like, from many cultures.

Not surprisingly, Gibraltar is a political football; in conversation with some Spaniards, it is interesting to note that it only rises to the top of the agenda when politicians wish to divert attention away from more pressing economic issues. Its future remains open, and discussions about joint sovereignty bubble to the surface from time to time. But what of the Rock's background? How did it come to resemble its current configuration? For an unbiased view, we turn to Samuel Langhorne Clemens, better known as Mark Twain, author of *The Adventures of Tom Sawyer*.

In 1867, Twain caught the cruiseliner *The Quaker City* from New York harbour. His trip was to be an exercise in package tourism from the New World to the Old. The account of his journey, *The Innocents Abroad*, is a fascinating and humorous take on American and European mores. Having given some explanations for the early bones found in caves on the Gibraltarian coast, the American soon proceeds to describe his first impressions of the Rock:

> There is an English garrison at Gibraltar of 6000 or 7000 men, and so uniforms of flaming red are plenty; and red and blue, and undress costumes of snowy white, and also the queer uniform of the bare-kneed Highlander; and one sees soft-eyed Spanish girls from San Roque, and veiled Moorish beauties (I suppose they are beauties) from Tarifa, and turbaned, sashed, and trousered Moorish merchants from Fez.

It is a description of an Afro-European melting pot, as viewed by an American used to his own version of mixed culture. That is not to say that Twain and the other tourists did not find this an exotic scene – a vision he calls a 'shifting panorama of fashion to-day'. Twain's satirical writing also takes a wry look at his fellow American passengers. One young gentleman, nicknamed the 'Interrogation Point', was fond of cornering the locals and bombarding them with questions. Whilst in Gibraltar, Mr Interrogation waylaid some British officers and badgered them with 'braggadocio about America and the wonders she can perform'.

This kind of swagger and high-mindedness was a trait more often associated with British travel writers during the era of colonial expansion. One such personality was John Galt, the Scottish novelist, entrepreneur and commentator. In his book, *Voyages and Travels in the Years 1809, 1810 and 1811*, he explored the Rock. After taking a turn around Apes' Den to see the famous barbary apes, he slips into pompous mode, declaring he could finally see the reason for British involvement here, having previously doubted its worth, even stressing that in order 'to render us effectually masters of the Straits, Ceuta on the African side must be made ours'.

If this self-righteous game of chessboard colonialism was not enough, his descriptions of the locals he encountered are breathtakingly racist: 'The motley multitude of Jews, Moors, Spaniards &c. at the Mole, where the trading vessels lie, presented a new scene to me; nor was it easy to avoid thinking of the odious race of the Orang Outang, on seeing several filthy, bearded, bare-legged groupes huddled together in shady corners during the heat of the day.' He even goes on to denigrate the Jews as, 'deplorably simple animals'. Such casual racism is shocking to twenty-first-century ears and in marked contrast to the more enlightened Mark Twain.

During John Galt's European travels, it seems he befriended Lord Byron and, like so many who crossed the path of the poet, he felt the need to record his impressions on paper. In fact, Galt was the first to write a full biography of Byron, which was published in 1830. The two appear an odd couple, given Byron's much broader mind and openness to the allure of the exotic – although he was far from being without his own arrogances.

Interestingly, Byron thoroughly disliked certain aspects of Gibraltar too, but he always did affect a dislike for places where too many of his countrymen had gathered. In a letter to Hanson, his lawyer, the poet described the Rock as 'the dirtiest most detestable spot in existence'. Byron's party stayed in the Three Anchors Hotel, now rechristened the Bingo Casino. His friend and travelling partner, John Cam Hobhouse, was equally unenthusiastic and surprised at the state of the accommodation: 'horrid and dirty, a shocking hotel' with 'very buggy' rooms.

True to form, Byron was disparaging of his compatriot landlord, a Mr Hawthorne, whom he labelled a 'fat, short man like the pictures of jolly Bacchus'. Hobhouse and Byron endured ten nights in this cockroach-infested den, sleeping on sofas in an attempt to avoid the predations of Gibraltar's worst insect life. Eventually, they caught the Townsend Packet headed for Malta, the same ship that carried John Galt.

Nineteenth-century Britons appear to have been less than enamoured of their colonial prize, but what of the Spanish? The book *Gibraltar Through the Spanish Eye* compiles an interesting series of snippets focusing on the Rock that hail from writers as varied as Vicente Blasco Ibáñez, Fernán Caballero and Pedro Antonio de Alarcón (whom we will meet later). Blasco Ibáñez has two entries in this anthology: one from his short novel *Luna Benamor* and a piece from his *Crónicas de Viaje* (best translated as *Travel Diaries*).

Blasco Ibáñez was not Andalucian, being born in Valencia in 1867. He was a much-respected novelist, initially writing in the *costumbrismo* style, presenting life without any trimmings and often laden with a didactic element. This was an approach he left behind for his more cosmopolitan texts and greatest successes, which include *Blood and Sand* (*Sangre y arena*) and *The Four Horsemen of the Apocalypse* (*Los cuatro jinetes del Apocalipsis*).

His travelogue reflects his surprise on arriving in Gibraltar: 'I must confess with a certain embarrassment, born of my weak patriotic feelings, that on entering Gibraltar and seeing the usurpers who were guarding it, I felt no indignation. If we were to be infuriated by every historic injustice throughout the centuries, we would spend our lives in a constant state of fury.' He goes on to describe his perception of the Rock's declining importance. To put things in context, Blasco Ibáñez visited Gibraltar in 1902, at a time when the Napoleonic Wars were a century distant.

That unassailable Gibraltar we have all heard about since we were children has passed into legend. During the time when artillery had less reach and it had to lay siege to nearby squares, Gibraltar was impregnable, owing to the necessity of approaching it by sea or from the land side of La Línea that joins the Rock to the peninsula.

Blasco Ibáñez assures his Spanish readers that 'the destruction of Gibraltar would be the work of weeks.' Not that the writer wished such an attack, even surprising his more ardent countrymen with the 'smiling amiability' and 'fraternal trust' that the people of Algeciras, La Línea and San Roque shared with perfidious Albion.

Arcos de la Frontera

We now leave the coast and head to the hinterland of the province. Our first stop is Arcos de la Frontera, a 40-minute drive north-east from Cádiz. The designation 'de la Frontera' is applied to several towns in the area and comes from the Christian reconquest, when the frontier between Moorish and Christian Spain wavered through the hills and plains of Andalucia. Situated atop a hill with a jaw-dropping cliff down to the Guadalete River, Arcos wears a whitewashed veneer, characteristic of many of the *frontera* towns. Nicknamed 'Arcos de los poetas', Arcos of the Poets, it has a long tradition in Andalucian verse.

It is probably best to start by listing those associated with the location: Julio Mariscal Montes, Antonio and Carlos Murciano, José María Pemán, Antonio Hernández and José Martínez Ruiz, aka Azorín. The town hall has taken ample steps to ensure that their legacy is not forgotten. In Calle Corredera, on the way up the hill to Arcos's high point is a bust commemorating Mariscal Montes. Born in the town in 1922, he formed part of the poetic group Alcaraván, a name recalled by a flamenco bar opposite the birthplace of the Murciano brothers, both poets and writers who coordinated the magazine of the same name.

To give a flavour of Mariscal Montes's poetry, we turn to this verse from his 1955 collection, *Pasan hombres oscuros* (*Shadowy Men Pass*), a book that reflects his love for a young woman and his feelings somewhere between carnal desire and protective love:

> The air was mistaken
> taking almonds for olives.
> It was an April of lazy clouds
> or a baroque September of promises.
> Desire was beating like a captive
> bird in the hands.

Antonio Hernández is a better-known poet in the Spanish arena, where he continues to contribute articles to the national press. In 2014, he received the National Poetry Prize and, unsurprisingly, he has been named a Hijo Predilecto (Favourite Son) of Arcos, somewhat equivalent to being given the key to the town. In *Habitación en Arcos* (*A Room in Arcos*), Hernández pays homage to his childhood in the vicinity. The room in question can be found at the Hotel El Convento, nestling in the folds of Calle Maldonado; the hotel is owned by a childhood friend of Hernández and has a room that bears his name.

Hernández also penned a *Guía secreta de Cádiz* (*Secret Guide to Cadiz Province*), in which he described Arcos as 'an absolution for the eyes'. He knows only too well the pueblo's poetic allure: 'Hundreds of poets have been lost for poetry in its streets, facing the unequal competition from its sleepwalking spectre of alleyways, niches, patios, gulfs, pavements and birds.'

Our final two poets have quite complicated relationships with Spain's recent history. José María Pemán was a supporter of the dictator, General Franco, and the Falange. José Martínez Ruiz, who took the pseudonym Azorín, was part of the Generation of '98, a grouping of writers and intellectuals active during the disastrous Spanish–American war of 1898 and its aftermath. Azorín veered from being a political radical to becoming a monarchist and conservative. At the outbreak of the Civil War, he adopted a progressive stance and thus had to flee to Paris. On returning, he tacitly accepted the support of Franco's regime in order to continue his writing career.

Azorín travelled widely throughout the peninsula and left many of his impressions in book form, including his journey in the footsteps of Don Quixote, *La ruta de don Quijote* (*The Route of Don Quixote*).

Amongst other authors, thanks to the good auspice of Arcos's local government, both Pemán and Azorín also find their words immortalised on tiles adhered to the limewashed walls of the town's streets. From the Plaza del Cabildo, with its spectacular open-air balcony, to the winding alleys spanned by arches, Arcos displays its literary history on its sleeve. It is easy to see why Azorín felt he had 'never seen a more expressive town. Standing on the rim of a mountainside, there in the depths slips away the river Guadalete. I spent some unforgettable days in Arcos.'

Jerez de la Frontera

Jerez is the most well known of the frontier towns. Considerably bigger than Arcos, it sits at the bend of a dog-leg, between El Puerto de Santa María and Sanlúcar de Barrameda, at the heart of the sherry triangle. If Sanlúcar is the birthplace of manzanilla, then Jerez is, of course, the capital of sherry, Andalucia's most distinctive fortified wine. In his *Handbook*, Richard Ford claimed that the town was called Sherish Filistin by the Moors as it was 'allotted to a tribe of Philistine'. Whatever the veracity of the assertion, the transcription of the Moorish word makes it is easy to see how English could derive the word 'sherry'.

Vineyards in the area have a long history dating back to 1100 BC, to the Phoenicians, who were also the originators of much wine production in that other fortified-wine district of Marsala in Sicily. Adopted by the Romans and refined by the Moors, who were partial to the grape despite religious practice, sherry production in the area was soon a European-wide asset. It was the British who really took the drink to their hearts, especially after Sir Francis Drake sacked Cádiz and stole the liquid booty. In fact, on one memorable occasion, the troops became so inebriated on the contents of the warehouses that they were unable to continue the siege.

British literary allusions to the grape and its product go as far back as Chaucer, who included it in his 'Pardoner's Tale'. Julian Jeffs, in his wonderful book simply called *Sherry*, has carried out some literary investigation of his own. He highlights Chaucer, who specifically mentions the wine of Lepe, west of Jerez in Huelva Province, a wine that was occasionally mixed with the town's more superior blends. Chaucer warns the unwary drinker of its potency:

> Now keep ye from the white and from the red
> And namely from the white wine of Lepe
> That is to sell in Fish Street or in Chepe.
> This wine of Spain creepeth subtilly
> In other wines, growing fast by,
> Of which there riseth such fumositee,
> That when a man hath drunken draughts three,
> And weneth that he be at home in Chepe,
> He is in Spain, right at the town of Lepe.

Andalucia, being what it is, needs no excuse for a fiesta, but Jerez has more reason than most. Every year at harvest time, the Fiesta de la Vendimia is dedicated to a particular personage or area connected to sherry. In 1956, the honour went to Shakespeare and his great imbiber of 'sack', Sir John Falstaff, who, in *Henry IV, Part II*, advises: 'If I had a thousand sons, the first humane principle I would teach them should be, to forswear thin potations and to addict themselves to sack.' Ford also quotes Falstaff when summing up the character of the local Jerezanos, who had a reputation for practical jokes and less refinement than the peacocks of Seville. As Falstaff says, all 'this valour comes of sherris'.

The bodegas dominate the town; the names González Byass, Domecq, Harveys and Sandeman are famous the world over. Falstaff's lusty downing of the drink has passed from fashion in his native land, where it is now often sipped by Great Aunt Maude before dinner. The atmosphere surrounding sherry is very different in Spain, where some bars backed with barrels of many varieties treat the beverage with due respect. From biscuit-dry finos served ice cold to the scented olorosos with their sweet, golden viscosity, the drink has many personalities.

In many ways, sherry is quintessentially Andalucian, but the names suggest a heavy British influence. One of the most well-known companies is that of the aforementioned González Byass, whose bodega runs the length of the street named after its founder, Manuel María González Ángel. The man himself stands on a plinth in a little square between the Alcázar and the Cathedral of San Salvador. With one hand in his pocket and the other proudly atop a Tio Pepe barrel, he looks towards the Alcázar, Jerez's former Moorish palace with its preserved mosque and attractive formal gardens.

6   *Statue of Manuel María González Ángel in front of the Cathedral of San Salvador, Jerez*

The British side of the equation came from Robert Blake Byass, who was first González's agent and then business partner. Although the Byass influence remains in the name, it is now only Manuel María's descendants who run the company. Two commonly seen icons dot the Spanish countryside – both have sherry-based origins. Anyone driving along a motorway in Andalucia is likely to pass the black silhouette of the Osborne bull on a hoarding; alternatively, the jaunty figure of a Tio Pepe bottle, sporting a guitar and wearing a Cordobés hat, is equally likely to make an appearance and has done since 1935 when González Byass adopted it as their logo. The same bottle indicates the direction visitors should follow if they wish to join a bodega tour.

Richard Ford, all in the name of research for his guide, was personally shown around the bodegas of Domecq and Charles Gordon, which he clearly thought the finest in the town. The Domecq establishment boasted some works of art, but it was the butts of sherry that impressed Ford the most. He gives us an idiosyncratic account of his wine tour:

> There the whole process of making sherry will be explained. The lecture is long, and is illustrated by experiments. Every cask is tasted, from the raw young wine to the mature golden fluid. Those who are not stupefied by drink come out much edified [...] the best wine is reserved for the last, the qualities ascending in a vinous climax.

He goes on to proffer his opinion of the qualities a great sherry should possess, namely it 'ought to unite fulness of body, a nutty flavour and aroma, dryness, absence from acidity, strength, spirituosity, and durability'. A good fino will fulfil all these qualities.

Benito Pérez Galdós was very aware of the Victorian Englishman's addiction to sherry; in his work *El doctor Centeno*, he puts these words into the mouth of his character Florencio: 'Well the day we want to put the wretched English into a tight spot, we can do no better than to tell them "Gentlemen, there is no more sherry."' We have already met Lord Gray, Galdós's Byronesque character from *Cádiz*, who also appears to have had a penchant for the golden wine of Jerez: 'Its generous fire, lighting flames of intelligence in our mind.'

The real Byron did pass through the town on his way to the coast, and like Ford, he met the same bodega owner: 'at Xeres where the sherry we drink is made I met a great merchant a Mr. Gordon of Scotland, who was extremely polite and favoured me with the Inspection of his vaults & cellars, so that I quaffed at the Fountain head.' Leaving Byron to make his way to Cádiz, we travel forward to the twentieth century and another poet who made the same journey to the coast, thus passing through the town.

Laurie Lee, as we know, immortalised his journey in the book *As I Walked Out One Midsummer Morning*, but he captured Jerez's essence far more sensuously in his verses. Most people associate Lee with travel literature and his paean to a lost rural Gloucestershire childhood in his memoir *Cider with Rosie*. However, his real passion and talent lay in poetry, which inevitability influenced his beautifully descriptive prose. In the poem 'Stork in Jerez', he crystallises the timeless atmosphere of a warehouse and its ungainly inhabitant:

> White arched, in loops of silence, the bodega
> Lies drowsed in spices, where the antique woods,
> Piled in solera, dripping years of flavour,
> Distil their golden fumes among the shades.
> In from the yard – where barrels under figtrees
> Split staves of sunlight from the noon's hot glare -
> The tall stork comes; black-stilted, sagely-witted,
> Wiping his careful beak upon the air.

Thanks to a Society of Authors' travelling scholarship, Lee was able to partially recreate his pre-war walk in the postwar era of the 1950s. The product of his travels was the third in the trilogy of his

Spanish adventures, *A Rose for Winter*. No stranger to a crowded bar, guitar or violin in hand, singing at the top of his voice, Lee loved the convivial atmosphere of the Andalucian local.

The picturesque scene would be complete when Kathy, his wife, took to the floor. The poet's biographer, Valerie Grove, in her work *The Life and Loves of Laurie Lee*, noted that Kathy had a Provençal childhood observing Gypsy dancers, which made her a consummate performer of Sevillanas, Malagueñas and flamenco dances. We are building a picture of Jerez, with its wine, music, dance, equine excellence and costume, as a cornucopia of Andalucian iconography. The reality of its musical connection is a little more earthy.

Jerez does have a reputation for producing quality flamenco, much of it based in the Santiago neighbourhood facing the cathedral. Traditionally a Gypsy barrio, it boasts a Gothic church, which lends its name to the quarter, and the Andalucian Flamenco Foundation in the Plaza de San Juan. Of course, dance is inextricably linked with the musical style. One of the purest forms of flamenco is the *cante jondo* or 'deep song', which also has an accompanying *jondo* dance form. One writer who has explored this world is a Jerez native, José Manuel Caballero Bonald. He was born in Calle Caballeros, a bodega-width from the Alcázar, where there is now a foundation dedicated to his works and those of local writers.

Moving back and forth between the New World and the Old, Caballero Bonald was given the great honour of the Miguel de Cervantes Prize in 2012, one of the Spanish-speaking world's most prestigious literary awards. In his book, *Sevilla en tiempos de Cervantes* (*Seville in the Time of Cervantes*), he describes himself as chiefly dedicated to the production of fiction; yet, as this and another of his books, *Andalusian Dances*, amply illustrate, he was more than capable of turning his hand to the capturing of history and tradition. This *payo*, or non-gypsy, really seems to understand the esoteric world of flamenco. Here he describes the secrecies of the *jondo* dance:

Jondo dancing is in itself a hermetically sealed world, an unfathomable abyss into which the ropes of logic cannot be lowered. It is by its very nature an elusive, anarchical thing. The understanding can only reach it along the dark channels of the most unconditional interpenetration. How can this identifying communication be achieved? For whether you like it or not, very few do actually manage it. This is a mystery and yet the most commonplace of commonplaces.

José Manuel suggests that anyone in search of the authentic should 'flee from theatres or commercial set-ups'. This is solid advice and something Giles Tremlett adhered to in his book, *Ghosts of Spain* (2007). In one chapter, this *Guardian* newspaper correspondent went in search of 'real' spontaneous flamenco, a search which took him to the infamous Las Tres Mil barrio of Seville where drugs mix perilously with high tensions and much unemployment. He was also directed to the capital of sherry which, he tells us, is part of the 'cradle' of flamenco.

Tremlett paints a picture of the art form that is almost unrecognisable to a tourist who has only seen the sanitised versions performed in coastal hotels. He stresses that it is constantly evolving and immune to attacks from over-commercialisation and those who turn their back in search of music from other shores. The many venues in Jerez, often hidden to all but the initiated, are testament to flamenco's enduring appeal.

5

MÁLAGA PROVINCE

Hilltowns and Hotels

Malaga, charming town, I feel myself at home in thee!
(Hans Christian Andersen, *In Spain*, 1870)

Málaga

The first-time visitor to Andalucia is more than likely to touch down at Málaga Airport and, for many, this will be all they see of the city as they travel on to the beaches of the Costa del Sol. They will, however, have missed an intriguing, multilayered city, second only to Seville in size. Like many places that have undergone rapid development, the outlying suburbs with their uniform high-rises are not easy on the eye, but the centre is altogether another story. Originally Phoenician, this harbour city was prized away from Carthage by the Romans. Its central location on the Andalucian coast was also key in providing the Moorish towns of the interior, particularly Granada, with a major trading port.

When history allowed it to flower, as it did during the flourishing years of the wine trade, Málaga attracted many admirers. Richard Ford praised its micro-climate, calling it 'almost tropical', enabling cactus, coffee, cocoa and sugar cane to be grown in the botanical garden. He was well aware of the city's commercial nature, stating that, 'As a mercantile residence, the town is agreeable. The better classes are well off, gay, and hospitable – the ladies are pretty, sprightly, and fascinating.' Not for the first time, Ford described the local women as if they were a tourist attraction.

A compatriot and contemperory of Ford, Henry David Inglis, delved further into Málaga's business world and came up with some very high-minded imperialistic opinions. Inglis, who was actually a Scottish businessman, could easily have been the one to coin the nefarious Elizabethan phrase, 'Spanish practices', given its whiff of financial irregularity. He wrote up his travels in the snappily titled *Spain in 1830*. In the book, he recounts the story of goods being deposited in the customs house but, when shipped, they had mysteriously diminished in size. In giving his opinion on the matter, he provides this gem of Anglo-Saxon, or in his case Celtic, phlegm: 'I relate this, not of course as an example of government oppression or injustice, but as a proof of the lax and unhinged state of the government and total want of integrity.'

Sadly, even the most ardent Hispanophile would have to admit that shadier corners have always existed where Andalucian money and power have mixed; Spain and its regions are by no means unique in this. Fortunately, not every traveller showed such interest in the murky world of business – many were just happy to soak up the atmosphere. Hans Christian Andersen overflowed with praise for the city and its people when he visited in the 1860s. By this time, Andersen was a well-known author, his first collection of *Fairy Tales* having been published in 1835. He is, of course, most famous for these stories, notably 'The Princess and the Pea', 'The Little Mermaid' and 'Thumbelina'. Although subtitled *Told for Children*, many of the tales were avidly read by adults who detected undercurrents of thought and morality that could be applied to everyday life.

Despite his international fame as a children's storyteller, Andersen was much more than this: a poet, a novelist and a travel writer. His inauspicious beginnings, especially losing his father at the age of 11, led few to believe he would achieve his goal of making a living from words; he was even bullied by a schoolteacher who held no faith in his desired aim. It was only thanks to the patronage of Copenhagen's theatre director that Andersen was able to reach a modicum of educational attainment. Tall, gangly – the ugly duckling of his stories – the 17-year-old Andersen stood out from his younger peers.

Taken under the wing of various prestigious families in the Danish capital, Andersen was eventually able to fulfil his dreams. Both shy and gregarious at the same time, and always uncomfortable in his own skin, he never married or had children. Biographers have identified passions for both sexes, albeit his male companionships were cloaked in the acceptable norm of ardent friendship. Steering away from sexual relationships, his infatuations were often unrequited. In many ways, his frequent travels were an escape from the social strains of his Danish life. However, that is not to say that he indulged in the more louche activities of the grand tourist – his sense of propriety kept him on the straight and narrow.

This did not prevent Andersen from admiring beauty from afar. He conjures a picture of Málaga's beach front where 'old, sunburnt seamen were sitting on the bulkheads smoking their cigars', and 'amidst all this there was beauty to be seen – here were Andalucian eyes and witching smiles'. At which point in his travelogue, *In Spain and a Visit to Portugal*, he breaks from the narrative and flows into verse:

> Can I believe
> These beaming eyes?
> Do they deceive
> With flattering lies?
> And round the mouth is not the smile
> Lingering there, but to beguile?
> Ah! those eyes,
> And those lies,
> And those smiles so sweet that seem –
> They are Satan's work I deem.

In fact, Andersen's whole stay in Málaga is brimming with enthusiasm. His hotel overlooked the Alameda – the city's thoroughfare, as popular today as it was in the nineteenth century. He paints a multicultural picture of the people strolling its length: 'there went bare-legged Bedouins in their white burnooses, African Jews in long embroidered kaftans, Spanish women in their becoming black mantillas, ladies of higher rank in bright-colored shawls, elegant-looking young men on foot and on horseback, peasants and porters; all was life and animation.'

The modern-day Alameda runs into the Paseo del Parque, the city's green lung. Joining the two is the Plaza de la Marina, which sports a jaunty, seated statue of Denmark's favourite storyteller. It was donated by the Danish government in recognition of his love for the city. These stretches of Malagueño boulevard do not lack for commemorative statuary. Shaded alcoves along the Paseo

7   *Statue of Hans Christian Andersen, Plaza de la Marina, Málaga*

del Parque reveal fountains and figures, including El Fiestero, a mulleted flamenco character complete with tambourine. There is also a donkey honouring the poet Juan Ramón Jiménez and his immortal beast of burden, Platero.

At the eastern end of the park, taking refuge under the shady palms, we meet again the Nicaraguan poet Rubén Darío, who eulogised Málaga with these words: 'This is sweet Málaga, known as the beautiful, from whence hail the famous raisins, the famous women, and the wine preferred for Communion.' This description, in the original, is also used by Nathalie Handal to head her poem 'Walking to the Alcázar' in *Poet in Andalucía* (2012), her book written as a homage to García Lorca after she had recreated in reverse the trip that Lorca recorded in the soul-searching text, *Poet in New York (Poeta en Nueva York)*, first published in 1940.

Handal herself has an interesting background, her family having been exiled from the Middle East due to the political upheavals. Her peripatetic childhood saw her live in Latin America and France. She now lectures at Columbia University, on the very same campus that housed Lorca during his North American sojourn. Her poetic style has been praised by Yusef Kumunyakaa, the Pulitzer Prize-winner, for its 'cosmopolitan voice' that 'belongs to the human family'.

Handal travelled extensively throughout Andalucia, visiting the major cities of Córdoba, Seville, Huelva, Granada and Cádiz, but it is Málaga, with its 'Poems of Soledad con Biznagas', that starts the collection. *Soledad* refers to solitude and a *biznaga* is one of the city's great traditions – a spherical floral adornment made of jasmine flowers. In one of the first poems in *Poet in Andalucía*, the aforementioned 'Walking to the Alcázar', Handal absorbs the sights and sounds of Málaga's castle whilst invoking the Nicaraguan Darío:

> Now facing the Gibralfaro
> I accept the moment,
> what will come.
> I ask about the rampart, the Coracha, the Alcazaba,

ask about the limestones, the Patio de los Naranjos,
the gunpowder, and the Airón Well.
Where are you Rubén?
What haven't you shown me,
what do you look like undressed,
what do the earth and the waters
have in common
when a woman presses her breast against them?

The *alcázar* in question is reached from a path at the end of the Paseo del Parque. A twisting, slowly ascending lane leads you up to what must have been an excellent defensive garret. It also provides some spectacular views over the urban and coastal landscape below: the twin arms of the port jutting into the Mediterranean, the Alameda cutting a swathe through the belle époque and, to the left, the once-proud bullring keeping the twentieth-century overdevelopment at bay. Handal is well aware of how monuments like the castle, with its Moorish origins, encapsulate the entire region. In her preface, she beautifully conceives the roots of her poetry and the region's mythic allure. It is worth quoting her at length:

Andalucía has always been the place where racial, ethnic, and religious forces converge and contend, where Islamic, Judaic, and Christian traditions remain a mirror of a past that is terrible and beautiful. *Poet in Andalucía* is a meditation on the past and the present. It renders in poetry a region that seems to hold the pulse of our earth, where all of our stories assemble.

Another writer, Victor Perera, this time from the Jewish diaspora, felt this convergence and contention whilst climbing the hill to the very same spot mentioned by Handal. He recounts the story in his 1996 book, *The Cross and the Pear Tree: A Sephardic Journey*. In essence, Perera, descended from the Sephardic Jews expelled from Spain in 1492, decided to retrace his family's footsteps across Europe and the Mediterranean to Latin America. Perera's mother still spoke Ladino, the medieval version of Spanish that migrated with the Jews as they moved away from the Iberian Peninsula to destinations such as Livorno in Italy and Salonika in northern Greece.

Originally spurred to explore Spain and its Sephardic heritage by a professor at his college, Perera first went to Málaga in 1958. Looking back on this visit in his book, he tells us of a series of meetings with a certain Canon Bandeña. On one occasion the pair met on the ramparts of the castle. Perera had decided to play along with the Canon's religious conversations out of curiosity. Little did the cleric know that his pupil was Jewish. The inevitable question eventually arrived as to his absence from Communion.

Initially, Victor pretended to be half Protestant. Pouncing on a potential convert, Bandeña went into a frenzy of suggestions and invitations – much reading material was proffered. During a subsequent meeting, when the writer rebutted the Canon with his own views on the real economic rationale behind the Inquisition, an irritated Perera confessed his Jewish ancestry. A rather smug Bandeña claimed he had known all along. It seems that Perera's fellow guest at a local pension had been doing a bit of Inquisitional spying for the Canon. The ultimate irony was revealed when the priest admitted his own surname was a variant on one of the names belonging to Perera's Jewish ancestors, Abendana. From which point onwards, the fervent cleric called him 'a kinsman'. The further these two dug into their common inheritance, the more they discovered Nathalie Handal's 'pulse of the earth' with its 'terrible and beautiful' past.

Málaga lays claim to one of the Iberian Peninsula's most recognised medieval Jewish poets, Solomon Ibn Gabirol. Descending from the Alcázar into Calle Alcazabilla, you come across a rather sad-looking bronze statue of a robed and turbaned figure with his eyes cast downwards. This is Gabirol, born in Málaga in 1021 or 1022. Not far from here, down an alleyway leading from the famous Bar El Pimpi, is also the Ben Gabirol Visitor Centre. Part of the poet's sadness must have been due to a crippling illness and a life that compelled him to live by his writing alone. The constant search for patrons sent him on a journey throughout the peninsula and saw him settle in Zaragoza.

Academics have categorised his poetry and prose work as a search for philosophy and wisdom, placing him in the neo-Platonic school. His most famous text was only finally attributed to him in the nineteenth century and is now known to us by its Latin title, *Fons Vitae (The Fountain of Life)*. Like his other poetic works, it is deeply concerned with religious and theological matters. For a time, Gabirol was on friendly terms with another of the greats of Judeo-Iberian poetry, Samuel Ha-Nagid, who once ran a spice shop in Málaga. One of Gabirol's non-religious poems praises Ha-Nagid: 'My friend, companion of my soul, you are a balm for pain, / You are the remedy and cure for every ill.'

Little remains of the city's Jewish quarter apart from the aforesaid Ben Gabirol Centre in Calle Granada, a tower built in the Mudéjar-style and recently renovated. Plans are afoot for further redevelopment, including the opening of a Sephardic museum. The Protestant community in Málaga has been more fortunate. The once-dilapidated Anglican Cemetery in Avenida Príes, to the east of the Alcázar, is now restored and run by a foundation dedicated to its upkeep. Before it was instituted in 1831, Protestants were buried on the beach in a standing position, eventually being swept away by the tides. This lamentable custom was stopped by William Mark, the British consul.

One of the first inhabitants of the graveyard was the Anglo-Irishman Robert Boyd, who took part in General Torrijos's liberal uprising in the December of the cemetery's creation and was shot for doing so. It could so easily have been the poet Alfred, Lord Tennyson, a liberal sympathiser who introduced Boyd to the exiled Torrijos. The burial ground is now a designated site of cultural interest; the foundation in charge presents the visitor with a detailed chart that maps out the more well-known graves, which include

8   *The Anglican Cemetery, Avenida Príes, Málaga*

those of Gerald Brenan and his American wife, Gamel Woolsey, who died in 1987 and 1968 respectively.

The couple were both writers and were respected by Málaga's populace; Brenan, in particular, was a noted Hispanist whose Andalucian story we will uncover in subsequent locations, including Churriana and the Alpujarras. In actual fact, Brenan did not ask to be buried in the cemetery, preferring to leave his body to scientific research. After his body had spent several years residing in the research facility of the local hospital, the doctors decided they were unable to dissect such a venerable friend of Spain. They laid him to rest in the upper tier of the graveyard, next to the original walled cemetery, beside his wife, whose tombstone poignantly reads, 'Fear no more the heat of the sun'.

The dappled shade cast on the white marble from the surrounding trees makes a tranquil location for visitors. Those climbing the mild slope at the entrance would be forgiven for thinking they were entering a botanical garden. Urns filled with vibrant flowers sit underneath olive trees, well-tended beds hedged with blossoming shrubs harbour burgeoning yucca and cactus. When Hans Christian Andersen visited the churchyard, he was taken with its 'strange power of attraction', and he could 'well understand how a splenetic Englishman might take his own life in order to be buried in this place'.

With his sarcastic wit, he tells us he had refrained from making an attempt on his own life, instead, preferring to wax lyrical about the

> myrtle hedge, covered with flowers sufficient for a thousand bridal wreathes; high geranium-bushes growing round the tomb-stones, which had inscriptions in Danish – Norse, it might also be called, as these were inscriptions over men from the north; there were English, German and Dutch to be read. Passion-flowers flung their tendrils over many grave-stones; pepper-trees waved their drooping branches amidst this place of repose.

Andersen was right about the nationalities; although designated an Anglican cemetery, it is, to all intents and purposes, a non-denominational Protestant one. A later incumbent from Scandinavia is the thriller and science-fiction writer, Aarne Viktor Haapakoski, who often used the pseudonym 'Outsider'. He died in 1961 and is buried just behind the Brenans.

One of the more surprising residents is the Spanish poet Jorge Guillén, another of the renowned Generation of '27, who hailed from Valladolid but who spent his twilight years in Málaga after returning from exile, dying at the age of 91 in 1984. Guillén admitted that the churchyard reminded him of Paul Valéry's *Le cimetière marin* (*The Graveyard by the Sea*), which he had translated years previously, providing one of the main reasons for his request to be interred within these confines. He also appreciated the cemetery's cultural melange and acceptance of a diverse range of rites and national outlooks. His motives may also have been related to his uneasy relationship with the Catholic Church.

Guillén is one of many from Spain's great wave of poets who have a connection with Málaga. We cannot leave this era without also mentioning Emilio Prados and Manuel Altolaguirre. Both were Malagueños, instigators of the publishers Imprenta Sur, and editors of the magazine *Litoral*, which has something of a mythical status for aficionados of those belonging to the Generation of '27. It was Prados who founded the Imprenta in 1925, which became a key location for this new wave of poets.

Originally situated at 24 Calle Tomás Heredia, the publishing company was lauded for its discerning selection of contemporary poets. Altolaguirre described the offices with barely disguised joy when he remembered the happiness to be found amidst flowers, pictures of Picasso, the music of Manuel de Falla and the books of Juan Ramón Jiménez. Animated conversation about poetry was at least as prevalent as the actual act of printing the verses. The list of contributors to the magazine reads like a who's who of early twentieth-century Spanish arts and letters; among the illustrious were García Lorca, Gerardo Diego, Rafael Alberti, Vicente Aleixandre, Picasso, Dalí and Jorge Guillén.

More than a few of the above would have made the pilgrimage to the offices in Tomás Heredia and to their subsequent location in Calle San Lorenzo. In addition to their publishing skills, Prados and Altolaguirre were both consummate poets. Perhaps not recognised in the same league as their admired Jiménez and trailing in the wake of Lorca's greatness, they were, nonetheless, held in esteem.

Prados had had a childhood that saw frequent bouts of illness, although his schoolfriend and fellow poet Aleixandre thought him happy, yet a daydreamer. Prados left two universities under something of a cloud, spent time at the famous student residence in Madrid with the likes of Lorca, and read voraciously during the two years he spent in Freiburg, Germany. All of these experiences were poured into his poetry, which is often full of symbolism and illusion. His childhood time spent recuperating in the Montes de Málaga had what his biographer P. J. Ellis called an 'almost Wordsworthian' impact on his verses and memory. In his autobiography, Prados recalls the countryside behind the city: 'After "La Venta", the road continued flat and bordered by magnificent cork oaks with blood-coloured trunks and wide leaves of dark green. All of this part of the road was full of silence and majesty.'

Altolaguirre, whose poems also have the hallmark of the Andalucian countryside, dedicated a 1926 edition of his verses to his friend Prados. In the poem 'Campo' ('Countryside'), we have echoes of those *montes*, Prados's mountains:

> That tree on the summit
> holds the bridles of the wind;
> its rider's cloak
> paints the heavens sky blue
> and the river's water flows away
> caressing reflections.

In common with Prados, Altolaguirre also spent time abroad, particularly in France, then England, where he established the magazine *1616*, so called in commemoration of the deaths of Cervantes and Shakespeare. Its intention was to strengthen the connections between Spanish and English literature through works published in the original and translation. The first edition saw him feature Byron's 'A Very Mournful Ballad on the Siege and Conquest of Alhama', which the aristocratic poet had translated from the Spanish, which in turn was a version of the Arabic original; the theme is very Byronic:

> I lost a damsel in that hour,
> Of all the land the loveliest flower;
> Doubloons a hundred I would pay,
> And think her ransom cheap that day.

Like so many of his age, Altolaguirre would feel this loss described in Byron's 'Ballad', as the Civil War forced him to live as an émigré, firstly in Cuba, then Mexico.

Our tour through the haunts of Málaga's poetic residents and visitors brings us to the heart of the city and the former Café Chinitas. It is to be found in a circular alcove along the Pasaje de Chinitas, an arched passageway that leads from the Plaza de la Constitución. A plaque commemorates Federico García Lorca and the café's former significance at the heart of Málaga's festive soul. It was here that Lorca set his eponymous poem in which Paquiro says to his brother:

> Soy más valiente que tu.
> Más torero y más gitano.
>
> I am braver than you.
> More of a bullfighter and more gypsy.

These lines were put on celebratory tiles that were fixed to the curved wall of the old bar in memory of the fiftieth anniversary of Lorca's death.

If Paquiro was proud of his bullfighter-like credentials, then the gentler fabulist Hans Christian Andersen was both appalled and mesmerised by the spectacle of the bullfight or *corrida*. He visited the bullring in Málaga and was relieved to obtain a more expensive seat in the shade, noting how those in the sun parried the heat with fans and parasols. The crowd was a mixture of cigar-smoking men in embroidered gaiters and brightly shawled women accompanied by their daughters. After seeing several horses gored and their riders dragged from the arena, he admits, 'it was scarcely possible to sit out this scene, and my blood tingled to the very points of my fingers.'

Despite Andersen's horror at this grisly sight, his aesthetic sense refused to let him leave the ringside. He thought there was 'something interesting and attractive in the skill and agility, the steady eye, and the dexterity with which the banderilleros and espada moved on the arena. It was like a game, or a dance upon the stage.' In his conversations with some Spaniards on the subject, he learned that the appeal of the *corrida* was far from universal and 'that latterly application had been made to the Cortes for the abolition of these fights'. Currently, some 145 years later, only Catalonia has actually banned bullfighting. News of the latest fights and the successes of the renowned *toreros* (bullfighters) continue to be published in the Arts sections of the country's national newspapers.

Clearly, the bullfight was an occasion for the locals to put on their Sunday best. Andersen's description of silk dresses and mantillas is redolent of an exotic image still fixed in the mind's eye of tourist brochure writers and souvenir hunters. Although such dress is as far removed from the everyday modern Spanish people as Morris dancing smocks are from the average English villager – strictly for festivals only – there is a true history to be discovered here, and we find it in the witty observations of Lady Louisa Tenison.

Having been holed up on the city's Alameda for a winter of Mediterranean sun, Lady Tenison later set down her experiences in the 1853 text, *Castile and Andalucia*. She had married E. K. Tenison, a captain of the dragoons, who went on to make a serious contribution to photography, particularly during these visits to Spain in the early 1850s which were designed to aid his wife's health. Lady Tenison was a free-spirited woman of independent means, breaking that Victorian taboo that forbade travelling without the appendage of a male chaperone. Her talent for letters and art enabled her to contribute some illustrations to her books.

She poured scorn on Málaga's nascent fashion for the bonnet, much preferring the traditional mantilla:

There is an elegance and a dressy appearance about the mantilla which create surprise at its not having been adopted by other nations; and if Spaniards could only be made to feel how unbecoming bonnets are to them, the rich masses of whose

splendid hair prevent the bonnet being properly worn, they would
cherish the mantilla as conferring on them a peculiar charm in
which they are safe to fear no rivals.

She was equally plain-speaking of the poetic male's fascination for
Spanish women – a stereotypical bubble that she was ready to burst.
She comments on the pretty faces bespoiled by gaudy dresses and
harks back to the age of black. She was looking for the exotic Spain
of myth and legend that so attracted northern visitors and feared it
was being lost.

On one of her visits to the theatre, the Malagueños were able to
turn the tables by presenting a satirical play called the *Mercado de
Londres* (*London Market*), in which the protagonist sells his wife, 'an
event which they seem to imagine is of the commonest occurrence
in "*soberbia Albion*"'. The theatre she attended is likely to have been
the Teatro de la Libertad, which sadly burned down in the latter
half of the nineteenth century. The current Teatro Cervantes was
inaugurated in December 1870; its Naples-yellow façade with a trio
of white arched doorways still presides over Calle Zorrilla.

Lady Tenison continued to observe the fashions in the theatre
and amongst the strollers in the street. She was particularly taken
with the habit amongst women from all classes of wearing a rose
or jasmine in their hair. A twentieth-century poet who beautifully
captured the city's jasmine was the Irishman Pearse Hutchinson;
in fact, one of his poems, 'Málaga', was chosen by the renowned
novelist and Hispanophile Colm Toibín as one of his favourites.

Hutchinson, also a translator of considerable skill, remained
engaged with poetry from this part of the world right up until his
death in 2012. He first travelled throughout Spain in 1950. Vincent
Woods, in his study *Jasmine and Lagarto*, which focuses on Pearse's
Spanish works, tells us that the young Irishman was much smitten
by the world of Lorca, Prados and Cernuda – so much so that he
vowed to return to live in the country on a permanent basis. He
may not have achieved this goal, but he certainly spent much time

in Spain. His translations of a selection of works from over 60 poets (including Spaniards) appeared under the title *Done into English*; the first work of his own poetry, *Tongue without Hands*, appeared in 1963 and contains many verses inspired by these earlier travels, including Toibín's favourite:

> The scent of unseen jasmine on the warm night beach.
> The tram along the sea road all the way from town
> through its wide open sides drank unseen jasmine down.
> Living was nothing all those nights but that strong flower,
> whose hidden voice on darkness grew to such mad power
> I could have sworn for once I travelled through full peace.

With a poet's sensibility, he beautifully described why Andalucia had so captured his imagination, not because of its architecture, its bullfights, its costume or its tradition, but because 'the light walked for me as it never had before, and I walked through the light I had always longed for'. He was clearly a long way from the mists of Ireland.

For Andersen, too, the light was key, 'the warm sunshine was a magic veil' that he liked to imagine covering the streets as he wandered from the old castle to the cathedral. The city's cathedral – or to give it the full title, the Santa Iglesia Catedral Basílica de la Encarnación – has not attracted universal admirers. Louisa Tenison, in her usual frank fashion, thought it unable to 'boast of much architectural beauty', even going so far as to say 'it offers nothing remarkable either in the interior or exterior.' Perhaps the most notable exterior feature is the lack of a second tower, the absence of which is attributable to the necessary funds having been diverted to the cause of American Independence from Britain.

This 'one-armed lady', as the cathedral is known, seemed to Andersen a 'mountain of marble' whose charms he thought lay in the sheer vastness of the structure, which must have been even more commanding without the city's twentieth-century development, although to a certain degree, Andersen's 'crooked, irregular streets' surrounding the cathedral still bear something of their original pattern. Strolling some hundred metres down the Scottish-sounding Calle Strachan to the west of the basilica leads you into Calle la Bolsa, where you are presented with a striking sculpture that appears both bird and open hand at one and the same time.

The bronze was created by the sculptor José Seguiri and is based on a sketch made by the Malagueño poet, Rafael Pérez Estrada. It is called the *Ave Quiromántica* (*The Chiromantic Bird*). More than once a finalist for Spain's National Literature Prize, Pérez Estrada found a passionate Anglophone supporter in the translator Steven Stewart, who, in a single-minded effort, sought out the writer's literary heirs after his death in 2000 and brought his poetry to an English-speaking audience in the book, *Devoured by the Moon*.

Another in a long list of legally trained poets, Pérez Estrada was a quirky exception in that he actually practised law, both in Madrid and at home. He was known for his enthusiasm and generous spirit, not to mention his ability to tell a good story – traits which no doubt helped in the courtroom – and his work, also including plays and prose, is rich in imagery. Two texts in *Devoured by the Moon* stand out as quintessential examples: 'Angels of Desperation and Abandonment' and 'When the Seagulls Take Flight'. Love, the fleeting nature of life, anxiety and mortality pierce the verses. In the first of the above two pieces, he enumerates a list of angels doomed to carry the weight of human suffering, a misery that sees no one accept 'the services of a murdered man's angel'.

Born two years before the start of the Civil War, Pérez Estrada would have grown up in a Spain much haunted by his 'murdered man's angel'. Málaga suffered more than many places. It was at this time that Gerald Brenan found himself in Churriana, now included as one of the 11 districts of Málaga; however, in the 1930s, it was very much a separate settlement. Brenan had come from Yegen in the Alpujarra mountains, accompanied by his wife, Gamel Woolsey, and his faithful staff consisting of Rosario, her sister María and her husband, Antonio. It had been in these mountains in 1920 that the Bloomsbury-affiliated Brenan had fallen in love with Spain, also hoping it would soothe his post-World War soul and make his meagre income go further.

The Brenans' Churriana bolt-hole was far grander than his Yegen residence. He had bought La Reina de los Angeles at 56 Calle Torremolinos in 1935 from Carlos Crooke Larios. The house and gardens were in a dilapidated state and took months to renovate. Years after Brenan's death, the house again fell into decay – its once-gleaming whitewashed walls peeling, doors bricked up and windows smashed. Fortunately, after much effort, 2014 saw the property reopen as the Casa Gerald Brenan, a space which now commemorates his work and promotes his vision.

Brenan's letters to friends from Churriana before the outbreak of war in 1936 shine with passion and contentment for his new home. Both Gamel Woolsey and Brenan were most enamoured of the garden, which he describes irresistibly in *The Face of Spain*, the book he wrote on returning to the house after the conflict had forced him back to England:

> Every day we paced round it a dozen times with Antonio or Rosario, touching, smelling, admiring, commenting: breathing in the calm and happiness that only southern gardens, bathed in perpetual sunlight, can give. The orange buds come out, the goldfinches chase one another among the branches, the flower of the avocado-pear tree gives off its summery smell, the datura its Cleopatra perfume. Then evening falls: every colour becomes transparent, every shadow filled with light, while in the sky above long pink and scarlet trails of cloud act the charade of another garden overhead.

His words make palpable his gratitude to Antonio and Rosario, who had kept the property in as good a condition as could be expected throughout the war. Brenan was, and continued to be on his return, a sympathiser with the anti-Franco cause, but this did not stop him sheltering Don Carlos, the Falange-supporting man from whom he had purchased La Reina, the individual being more important than their beliefs. Clearly, Brenan's experiences in the First World War had shown him that fighting was never going to be the solution.

In the early stages of the Falangist uprising, Communist troops came to the house to search for weapons, but Brenan's privacy was respected, especially when the housekeeper, Rosario, somewhat flippantly produced the cosh Brenan had carried in the First World War. It was a difficult time for all concerned. Gamel recalled these early moments in her memoir, *Death's Other Kingdom*, now retitled as *Malaga Burning*. Trucks rattled past the property packed with itinerant soldiers recruited on the hoof for the likes of the Socialists, Anarcho-Syndicalists and Anarchists. As Brenan later told the world in his masterwork, *The Spanish Labyrinth*, the Republican side was made up of a confusing mass of groupings and sub-groupings ranging from the centre-left to the extreme.

On the horizon, Gamel could see that the distant centre of the city had been attacked: 'Malaga lying spread out across the bay was under a pall of smoke. The city was hidden and the smoke drifted far out over the sea. Malaga is burning down.' As she stood with her friend Enrique, he scornfully prophesied, 'Someone will get killed soon.' The sad fact is that this statement was fulfilled thousands of times over, with many dying in Málaga. Before we pick up the thread of the city under siege, we will first follow Brenan during his more tranquil postwar years in La Reina de los Angeles.

Surprisingly, on the couple's return, both right and left appear to have accepted and welcomed them back. The novelist Silvia Grijalba, who now oversees the foundation, has stated that the aim of the newly refurbished space is to unite the cosmopolitan with the local, which is something she rightly claims Brenan managed to achieve. He was equally at home chatting with his neighbours and the baker or hosting the likes of the philosopher Bertrand Russell, the orientalist Arthur Waley and his Bloomsbury friends, or, most notably, Ernest Hemingway. He also struck up a close friendship with Julio Caro Baroja, the anthropologist and historian who was the nephew of the famous novelist Pio Baroja.

These were years of furious writing, not all of which managed to see the light of day. Like Patrick Leigh Fermor, Brenan was an inveterate note-taker and tinkerer with his texts, constantly revising and rewriting so that a book could take anything up to five years to finish. Unlike Leigh Fermor, who was championed at home and abroad, it is perhaps true to say that Brenan was more well known in his adopted country of Spain. His sometime guest Hemingway had already become synonymous with the country owing to his journalism from the front and his Civil War novel, *For Whom the Bell Tolls*, not to mention his fascination with bullfighting in *Death in the Afternoon*.

On what was to be his penultimate birthday, Hemingway celebrated at the house of Bill Davis, a very wealthy American who owned La Cónsula, a property in Churriana next to the Alhaurín de la Torre road. It is a rather grandiose affair with arches upon arches and balustrades aplenty. Luckily for the curious, this *finca* is now more accessible as it is Málaga's Catering College. Other regular visitors to Davis and his wife were the bullfighters Antonio Ordóñez and Luis Miguel Dominguín, whose rivalry Hemingway was then writing about – a story which would ultimately form the basis of his last book, *The Dangerous Summer*. Pictures of a ruddy, worn-looking Hemingway still exist from his time at La Cónsula, showing him dining with friends, reading in one of the bedrooms and, alongside Ordóñez, indulging in his passion for shooting.

The birthday party in question was a breath-taking affair, as A. E. Hotchner's biography, *Papa Hemingway*, points out. There was champagne from Paris, Chinese food from London and salt cod from Madrid. Fireworks came from Valencia, flamenco dancers from Málaga and musicians from Torremolinos, which was still yet to earn its dubious reputation for low-rent package tourism. Incredibly, it seems that the maharajas of Jaihpur and Cooch Behar turned up, and Hotchner assures us that Hemingway shot cigarettes from the lips of his bullfighter friend and one of the more foolhardy maharajas.

The alcohol-fuelled whimsical mayhem was a great success until one of the Valencian firecrackers set a palm tree on fire. No harm was done, thanks to the skills of the local fire brigade, who were immediately assimilated into the party. In many ways, this was Hemingway's last hurrah before returning to the Americas and ultimately ending his life with a shotgun at home in Ketchum, Idaho; a ticket for next season's Spanish bullfighting was found amongst his effects.

It is easy to imagine lively conversations between Hemingway, Brenan and their Spanish friends. The Civil War and its aftermath must have figured large, seeing them talk into the night over Jerez brandy. These two were by no means the only foreign wordsmiths to portray the evils of this fratricidal conflict. Arthur Koestler, the Hungarian-born journalist and writer who spent the last 43 years of his life living in Britain, was witness to the fall of Málaga. He had gone to Spain as a journalist for the UK-based *News Chronicle* and had previously infiltrated the Francoist headquarters in Seville on behalf of Comintern, the international Communist organisation originally created in Russia. It is clear where his sympathies lay, although disillusion with Stalin did see him resign his German Communist Party membership in 1938.

On 28 January 1937, Koestler found himself in the capital of the Costa del Sol. His description of what ensued is to be found in his book *Spanish Testament* (an English adaption of *Menschenopfer unerhört*). Franco's troops, backed by German and Italian air and sea forces, had swiftly swept along the Mediterranean, encountering little resistance until they reached Málaga, a bastion of Republican sentiment. Joined by Moroccan regulars and Italian tanks, on 3 February the Nationalists started a ground attack from the north that would take less than a week to complete, reaching the heights above the city on 6 February.

Koestler had previously received news from the British Consul in Almería – whom he had compared to a pillar 'in the apocalyptic flood: dry and solid' – that the siege of Málaga would be butchery and that the Republicans would attempt to defend to the last gasp. It seems that the Consul's sangfroid had led him to suggest that British warships in the harbour might provide an escape route. To add to the catastrophe, torrential rain had flooded the roads, creating yet another barrier. Koestler's impressions prior to the ground offensive were of a city damaged by some seismic event, with whole streets bombed into ruin.

He stayed in the Regina Hotel, where the only food he could get was fried fish, the waiter informing him that the establishment had escaped destruction by a whisker when a neighbouring house had been flattened by a hefty shell. To his dismay, on the following morning, he discovered that the last British warship had left. He noted that 'Europe doesn't seem to be interested'. This was swiftly followed by an air raid that saw panic and confusion amongst the populace. He can barely disguise his consternation when he encounters a guard post with no fortifications and only two soldiers, the rest being back at barracks.

In a quirky aside, he tells the reader that, the day before the main offensive, he went to visit Sir Peter Chalmers-Mitchell, the creator of Whipsnade Zoo, who had bought a house in the city so he could retire in peaceful surroundings. Koestler has no need to point out the irony, as he looks out on the 'enchanted isle' of Sir Peter's garden. The havoc of the ensuing days made this haven of tranquillity a distant memory. On 6 February, panic and implausible propaganda are evident at the Governor's Residence, and the whole city is a rumour mill of anxiety and fear. Koestler finds himself in the exodus to Vélez, being told by his driver to flee to Valencia and not to come back. He ignores this wise advice and, on returning, he finds the Republican headquarters resembling a 'night refuge'. Defeat is imminent.

The flow of refugees and retreating militiamen from the city was directed towards Almería and became known as the 'Caravan of Death'. Thousands fell en route, and those Republicans left in Málaga faced an equally grisly fate, some being shot in reprisal for the treatment of Nationalist prisoners, whilst others were randomly executed and buried in mass graves. This was a fate that Koestler only just escaped, thanks to a prisoner exchange with a prominent Falangist. Amidst this mayhem of death and destruction there are some stories of true altruistic heroism. One such account is told by Paul Read in his booklet, *The Ambulance Man and the Spanish Civil War.*

Read, the self-styled Gazpacho Monk, blogs and writes about Spain and has also published pieces on Orwell and Ethel MacDonald, the anarchist reporter from Scotland. *The Ambulance Man* is about Norman Bethune, who joined a Canadian variant of the International Brigades fighting for the Republic, although his vocation in the war was obviously medical. On hearing about the flight of thousands from Málaga, Bethune and colleagues stocked up their makeshift Renault ambulance and headed for the coastal road connecting the city with Almería.

Paul Read describes what Bethune and his friends saw when he encountered the first refugees:

> Climbing a hill they looked further on and saw a serpentine line that filled the whole width of the road as far as the eye could see. At least 30 kilometres of slumped and exhausted bodies were dragging themselves automatically onwards. So compact were the groups of terrified Malagueños that they trod on each other's feet as they stumbled forward.

Realising the ambulance crew could do little for Málaga, Norman and a friend, Size, decided to clear out their ambulance and turn it into a passenger transport in order to drive the vulnerable people to safety, avoiding the shelling from the sea. Over a period of four days, the crew ferried the bedraggled to Almería and came back for more, 30 at a time.

For those who thought they had found safety at the port city of Almería, subsequent attacks meant they had walked or been driven to a similar fate. That is not to deny the heroic efforts of the ambulance man and his companions, although, as Read tells us, Bethune became something of a forgotten man in Spain during the Franco years, even being besmirched by the Communist Party during the war for supposed moral faults and the passing of maps to an infiltrator. The alleged spy was, in reality, his Swedish girlfriend and extremely unlikely to have been a Fascist sympathiser.

The epilogue to Read's text contains details of a conversation the author had with a man from the mountains who had been part of the convoy. As a boy, he had left his quiet, simple hillside village to join others escaping from the Falange. It is easy to forget that these events only took place close to 80 years ago as the hills, valleys and the coastal strips have changed beyond recognition. Yet Spain is only just now coming to terms with its *pacto del olvido*, its tacit 'agreement to forget' that saw the country through the transition to democracy. Recent years have seen relatives clamour to rebury their dead with dignity, reclaiming them from their roadside graves.

The Costa del Sol

Málaga sits at the geographical centre of the Costa del Sol, which radiates out to the west as far as Manilva, passing through the very familiar-sounding resorts of Torremolinos, Fuengirola, Marbella and Estepona. To the east, the Costa del Sol spreads as far as Torrox and Nerja, where the Costa Tropical begins. As intimated above, the area has undergone a transformation in the latter half of the twentieth century that has seen the small fishing villages and agricultural hamlets give way to the kind of mass tourism that is so synonymous with this part of southern Spain. A coastal highway that starts in the west with a toll road links all of the towns mentioned. In many ways, the strip has become one long line of development, where each new *urbanización* with its homogenous whitewashed villas vacuums up the remnants of individuality still clinging to the original settlements. Given this expansion, it is hard not to treat the Costa del Sol as one entity.

If one were to put this entity on the psychologist's couch, it would be very easy to make some initial diagnoses on a superficial level that tend to sweeping and condemnatory judgements but, as all good psychologists know, the truth is never that simple. What created this behemoth of package tourism and expat society, labelled by the locals as Guirilandia (Foreignerland)? To start at the beginning, romanticising the pre-tourist village is remarkably easy from an outside perspective – quaint scenes of pastoral simplicity laced with exotic tradition, all held together by sunshine and family. Yet the reality was far from these facile observations: no electricity, often a lack of running water, a reliance on harvests that could easily fail, day labourer wages and a hand-to-mouth existence.

Contrary to expectations, the first tourists and expats in the area were not of the packaged variety, but a far more adventurous and bohemian type. In his book *Pueblo*, Ronald Fraser took a look at the village of Tajos, whose real-life counterpart was Mijas, some seven kilometres (five miles) behind Fuengirola. Fraser specialised in oral histories, taking the testimonies first hand from people who had experienced some of Spain's most momentous events. Fraser is particularly known for *Blood of Spain: An Oral History of the Spanish Civil War* and *In Hiding: The Life of Manuel Cortes*, the latter focusing on the Republican mayor who hid from the end of the war until Franco's amnesty in 1969.

Pueblo was published in 1973 but draws on accounts before this date, when Tajos/Mijas was a working settlement. In one chapter, Fraser tells the stories of some of the first foreigners to put down roots in the area. One such was John Bertorelli, who found himself spellbound by the scenery when he stopped off to visit on the way to Italy from New York – so much so that he never left. Bertorelli was a commercial artist-turned-silversmith who was able to make a living by supplying shops on the coast.

It is clear from his testimony that the mountain and sea views were the main draw. Experience taught him that the village was less attractive to a cosmopolitan city-dweller more used to living in a degree of anonymity. He found superficial conversations and friendships easy, but hit a barrier with anything deeper. In many ways, this dilemma is central to village life everywhere, where gossip forms part of the daily routine but remains relatively shallow, enabling everyone to rub along in a degree of harmony. In such societies the world over, strangers will inevitably be something of a curiosity and seen in a different light.

That is not to say that he felt isolated but, rather, frustrated. He almost felt that a kind of paranoia had set in, something he detected most strongly when strolling through the village on his own, supposing eyes to be upon him. Interestingly, he noted that Spaniards from other regions who had settled in the area sensed a similar atmosphere. In reality, this must have been the dawning realisation that the villagers' future was to depend on these tourists and long-term residents, creating an inevitable love–hate relationship and interdependence that is now likely to continue for generations to come.

Bertorelli's solution, rather than attempt further integration, was to consider a move out into the countryside, where he could feel freer. In so doing, he represents the escapist tendency of a particular type of expat, the one who wants to live in isolated splendour in the Andalucian hillsides, away from the locals and other expats. Others choose the opposite tendency and cluster together in like-minded communities fuelled by the development of the *urbanización*.

Returning to the psychologist's waiting room, Karen O'Reilly in her study, *The British on the Costa del Sol*, has put a whole nation of expats on the couch. Prompted by increasing media headlines in the 1980s, most of which were negative, she decided an in-depth study was in order. One of her text's first inclinations is towards the role of nostalgia and the large part it plays in the residents' desire to recreate a supposed version of Britain in the 1950s, when notions of community and family were stronger; the ultimate irony being, as O'Reilly indicates, that the majority who feel this way have left family behind in order to make such a life for themselves.

One of the chapters is entitled 'Betwixt and Between' – an apt description of the position in which many who have moved to the Costa del Sol find themselves. The terminology used is most revealing, with the word 'expatriate' being loaded with many connotations that do not evoke anything related to 'migrant'. The former is nuanced towards a lack of integration which leads to a form of self-ghettoisation, the Guirilandia of popular Spanish imagination. One of O'Reilly's interviewees was a local official who admitted that these new residents had been welcomed as they brought prosperity, but it was at a price. The prosperous nature of today's expat is only likely to decline as age and all its attendant issues have an impact on the society in which they live, something which O'Reilly alludes to in her study.

Fuengirola, just half an hour's drive from Málaga, is a case in point. It was a poor fishing village before the arrival of the tourist, and the opinion among many newcomers is that the Andalucians were happy to embrace the wealth arriving with the transient and resident foreigner. Some of the populace now complain of the damage to the environment, which is so evident in terms of the acres of concrete poured all over the virgin coastline, yet expats in Karen O'Reilly's study note that people were not complaining at the time. This may be true, but everyone, *guiris* and locals alike, sold their souls in the pursuit of a dream.

And just a dream it may have been, for some at least. The isolation that comes with uprooting from a familiar culture and implanting yourself 'betwixt and between' can lead to loneliness and boredom. A frightening step further into an imagined realm of a life without purpose was taken by the author J. G. Ballard in his 1996 book, *Cocaine Nights*. Ballard's reputation has become so embedded in British letters that the adjective Ballardian is now common currency. It refers to dystopias and the psychological effects of technology or landscapes carved out by man. In essence, *Cocaine Nights* tackles these themes head-on as Charles Prentice, the travel writer protagonist, makes his way to the Costa del Sol to help his brother, who has been imprisoned for arson and causing the deaths that resulted from the fire. Prentice finds an expat community that is being roused from its catatonic state by a psychopathic young man driven by his desire to shake the municipality awake; his methods are dark and destructive.

Prentice's opinion of the roadside developments and their numb cocoons appear in this nightmarish vision:

The retirement pueblos lay by the motorway, embalmed in the dream of the sun from which they would never awake. As always, when I drove along the coast to Marbella, I seemed to be moving through a zone that was fully accessible only to a neuroscientist, and scarcely at all to a travel writer. The white facades of the villas and apartment houses were like blocks of time that had crystallized beside the road. Here on the Costa del Sol nothing would ever happen again, and the people of the pueblos were already the ghosts of themselves.

Charles finds himself drawn into a web of drugs, sex and violence, the underbelly of the civilised surface, actively provoked by forces he cannot control. As he learns the truth behind his brother's imprisonment, he falls into a similar trap. Compelling and excruciating, Ballard's portrait of the Costa del Sol, whilst fantastical, contains something which the reader will find uncomfortably close to a potential reality.

Giles Tremlett's book, *Ghosts of Spain*, has a whole section dedicated to 'How the Bikini Saved Spain', an ironic title focusing on the happy injections of wealth and their not-so-pleasurable consequences. He quotes a study undertaken by Málaga University that highlights some shocking statistics on the nature of corruption, which was at its most rife when the housing bubble had yet to burst. The coast has had its fair share of locals with their fingers in the metaphorical pie and a good few expats hiding out from justice back home, giving rise to its nickname as the Costa del Crime.

The transnational nature of crime and drug trafficking forms the backdrop to Arturo Pérez-Reverte's novel *The Queen of the South*. The queen in question is Teresa Mendoza, who escapes the wrath of the Mexican Sinaloa drug cartel, fleeing to the Spanish enclave of Melilla on the coast of North Africa. From there, she becomes mixed up in trafficking across the Straits of Gibraltar. The work is a hectic mix of double-dealing, corruption and what would be labelled in Italy as the Mafia. It was almost tailor-made for the small screen and was indeed adapted by Telemundo and Antena 3 in 2011. In the United States it out-rated English-speaking programmes put up against it.

The literary output centring on the Costa is mostly negative in nature, yet there are more than a few glimpses of light that give balance to this area's destructive reputation. Estepona, for example, has managed to maintain a degree of its original character, with twisting lanes, bars that serve more than Americanised fast food, and shops that provide something other than tourist tat. In these towns, the fervent sun that drugs the unwary in Ballard has a healing effect on some expats who have found their dream living up to reality. Those who have succeeded are the people who have adapted, tried to integrate and found a niche. Tales of relocation abound – one of the more heart-warming ones is Jackie Todd's *Dog Days in Andalucía*.

The Todds moved to the region in 1997, specifically to the hamlet of La Molineta just below the brilliant white façades of Frigiliana, which lies about half an hour inland from the coastal town of Nerja. Frigiliana is the quintessential Andaluz pueblo, a settlement clinging to a soft hilltop like crenellated icing on a tiered wedding cake. The houses have spectacular views but seem to turn inward towards their trusted neighbours. It was this sense of community that attracted the couple, who openly rejected the 'tourist ghettos' on the coast. They bought an old mill complex with Moorish origins and eventually acquired the next-door property that had been the bakery.

The original idea was to rent out the mill whilst living in the other building. So far so typical of many expats with dreams of making a living from a more cultured tourism. What happened next draws on the beloved stereotype of animal-loving Britons, but it was a cliché that turned into a concrete reality for this kind-hearted couple and embedded them further in the affections of the locals. Jackie and her husband, Stephen, adopted a stray dog, yet this one act of kindness proved to be more than an isolated case; other dogs followed, as did cats. Their intention was always, in the initial stages, to foster strays until they were well enough to be taken to the local animal charity where owners would be found. Inevitably, some found their way into the Todds' ever-growing family.

Jackie stresses in her account the need to embrace the local community and culture, which the pair had clearly achieved – in the process demolishing the expat myth and instead building on their status as migrants:

> So there we were: the years had flown by, we had three dogs, three cats and three houses. Still not a Spanish pointer or Mediterranean tabby, but the village had adopted us and it certainly felt like home. English people living here would sometimes ask 'do you go home often?' and didn't seem to understand our response that we went home every day.

From three dogs and cats, their pack grew to ten canines and eight felines, a mammoth undertaking, but a happy one. After years creating their own version of a Frigilianan Noah's Ark, sadly Jackie Todd died in 2010.

Ronda

Over 60 kilometres (37 miles) safely north of the kitsch glitz of Marbella and 100-plus kilometres to the west of Málaga, Ronda is famed for its spectacular location. The gorge, known by the name of El Tajo, literally slices through the heart of the town. The iconic Puente Nuevo or New Bridge spans the vertiginous drop, its arched brickwork pushing back against the sides of the chasm. The views out over Ronda's surrounding mountains are an obvious draw for the visitor, particularly when the long shadows at dusk chisel the contours of the gorge into luminous red corrugations.

The bridge has not always had such picturesque connotations. Terrifying events that took place on this very spot during the Civil War were portrayed in Ernest Hemingway's *For Whom the Bell Tolls*, albeit transferred to a more northerly location. The main protagonist, Robert Jordan – whose adventures were loosely based

9   *The Puente Nuevo, Ronda*

on Hemingway's own Civil War experiences – listens to Pilar, the lover of Pablo the guerrilla leader, as she recounts the events that took place in the town square. Pablo had blocked the exits to the plaza, thus trapping the remaining Fascists, who were offered final confession by a local priest.

Awaiting the doomed Falangists were two solid lines of people, two metres apart, armed with flails that were usually used for threshing grain; clubs and pitchforks were added to the gruesome methods of execution. The Mayor, the first Fascist made to walk through the lines, continued for quite some time before anything happened. Once the blows had started to land, the unfortunate Mayor was then taken to the walk by the edge of the cliff and thrown over into the river. A similar procession of other local Fascist luminaries continued until 20 men had met the same fate. In fact, Hemingway underestimated the numbers that were actually involved. A house by Ronda's cliff-face was used as a gruesome springboard, according to some testimonies, for hundreds of right-wing sympathisers who met their deaths in the gorge below.

In one pithy anecdote, again recounted by Pablo's lover, a certain Don Faustino was killed by the mob. He was the quintessential little rich kid, a pretend womaniser and vain popinjay who liked to play at bullfighting. It is with scorn that Pilar tells us of his delight in dressing up as an Andalucian *rejoneador*, the bullfighter who faces his foe on horseback. We can almost hear Hemingway's contempt for this pseudo-matador, given his own passion for the *corrida* and its place at the heart of Ronda's traditional social calendar.

The bullring is a short walk from the Puente Nuevo along the Calle Virgen de la Paz. Its traditional whitewashed curved walls are topped with terracotta tiles. For those with an interest in the *toros*, there is a museum attached which guides the visitor through the history of bullfighting, including the animal's place in cultural history, the *corridas* in the era of Goya, as well as details on Ronda's *torero* dynasties, notably the Ordóñez. There is more than one bloodstained *traje de luces*, the suit of lights worn by the matador, occasionally accompanied by photographs of Hemingway or Orson Welles grinning next to the bullfighter in question.

The film director and actor Orson Welles, like his American comrade, was also a regular visitor to Ronda. He formed a friendship with Antonio Ordóñez, the instigator of Ronda's Feria Goyesca, the season of fights staged in period costume, reminiscent of the taurine paintings of Francisco Goya. In fact, the museum holds an edition of Goya's famous Tauromaquia collection, depicting this style of costume. Welles was so taken with the atmosphere of the area and its traditions that it seems fitting his ashes were buried in a flower-covered well on the estate of his friend Ordóñez, close to his beloved Ronda.

As we know from his time in Churriana, Hemingway also had a connection to Ordóñez. During that last trip to Spain in 1959, he was writing the articles that would form the basis of *The Dangerous Summer*, his account of the rivalry between Dominguín and Ordóñez. It took his love of bullfighting one step further, expanding upon the emotion and ritual he had previously described in *Death in the Afternoon*. Inevitably, some find the bullfight abhorrent, your authors included, but that does not detract from Hemingway's obvious passion for his subject and his ability to convey its nuances to a new audience.

Gazing across El Tajo towards the bullring from the other side of the Puente Nuevo is the Palacio de Mondragón, situated in the square of the same name. Now a museum, it was once home to the Moorish ruler Abbel Mallek, and although much renovated, it still retains some original features evident in the Arab archways, tiling and, most poignantly, in the gardens that are redolent of the Moors' delight in playing with water in all its soothing aspects.

The palace and its adjoining casa have a very British literary connection which centres on the lives of Alastair Boyd, Hilary Amis, her former husband, Kingsley, and their writer son Martin. After meeting in Oxford, Hilary and Kingsley were married in 1948. It was a partnership that lasted until 1963, with both subsequently remarrying: Hilary to Shackleton Bailey, a Cambridge academic. This marriage also hit the rocks when Hilary decided to stay in Ronda during a holiday the couple had taken in southern Spain. It is at this point that Alastair Boyd enters the scene, a former City of London businessman and Scottish aristocrat who had sought a new life in the town.

Boyd was running a language school in the Mondragón complex; the stage was set for a relationship to form between the pair, which eventually led to marriage. Hilary's son, Martin Amis, picks up the story in his book *Experience*. Amis's first novel, *The Rachel Papers*, had won the Somerset Maugham Award and, as he notes, the terms of the prize required the author to spend some time abroad. He headed for Spain and his mother's house, the Casa de Mondragón, next to the palacio. Amis calls Spain his other European country, a feeling he tells us his mother shared. At the time, she was dabbling in the running of a local bar, flushed with the success of the fish and chip shop she had set up whilst living with her second husband in Michigan.

During his stay, Martin established himself in one of the palace bedrooms, smoking his way prodigiously through the typing of the manuscript for his second novel, *Dead Babies*. He admits he filled two litre bottles with cigarette butts. Whilst not smoking and furiously typing, he used to stroll across the bridge into the centre of town and play the pinball machines. In *Experience*, he uses his sardonic wit to pierce the Hemingway bubble, commenting on the preponderance of bars sporting photographs of a partially pickled Papa Hemingway imbibing with the owner of the establishment. He was equally unimpressed with the American's recommendation of Ronda's casino in the main square as a good place for an elopement. He was, however, awed by the gorge and the birds flying below.

Dead Babies, the novel Amis was working on at the Mondragón, has no specific connection with Spain, rather being a darkly humorous satire of a drug-fuelled group of friends who convene at a country house for a weekend of debauchery. His stepfather, Alastair Boyd, wrote more directly about the region, penning *The Road from Ronda*, published in 1969. In its early pages, he gives us the actual moment at which he decided the town was going to play a part in his future: 'Leaving my luggage in the Hotel Royal, I walked across the street into the *alameda* and knew at once, as one instinctively does, that I had reached a place of great significance in my life.'

It was the November of 1957 when Alastair and his first wife took up residence during a period of transition for Ronda that witnessed the first influx of package tourists on day-trips from the coast. Boyd recognises the town's slightly schizophrenic existence with one eye on the easy money and the other on its much-vaunted past, a past epitomised by the house he lived in, the Mondragón:

> [T]he locals call it Casa de Piedra, the Stone House, a name deriving from its all-stone façade unbroken except by a great Renaissance portico and the three long windows of the saloon on the first floor. The staircase leading up to this floor has a fine plaster vaulted ceiling painted with heraldic achievements, among which three severed Moors' heads figure prominently [...] Beyond the front patio, which dates from about 1570, lies the oldest part of the house, known as the Patio Arabe, and beyond this again the garden hanging over the gorge.

On reading this, we wondered at his ability to afford such a property, especially as his second novel had received a short sharp rejection from the publishers, but Boyd explains that English teaching was the remedy that opened the doors to his paradise.

The Serranía de Ronda also proved attractive to Xan Fielding and his partner, Magouche Phillips. Fielding had been a Special Operations Executive agent in occupied Crete during the Second World War, becoming a translator and writer in later life. He shared all these merits with the far more famous Patrick Leigh Fermor. Aside from writing about his wartime exploits, Fielding also published *Images of Spain* in 1991. A happy reunion between the old wartime buddies is recalled in Leigh Fermor's *Words of Mercury*. Paddy, as he was always known, found the Fielding residence, Tramores, a splendid sight, built in a ruined Moorish tower high in the Ronda mountains. Leigh Fermor and his wife were treated to excursions throughout Andalucia, including visits to Gerald Brenan. Yet Ronda remained the place that most engaged his effervescently fluvial prose:

> [T]his wonderful Roman-Moorish-Spanish town, lifted into the sky, complete with bullring and churches and palaces on tremendous cliffs sundered by a narrow chasm from top to bottom, right in the town's heart, so that one peers over the bridge and down through the layers of choughs, jackdaws, ravens, swallows and crows to a cascade that looks a mile below.

This sensibility to place would have appealed to Rainer Maria Rilke, the Austro-Bohemian poet, who described the town in a letter to his sculptor friend, Rodin, as 'an incomparable spot of earth, a giant of a rock which bears a small white-washed town on his shoulders'. Rilke initially travelled to Spain in 1912 with the intention of viewing art, being particularly taken with El Greco and Goya; in reality, he was escaping money worries and trying to shake off the black dog of depression. After Toledo, he headed for Seville; originally it was his aim to settle in the city for a few months. The Andalucian capital was not to his taste and, on the advice of an acquaintance, he moved to Ronda. As we can see from the above, he was immediately smitten.

Rilke was delighted to find that the off-season Hotel Reina Victoria was a haven of peace and tranquillity, being virtually empty. In fact, he is still there today, frozen in time, gazing towards the horizon, book in hand. As well as this statue in the hotel gardens, you can visit his room, which has been turned into a small exhibition in his honour. He liked nothing more than to wander the narrow, crooked streets, turning his back on the famous bullring and making, instead, for the fields full of trees: the oak, the olive and the fig, the latter of which found its way into the 'Sixth Elegy' of his *Duino Elegies* actually written in the town.

Rilke's poetry is complex, centred on his own particular interpretation of spirituality and laced with mysticism and an existential angst that stemmed from his struggles with depression. Throughout the period in Ronda, his poetic output increased as his mood fell. He also worked on what would become known as the *Spanish Trilogy*, in addition to a series of individual poems. One of his more accessible offerings is 'The Spanish Dancer':

> As a lit match first flickers in the hands
> Before it flames, and darts out from all sides
> Bright, twitching tongues, so, ringed by growing bands
> Of spectators – she, quivering, glowing stands
> Poised tensely for the dance – then forward glides
> And suddenly becomes a flaming torch.
> Her bright hair flames, her burning glances scorch,
> And with a daring art at her command
> Her whole robe blazes like a fire-brand
> From which is stretched each naked arm, awake,
> Gleaming and rattling like a frightened snake.

This evocation of the flamenco dancer catches the elusive *duende* spirit through the metaphorical flames that ignite as her dress swirls in time to the music. For a melancholic northern European, this is a valiant evocation of a very southern art.

Another traveller to Ronda was even more attuned to the music and Gypsy culture of Andalucia. We are referring to that latter-day George Borrow, Walter Starkie, who died in 1976. The title of his Spanish books, *Don Gypsy: Adventures with a Fiddle in Barbary, Andalusia and La Mancha* and *Spanish Raggle-Taggle*, speak for themselves. Unlike Borrow, the Irish Starkie was not an autodidact. He was an academic, holding the professorship of Spanish and Italian at Trinity College, Dublin, where one of his pupils was Samuel Beckett. He had initial authorial success with a book on the Sicilian playwright Luigi Pirandello which led to his appointment as director of the Abbey Theatre. During the Second World War, he was sent to Spain as a cultural representative of the British Institute.

Given his interest in Romany culture, it is no surprise that Spain, especially Andalucia, became something of a second home. He spent the long university holidays literally living the life of Riley. This vagabond existence was combined with the scholarly pursuit of literary translation, notably his versions of *Don Quixote* and the plays of the Spanish Golden Age. On one of his hobo excursions with his fiddle slung on his back, Starkie was bowled over by Ronda, adding to the ecstatic praise so many have heaped upon this unique location with the now oft-repeated description: 'Ronda is a town which hangs from the sky atop a mountain split in two by the Gods.'

To close our meandering through the streets and fields of Ronda, we combine Rilke's trees and Starkie's nomads in George Eliot's *The Spanish Gypsy*, originally written in the winter of 1864–5:

> 'Tis the warm South, where Europe spreads her lands
> Like fretted leaflets, breathing on the deep:
> Broad-breasted Spain, leaning with equal love
> On the Mid Sea that moans with memories,
> And on the untravelled Ocean's restless tides.
> [...] This deep mountain gorge
> Slopes widening on the olive pluméd plains.

Wilder speculation attributes distant Judeo-Spanish ancestry to George Eliot (Mary Ann Evans), the author of *Daniel Deronda*, maybe owing to the character's own roots: a Sephardic Jew brought up as an Englishman.

Antequera

An easy day trip from Málaga, 52 kilometres (33 miles) in a northerly direction, lies the market town of Antequera. Just to the south of the town, approaching from the Málaga road, is the noteworthy El Torcal nature reserve formed from glaciated limestone. The rocks have been weathered over the years and softened by vegetation, giving rise to some spectacular formations composed of striated and creased boulders, rounded at the edges. The shapes provide fanciful resemblances for those with a lucid imagination.

Even closer to the town is the quaintly called Montaña del Indio, owing to its profile, which supposedly mimics that of a Native American. If you squint into the sun, you can make out the 'nose' of this mound. It has also been called the Peña de los Enamorados, or Lovers' Rock, in honour of a possibly apocryphal story centring on two Moorish lovers from rival families. Whilst being pursued by the girl's angry father, they threw themselves to their death from the end of the nose. Some versions of the story have the couple divided by religion, with the young lady's lover being a Christian soldier named Tello.

This tale appealed to the English poet laureate, Robert Southey, who immortalised the tragedy in his poem, 'The Lover's Rock'. Southey used to visit Spain for 'poetic inspiration'. In a letter sent to his brother Thomas, dated 1802, he quotes, or possibly misquotes, a local ballad at length, including these evocative lines: '"Yo me estaba en Antequera/En bodas de una mi hermana; (Mal fuego quemen las bodas …)" [I was in Antequera / At my sister's wedding; (The fire of misfortune destroyed the celebrations …)].' The tale speaks of the marriage of the narrator's sister and its fiery fate.

He implores his brother to study the ballad, even if he needs a dictionary. Clearly, Southey found Antequera fertile ground for his 'inspiration'. 'The Lover's Rock' is written in rhyming couplets and has a balladic rhythm that seems frothy to the modern ear, particularly given the couple's ultimate destiny, which Southey gives us in these final verses:

He clasp'd her close and cried farewell,
In one another's arms they fell;
They leapt adown the craggy side,
In one another's arms they died.

And side by side they there are laid,
The Christian youth and Moorish maid,
But never Cross was planted there,
Because they perish'd for despair.

Yet every Moorish maid can tell
Where Laila lies who loved so well,
And every youth who passes there,
Says for Manuel's soul a prayer.

Walter Starkie, the twentieth-century wandering philosopher, also drifted into town from Ronda. He tells us in *Don Gypsy* that he found Antequera impressive, built as it is, around the ruins of its castle. Starkie was also fortunate enough to earn his keep by playing the violin at café tables in town, thereby making sufficient money to find a bed in a reasonable *posada*. The scholar would have been taken with the many fine buildings that rose from the prosperity experienced by the town between the sixteenth and eighteenth centuries when Spain was at its colonial height. There is a plethora of churches representing the various religious orders that established themselves in Antequera. The Real Colegiata de Santa María Mayor is a fine example.

Santa María Mayor is opposite a square, just beyond the Arco de los Gigantes, the arch built in 1585 on the street leading to the Alcazaba. The church has a plateresque façade, constructed to mimic the work of a silversmith, and is recognised as one of the most outstanding examples in Andalucia. Robert Dundas Murray, who wrote *The Cities and Wilds of Andalucia*, published in 1853, clearly felt that Antequera, with these grandiose religious and aristocratic buildings, could not possibly warrant the reputation of a town full of bandits – an infamy he had been warned about when approaching the outskirts:

> I had, however, been accustomed to connect Antequera in my thoughts with associations of a very different and more pleasing character than those suggested by such stories as the preceding, and could not so readily bring my mind to admit the idea that it was little better than a den of thieves and kidnappers.

Like Murray, the opinionated Lady Louisa Tenison found this aristocratic little town to warrant a far better reputation than had been suggested. Tenison's one complaint concerned the food: 'Oil and garlic seemed to be the staple products of Antequera, and garnished the dishes to an extent even rare in this land, rendering still more unpalatable the tough, fibrous chickens.' She was far more favourable towards the town's antiquities and, as so many before and since, makes reference to yet another version of the Lovers' Rock story; perhaps the one more associated with Rodrigo de Carvajal y Robles, the Antequeran born in the second half of the sixteenth century, who penned the *Poema heróico del asalto y conquista de Antequera (The Heroic Poem of the Assault and Conquest of Antequera)*. The poem contains many local legends, including a representation of the Christian/Muslim couple doomed to their tragic end.

Tenison's most interesting historical allusion refers to the dolmens found on the fringes of the town. One of these prehistoric stone structures is the Cueva de Menga, yet it is not a natural cave, but a megalithic burial chamber, which Tenison describes as 'a Druidic temple, a chambered mound'. She had no end of problems finding the edifice, as did your writers, but for Lady Tenison a letter to the Mayor bore fruit, resulting in him sending her a guide. After a long-winded introduction paraphrasing the first pamphlet written by a Spaniard on the subject, Tenison cuts to the chase:

It presents a perfect porch, symmetrical in shape, but composed of rough stones of gigantic magnitude. This porch is an oblong square, seventeen feet in depth, nine wide and eight high. Its roof is composed of a single stone, nearly fifteen feet square, and over four feet high, [...] an inner chamber lies before you, but of a different form.

After a flurry of further statistical analysis worthy of an architect's plan, she remarks on how the structure bears no evidence of human manufacture:

There are no traces upon them of chisel marks, nor any lines whatever; nor are there around the base of the hill, as is generally the case in Ireland, any remains of a stone circle. The structure is just under the surface of the summit, the conical shape of which is still preserved.

Visiting the dolmens is a delightful way of ending a visit to Antequera. Despite much subsequent academic study, the area still retains that prehistoric mystery that so fascinated nineteenth-century travellers. Perhaps the best view is at the entrance porch of the Menga Cave; turn inwards to contemplate the burial chamber of a long-forgotten dignitary, or turn outwards to see the Lovers' Rock perfectly outlined in the doorway – a framed portrait that cannot have been an accident.

✿ 6 ✿

GRANADA PROVINCE

The Moor's Last Sigh

The distant mountains surge and ripple lazily like a serpent.
An infinitely crystalline translucency reveals matt splendour on
    all sides.

(Federico García Lorca, *Sketches of Spain*, 2013
(*Impresiones y paisajes*, 1918))

Granada

Home to the magnificent Alhambra Palace, the last redoubt of
Moorish Spain, Granada is uniquely situated, both geographically
and historically. The city's way to the coast is blocked by the snow-
capped peaks of the justly named Sierra Nevada (literally, the snowy
mountains), and it is these very peaks that provide the meltwaters
so adroitly channelled by the Arabs into the paradisiacal gardens of
the Partal and Generalife. The waters still run along the channels
created by the Moors before their final defeat in 1492 at the hands
of the Catholic Monarchs Ferdinand and Isabella.

The world renown of the Alhambra is more than warranted; it is
the only example of a medieval Muslim palace still to be found in
Western Europe. A stroll through its environs will soon show the
diversity of the visitors that come from all corners of the earth. We
will join them later in the company of many notable writers and
poets. The Granadine poet Federico García Lorca's reputation has

also spread far and wide. Like the Alhambra's, his story is laden with tragedy and the portents of a doomed future.

In many ways, Lorca has been striding through these pages like a colossus; even if unmentioned, his presence has cast a long shadow over Andalucia's literary and historical landscape. Before we go any further, we must acknowledge a profound debt to the writer, biographer and historian Ian Gibson, whose award-winning works on Lorca have been invaluable in leading us to many hidden corners of the poet's city. For those who want to investigate Lorca more deeply than space allows us to do here, we can do no better than recommend Gibson's practical guide, *Lorca's Granada*.

Federico was a product of the Granadine Vega, the fertile plains that surround the city, many references to which are found in his work. His family, having made their fortune from sugar beet, moved to the province's capital in 1909 when the would-be poet was 11 years old. In fact, his first love was music, and his original tutor, Antonio Segura Mesa, thought he had the makings of a professional musician. He grew into the role of poet and dramatist, much to the detriment of the official university studies that his parents were so keen he undertook, refusing his wishes to study music in Paris. After much cajoling and prompting, he eventually graduated in Law from the city's university but dropped his other course in Philosophy and Letters.

It was during his university years that Lorca wrote his first book, quoted from at the head of this chapter. It was inspired by trips to the rest of Spain and the hidden corners of his own city. Now available in English as *Sketches of Spain*, and wonderfully illustrated by Julian Bell, it is, as Gibson notes, the early work of a great poet, which contains some vibrant observations on his hometown. The poetic prose evokes the sights and, particularly, the sounds of a Granada still straddling two worlds, the medieval and the modern:

Seen from this tower, the night is an array of wonderful, magical sounds. If moonlit, a vague, deeply sensual mood invades the chords, if there is no moon … the river sings a unique, dreamy melody … but it is twilight that generates the most original, intense variations where colour assumes the haziest of musical expressions. The ground has been prepared from mid-afternoon … Shadows slip over the bonfire that is the Alhambra … The Vega lies flat and silent. The sun hides and infinite waterfalls of musical colour burst from the hillsides and hasten soft and velvety over the city and mountains.

In this passage, we can see Lorca's musicality and the sensuous imagery of his subsequent poetry. He infuses the view from the tower with an almost synaesthetic sense of the Granadine nightfall. These *Sketches* were well received but would not have seen the light of day if it had not been for his father's money, which allowed the first copies to be printed. It would be more than a few years before Lorca's greatness became evident to a much wider public.

His family's first residence in Granada was at 46 Acera del Darro, next to what is now the Hotel Montecarlo. Its cream-coloured clapper-boarded façade was once elegant, with its balconied windows looking down on to the promenaders below. Gibson tells us, via Lorca's brother, that the house, like so many in the city, hid a patio filled with flowers and even had a garden complete with a magnolia. It was not long before the family swapped this building for even grander accommodation, literally opposite the hotel. Now totally demolished and replaced by a bank, it had impressive wrought-iron bowed balconies, underlining the windows set out from the escutcheoned walls.

Not far from the Acera del Darro is the Plaza del Campillo, an important location in the development of Lorca as a person and a poet. The building, now home to the Restaurante Chikito, was once the Café Alameda. A plaque to the right of the entrance reads: 'En esta Casa antiguo "Café Alameda" se reunía entre 1.915 y 1.929 la Tertulia Literaria de "El Rinconcillo"' ('In this old establishment "Café Alameda", between 1915 and 1929 the literary group "The

Little Corner" used to meet'). The literary gathering in question, who met between the years indicated, was known as the 'Little Corner' because they made their home at the same set of tables in a corner of the café. Lorca, one of the chief members, would sit and discuss with his friends the state of artistic endeavour in the country. Principal members of the group included Melchor Fernández Almagro, Manuel Angeles Ortiz and José Fernández Montesinos, people who would continue to play an important part in Lorca's life.

The Chikito today serves some excellent tapas, including snails in an almond broth and sardines with a fresh avocado salad. In warmer weather, the four plane trees that punctuate each corner of the square provide the Chikito's terrace with much-needed shade. Sit there or inside and you can almost hear the lively chatter that would have passed between the members of the Rinconcillo, who occasionally added a visiting alumnus, most notably the Englishmen H. G. Wells and Rudyard Kipling, and the Polish pianist Artur Rubenstein.

A small alleyway at the top right of the Plaza del Campillo leads to the Plaza Mariana Pineda, named after the historical figure who resisted the absolutist regime of King Ferdinand VII. A search of Pineda's house in 1831 revealed a hand-stitched flag in support of the liberal cause and she was arrested. Refusing to divulge the names of her accomplices whilst on trial, the unfortunate Pineda was executed by the medieval method of the garrotte. The pretty little square is dominated by a statue in her honour: a wistful woman, with eyes downcast, holds one hand to her breast while the other clutches the flag of freedom. The plinth commemorates her heroism.

This story would have been known to Lorca from an early age, fixed as it is in Granadine folklore. He turned the events into a play of his own (*Mariana Pineda*) at a time when Spain was under the dictatorship of Primo de Rivera. Perhaps because of the play's slightly inflammatory content, it was not staged until 1927, when it was performed in Barcelona, where it received rapturous applause. Salvador Dalí, then Lorca's intimate friend, designed the set. Towards the end of his life, Lorca liked to say that this was his first theatre work, conveniently forgetting the disastrous reception of his first attempt, *The Butterfly's Evil Spell* (*El maleficio de la mariposa*).

In addition to attending the University of Granada, Lorca also spent much time at the innovative Residencia de Estudiantes in Madrid – a college residence specifically set up to mimic the style of education received in Oxford and Cambridge colleges, with their in-house accommodation and stimulating interdisciplinary environment. It was at the 'Resi' that Lorca met Dalí, the aspiring filmmaker Luis Buñuel, and Rafael Alberti, who dropped in to meet his Andalucian compatriot. Alberti gifted Lorca one of his paintings, *The Virgin of Sorrows*, which he dedicated to Lorca at the start of their friendship. This painting now hangs in Lorca's bedroom at the Huerta de San Vicente, the summer house of the poet's family on the outskirts of Granada.

The Huerta de San Vicente, once part of the city's surrounding fields and orchards, is enclosed by a park filled with roses and named in his honour. Mercifully, the house remains untouched, and a visit feels spine-tinglingly close to Lorca's spirit that was given free rein in these happy surroundings. The poet delighted in returning to the Huerta most summers and would write many of his poems and plays in his humbly furnished bedroom. At the foot of the bed is Alberti's picture. Light streams through the green-shuttered windows onto the original coloured floor tiles, cool underfoot. Eyes immediately turn to the large heavy wooden writing desk, above which is a poster celebrating the La Barraca theatre company directed by Lorca. La Barraca, instituted by the Spanish Republican government, toured the provinces with classic works from Spanish literature.

The lower floor is equally evocative, with the family's piano dominating the main salon. Lorca's hard-won university degree hangs on the wall below the teaching diploma gained by his mother.

10   *The Lorca family summer residence, the Huerta de San Vicente,*
Granada

The kitchen, complete with original range, is where Lorca would chat with the devoted servants, picking up dialogue and stories from the myth and folklore of Andalucian country life. Perhaps the most romantic part of the whole property is the balcony terrace to the right of the building on the first floor, from which Lorca would have been able to see the Alhambra, a view now sadly blocked by developments along the massive swathe cut through Granada known as the Camino de Ronda.

Balconies at the Huerta have a significance in the poet's work. Gibson, his biographer, is sure that the little green shutters in his bedroom opening onto the balcony are the ones referred to in the poem 'Leave-taking' ('Despedida'), taken from Lorca's book *Songs* (*Canciones*). The verses could almost be a prescient impression of his own tragic demise. It is worth quoting the work in both Spanish and English:

Si muero,
dejad el balcón abierto.

El niño come naranjas.
(Desde mi balcón lo veo.)

El segador siega el trigo.
(Desde mi balcón lo siento.)

¡Si muero,
dejad el balcón abierto!

If I die,
leave the balcony open.

The boy is eating oranges.
(From my balcony I can see him.)

The reaper is reaping the wheat.
(From my balcony I can hear him.)

If I die,
leave the balcony open!

On a lighter note, letters survive that were sent from this paradise of Mediterranean vegetation in which Lorca extols the virtues of the garden surrounding the property, exclaiming, in particular to his poet friend Jorge Guillén, how they all wake up with 'lyrical headaches' owing to the heady scent of jasmine.

The garden and terrace immediately surrounding the house still bear a strong resemblance to how they were in Lorca's time there, evidenced by photos on display in the upper rooms of the Huerta that show the poet with family and friends. Wisteria drips from the balcony rails and trees cast their shadow across the brilliant white façade.

The visitor is free to wander around the perfumed garden but a guided tour is essential to see the interior of the building. One poet who fulfilled the role of guide at the Huerta was Javier Egea. Born in 1952, he was one of the co-originators of the poetic movement known as La Otra Sentimentalidad, a search for a new or alternative sentimentality that encompassed feelings that any reader could appreciate and not just those of the poet.

Along with Luis García Montero, who shared his ideas, Egea delivered a presentation in 1982 honouring Lorca's friend Rafael Alberti, which was subsequently published as *El manifesto albertista* (*The Alberti Manifesto*). The pair noted that 'Alberti seas were always in Granada', an allusion to the fact that the poet from coastal Santa María was appreciated by literary friends in landlocked Granada. Egea's best-known work is arguably the 'Paseo de los tristes', from the collection of the same name, so titled for its melancholic associations with the eponymous street that runs between the Alhambra hill and the Albaicín, where he speaks of a condemned life, 'a lost history of exploitation and loneliness, of beloved death'.

Egea's disillusionment with a materialistic society, exemplified by stock markets and banks, must have contributed to the depression that led to his suicide in 1999. In many ways, the preoccupations of the 1980s Granadine generation presaged the housing bubble that blew up in the face of Spanish society some 30 years later. García Montero, Egea's ideological companion, has infused his poems with the emotional impact of these disastrous events, showing how the wider world always has consequences for the individual. In his prose poetry, *A Form of Resistance* (*Una forma de resistencia*), he focuses on the little things we cling to in times of trouble. The book starts with the following: 'Bankers count their profits, politicians count their votes, and poets count their mementos.' Lorca, increasingly concerned for the parlous state of his country's poor in the days leading up to the Civil War, would have recognised these words.

Lorca often claimed that he was rooted in the soil of the Vega, yet his poetry is far more complex than the simply bucolic.

Francisco Umbral wrote a book in 1968 entitled *Lorca, poeta maldito*, which could be loosely translated into English as *Lorca, the Cursed or Damned Poet*. This seemingly dramatic title reflects the conflicts and portents of the poet's life. Umbral says that he could have just as easily named the book *Sex and Death in García Lorca*, because he believes the two to be key elements in his work and inextricably linked.

Lorca was homosexual at a time when attitudes in Spain were conservative in this regard. Many of his poems reflect a thwarted eroticism, unfulfilled desires and repression. Some of the women in his plays equally show these traits. In *The House of Bernarda Alba* (*La casa de Bernarda Alba*), the eponymous Bernarda rules her family of daughters with a rod of iron. The sexual tension in the house is palpable as one of the daughters, Adela, yearns for the shadowy Pepe, who never actually appears on stage. The tragedy unfolds when their affair is discovered and Adela kills herself, believing Pepe to have already died. Throughout, Bernarda's overwhelming preoccupation is with the family's supposed honour.

The themes in the poet's work, although universal, are completely infused with Granada and its surroundings. It would be easy to quote Lorca at every corner, but a choice has to be made. We know that Lorca once had the spectacular view of the Alhambra from his terrace. Although the Moorish palace is on the opposite side of the city, it is no more than a vigorous half-hour walk to the foot of the Cuesta de Gomérez which climbs from the Plaza Nueva up to the Alhambra. This was a regular walk for Lorca, who was always charmed by the wood that spreads out on either side of the Cuesta.

The Alhambra wood starts at the Puerta de las Granadas, a grandiose stone arch created by Pedro Machuca for Carlos V. The trees provide welcome shade from the more aggressive aspects of the city's weather and seem to envelop the stroller in a contemplative solitude that presages the sights to come. Senses are further soothed by the constant murmur of water, which rises in the most unexpected places, fed by the surrounding sierras.

More than one commentator has suggested that Lorca's favourite 'Sleepwalking Ballad' ('Romance sonámbulo') from *The Gypsy Ballads* (*Romancero gitano*) took part of its inspiration from this forest haven:

> Green oh how I love you green.
> Green wind. Green boughs.
> Ship of the sea,
> horse on the mountain.
> With waist of shadow,
> she dreams at her rail,
> green flesh, green hair.

The implicit melancholic longing in these evocations of fertility defy logical explanation, leaving the poem to turn to images of death with the arrival of the wounded *compadre* in subsequent verses. Lorca was always equivocal and evasive about the meaning.

At the point where the Calle Real de la Alhambra meets the Cuesta, which then turns into a gravelled path, there is a curious monument to one of Lorca's Granadine heroes, Ángel Ganivet. The poet was not always complimentary about his fellow citizens, particularly the bourgeoisie, but he admired Ganivet's architectural and philosophical sensibilities. The monument itself is a rather hybridised combination of the real and the mythical. Ganivet's bust sits on a plinth looking down on a naked Pan-like figure wrestling with a billy goat. The goat's head is tilted back, shooting a spout of water at a rather unfortunate angle, into a square, shallow pool.

Discussions about the merits of this ensemble have not detracted from the man it celebrates. Ganivet was a brilliant scholar, achieving his doctorate with a thesis on Sanskrit. He initially entered the Archives, Libraries and Museums Service, from which he moved to the Diplomatic Corps, being sent to Antwerp, then Helsinki. It was in these northern climes that he wrote most of his respected works. The particular tract that Lorca read as a young man, which chimed with his own opinions, was *Granada la bella* (*Granada the Beautiful*), within which Ganivet set out some thoughts on his native city at the turn of the twentieth century.

From the very first page, the work makes clear its author's views on the way the city should be developed – 'My Granada is not the one you see today: it is the one it could be or should be, the one I am uncertain it will ever come to be.' The diplomat's Granada is exemplified by districts like the Albaicín, opposite the Alhambra, with its winding narrow lanes typified by the *carmen*, that inward-looking Granadine institution which has nothing to do with Mérimée's heroine. A *carmen* is often built around a beautiful garden and was best described by the seventeenth-century poet, Soto de Rojas, in the title of his poem 'A Paradise Closed to Many, Gardens Open to Few'.

Ganivet loved the small, intricate and intimate Granada he saw in these buildings and lamented what he described as 'street sacrifice'. It was during the latter part of his life, towards the end of the nineteenth century, that Granada started its Parisian habit of sweeping away the twisting medieval street plan in favour of the grandiose boulevard. In 1895, the Gran Via de Colón was created, lined with its belle époque buildings, complete with windowed balconies. To the uninitiated viewer, the street seems impressive enough, but Garnivet was horrified and not shy of telling his fellow citizens so in print.

His final posting as a diplomat was to Riga, acting as the Spanish consul. Suffering from syphilis, weighed down by a complicated love affair and profoundly depressed, the unfortunate Ganivet attempted suicide by throwing himself into the river Daugava that flows through the Latvian capital. A desperate bid to save him from his fate did not stop Ganivet from a subsequently successful effort. Never returned to his 'beautiful Granada', he remains buried in the cemetery of St Mark in Riga.

One of the best examples of a Granadine *carmen* is the one that used to belong to the composer Manuel de Falla in Calle

Antequeruela Alta, just a short walk from Ganivet's monument. The building is now a museum in honour of the musician, who was a great friend of Lorca's. The composer adopted Granada in 1921 when he moved into his beloved home. One English writer who came to know de Falla was the Hispanist J. B. Trend, who thought music the best way of capturing the city's essence. In his book, *A Picture of Modern Spain: Music and Men*, published in 1921, he wrote:

> Granada is a thing for painting or for music. Words are not the proper medium in which to express it, for it is impossible to write two lines without falling back on the stock phrases of romanticism. The old clichés can hardly be avoided, for in Granada they are all true. You cannot avoid saying, for example, that it is enchanting. All Spaniards pronounce it *encantadora*, and they are quite right.

It is to Lorca's credit that he achieved what Trend thought impossible, yet the English academic does have a point, and he thanked de Falla for introducing him to the city's music, which had increased his 'imaginative perception'. On one memorable stellar night, in an Albaicín *carmen*, Trend listened to the music of de Falla and a recitation from a local poet praising the virtues of the Moorish city; the poet turned out to be none other than Federico García Lorca. Trend crystallised the whole affair in this one sentence: 'Moorish art is only made intelligible by moonlight; Granada is only explained by its gardens and its guitars.'

The Alhambra, translated as the Red Fort, is special at any time of day, but displays its sublime virtues under Trend's moonlight. For de Falla, the grounds and their manifest displays of aquatic theatre provided the inspiration for his orchestral work *Nights in the Gardens of Spain*. The Puerta del Vino gate is a short walk downhill from de Falla's *carmen*. Its unmistakable Arab arch was a distant muse for another of Lorca's favourite composers, Claude Debussy. Although the Frenchman never visited the site,

Lorca considered his composition named after the arch to be the quintessential evocation of his city.

To the left of the gate is the Alhambra's only sandy square, which sits in front of the cubic towers of the Alcazaba Armoury. In this dusty arena, Lorca and de Falla put together one of the first great competitions lauding the virtues of *cante jondo*, the deep song of flamenco that seems to drag vocals from the very souls of the performers. On the first evening of the contest, an old Gypsy who had walked most of the way from Córdoba Province came away with the prize. After a day of drinking the profits, the second evening's performance by the old-timer was less heart-stopping.

Behind the square, and to the left of Carlos V's Renaissance palace, is the entrance to the halls and patios created by the Nasrid dynasty prior to the Christian reconquest. Robert Irwin, the Arab scholar, in his book simply titled *The Alhambra* (2004), gives a fascinating overview of the Nasrids. He calls the environs of the Red Fort a 'poisoned paradise' where blood flowed as often as water and wine. Rare was the peaceful transference of power, as exemplified by Muhammad III, who poisoned his own father with a deadly doughnut. The epithets 'poet' and 'architectural enthusiast' are not usually joined with the word 'sadist', but Irwin assures us that, together, they give us an accurate picture of someone so capable of patricide.

Muhammad III met his end in one of the Alhambra's water features, seemingly at the hands of his brother Nasir, who, remarkably, abdicated in 1314. He was succeeded by Ismail, who is thought to be responsible for the Mexuar, once home to the council chambers of the fort, one of the first rooms that you enter. It is not long before you come to the true glories of Alhambran architecture, many of which were instituted under the reign of Yusuf I, apparently a handsome ruler who loved the arts. It is thanks to his sensibilities that we have the Hall of the Ambassadors and the neighbouring Comares Palace, which is so beautifully reflected in the Court of the Myrtles. Unsurprisingly, Yusuf also met a sticky end, stabbed by a mentally unstable slave in the city's mosque.

For a more fanciful and less gruesome history of the buildings and gardens, we turn to Washington Irving and his *Tales of the Alhambra*. It was in 1829 that the American decided to make a 'rambling expedition' from Seville to Granada, accompanied by a friend from the Russian Embassy. The ultimate goal of his trip was the Red Fort 'so inseparably intertwined in the annals of romantic Spain'. Perhaps against advice, Washington decided the only way to truly experience the location would be to live in it. In so doing, he befriended the various characters who had taken up residence in its then-decaying halls and towers. The *Tales* are full of Irving's experiences and a sequence of overheard, and possibly embellished, stories; they made the palace's reputation in the Western world of letters.

The most iconic of all the courtyards is the Court of the Lions with its central fountain supported on the backs of the stylised felines. The marbled floor spreads out in a rectangle to the arched corridors and rooms, laden with delicately incised patterns and inscriptions from the Qur'an. Washington's echoes from the past still resonate with the modern visitor – 'Here the hand of time has fallen the lightest, and the traces of Moorish elegance and splendour exist in almost their original brilliance.'

The phrases on the walls are not always religious. The words of poets, including the fourteenth-century Ibn Zamrak, are also found dotted throughout the Alhambra. Much of Zamrak's work has been lost, no doubt some of it in the zealous bonfire set by Cardinal Cisneros after the taking of the city by the Christians; yet enough survives on paper and in stone to attest to his talent:

> Granada's breeze is languid, but cures the languishing;
> Its gardens are verdant with well-watered flowers all around,
> Water enough to quench a fiery thirst.
> An early cloud floated over its hills
> And sent a shower down to the prayer-place.

His verses are also found on the fountain rim shouldered by the lions.

11 *The Court of the Lions, the Alhambra, Granada*

It is more than likely that Irving had heard tell of Ibn Zamrak and it would have been a short leap for his lively imagination to have conjured the Moor in situ. On one occasion, Washington had no need to call on mental pictures. Standing next to the fountain in the Court of the Lions was a turbaned Moor breaking the 'spell of centuries'. As both spoke Spanish, the American was able to discover that he was nothing more than a seller of rhubarb and perfumes, although one who could decipher the Arabic carving. Ignoring the more bloodthirsty past that supposedly turned the fountains red, Washington has the merchant recounting a poetic history:

> 'Ah, *señor*,' said he, 'when the Moors held Granada, they were a gayer people than they are nowadays. They thought only of love, music, and poetry. They made stanzas upon every occasion, and set them all to music. He who could make the best verses, and she who had the most tuneful voice, might be sure of favour and preferment. In those days, if anyone asked for bread, the reply was, make me a couplet; and the poorest beggar, if he begged in rhyme, would often be rewarded with a piece of gold.'

Although there may be a nugget of truth in this, Irving and his latter-day Nasrid are clearly waxing lyrical. The American was not the only foreign writer to fall under the palace's charms or, for that matter, to live within its walls. Both Richard Ford and Théophile Gautier stayed in this sublime setting. Gautier tells us that he was not satisfied with simply visiting but wanted to spend some nights there. He persuaded the Granadine authorities to turn a blind eye, giving him four days and nights 'which constituted, without any doubt, the happiest moments of my existence'.

Gautier, thus enraptured, was blind to the worst excesses of the city's climate, when summer temperatures can reach extreme numbers; although he is right in noting the mitigating effects of water: 'This mixture of water, snow and fire renders the Granadian climate unparalleled throughout the world, and makes Granada a real terrestrial paradise.' His Alhambra utopia was also filled with light, especially the crepuscular rays of a setting sun, which he felt unworthy to describe; yet, once again, in defiance of the words of J. B. Trend, he made a valiant attempt:

No pen or pencil will be able to give a true idea of that brilliancy, of that light, of that vividness of hues. The most commonplace tones assume the appearance of jewels, and everything is on the same scale. Towards the end of the day, when the sun is oblique, the most inconceivable effects are produced: the mountains sparkle like heaps of rubies, topazes and carbuncles.

With his exuberant facial hair and flowing locks trapped under exotic headwear, the Romantic Gautier is somewhat reminiscent of a 1960s hippy wanderer. In the Court of the Lions, now so tightly regulated and sparklingly renovated, this nineteenth-century visitor was able to take the kind of liberties the modern tourist can only dream about, leaving his sherry bottle to cool in the trickling waters of the cascade whilst studying Ibn Zamrak's poetry: 'the basin of the fountain is like mother-of-pearl beneath the clear sparkling water; the flowing stream resembles melting silver, for the limpidness of the water and the whiteness of the stone have no equals.'

Even the more pragmatic Richard Ford, less prone to effervescent prose, could not help but litter his descriptions with poetic imagery. On first entering the palace, he gives us this vivid impression: 'The severe, simple, almost forbidding exterior of the Alhambra, gives no promise of the Aladdin gorgeousness which once shone within, when the opening of a single door, as if by the tap of a fairy's wand, admitted the stranger into an almost paradise.' His guide pointed to a stain near the lion fountain, claiming it to be the blood of the massacred Abencerrages dynasty killed by Boabdil (Muhammad XII, the last of the Nasrid dynasty). Ford laments that such beauty could have been marred by scenes of carnage but, with his tongue firmly in his cheek, he feigns to believe such tales – 'deem not these spots ferruginous, for nothing is more certain than that heroic blood never can be effaced, still less if shed in foul murder.'

Water is present not only in these inner precincts of the Nasrid court, but also in the adjoining Partal gardens and the more distant

Generalife. To untrained English ears, the name of this Moorish pleasure garden sounds more like an insurance company; in fact, as Ford tells us, it derives from *jennatu-l-'arif* (the garden of the architect), and what an architect he was. The Generalife is set slightly apart from the main Alhambra complex; its rectangular beds, filled with colour, look across to the Red Fort.

In the 1950s, a Lancastrian writer rejoicing in the name of Henry Canova Vollam Morton, visited Granada. His fame as a travel correspondent reached dizzy heights when he scooped the embedded *Times* reporter to reveal Howard Carter's discovery of Tutankhamun's tomb. His renown was later tainted by fascist sympathies. To such an orientalist, the Alhambra was an essential part of the itinerary. Morton, who mercifully published only using the initials H. V., tells us his impressions in the book *A Stranger in Spain*. He name-checks the usual authors and reflects on the extent to which the lamentable state of Richard Ford's Alhambra had now been changed by restoration. Modern tourists would also find it hard to believe that the sparkling marble floor in the Lion Court had once been full of plants.

Morton's most interesting anecdote concerns the Generalife. On one occasion, he found himself in the hotel lift, standing next to a young woman holding a ballet dress. To his surprise, it was none other than Margot Fonteyn, who told him that she was to dance in the Alhambra's gardens, where they had erected a temporary stage. She was referring to the Generalife and Morton was bowled over by the idea of seeing the grounds lit at night in the presence of such a dancer. He immediately went to the hotel desk, pleading with the concierge to find him a ticket, but to no avail.

Undeterred, the journalist decided to draw on his extensive list of contacts, including the British consul, the mayor and the provincial governor. Rather suspiciously, everyone was out of the office. Morton went back to his hotel room, resigned to missing the performance. Answering a knock on his door, he found a diminutive pageboy who, with a nod and a wink, suggested that he might like to buy a ticket to see La Fonteyn. Being asked for a paltry ten pesetas over the normal selling price, Henry jumped at the chance. The whole experience more than lived up to expectations; the lighting lowered into the fishponds and hidden in the hedges created a magical atmosphere. Guitars serenaded the spectators to their seats as the floral fragrances of the night assailed their senses.

Morton was sure that Gautier would have been just as overwhelmed as he was himself. The performance, the setting and the night had been perfect. Clearly, the idea of presenting artistic endeavour in these surroundings has taken root, given the fact that there is now a permanent open-air stage within the confines of the Generalife. Interestingly, Morton spoke to Margot Fonteyn after the performance, and she was less confident of her connection with the audience in such surroundings. Indeed, the gardens are theatre enough – witness the Water-Garden Courtyard (Patio de la Acequia), a Moorish evocation of paradise with its colonnade of fountains in perfect symmetry playfully rippling the surface of the elongated channel that cleaves through the scented planting.

Given the unique atmosphere that we sense from a distance of centuries, it is no surprise that Moorish Granada has been the inspiration for more than factual accounts. The list of novels and short stories that derive their plot and character from this era is a long one. The work of the French aristocrat François-René, Vicomte de Chateaubriand, provides an example of the romantic extravagance that the city encourages. In *The Last of the Abencerrajes* (*Les Aventures du dernier Abencérage*), Chateaubriand fictionalises the banishment of the eponymous dynasty; the book still appears on the shelves of the Alhambra's gift shop today.

The Breton Viscount, born in Saint-Malo in 1768, is considered by many as the father of French Romanticism. The author André Maurois considered Chateaubriand to be a significant literary role model for Lord Byron, if not a political one, for the more liberal young Englishman. Both were inveterate wanderers who drew upon their experiences for their works. No doubt Byron would have been thrilled by Moorish Granada – sadly, he never visited. Chateaubriand, however, stayed in the city in 1807 as the finale to his own Mediterranean odyssey.

The last Abencerraje is Aben-Hamet, forced into exile and in love with a Spanish duke's daughter, Bianca. Some commentators, notably John Clubbe in his article for the Byron Society of America, have claimed that Bianca is based on Madame de Noailles, the mistress whom Chateaubriand went to visit in Spain. The fictional lovers are parted by religion and distance but retain their longing for each other. Chateaubriand's book starts with an evocation of the last Nasrid, Boabdil, who famously stopped on the heights outside Granada to turn and look at his beloved city for the last time. This supposedly true and much mythologised story has the former ruler crying whilst his mother looks at him and says, 'Do not weep like a woman for what you could not defend like a man.'

The location of this legendary moment has now been christened El Puerto del Suspiro del Moro (The Pass of the Sigh of the Moor). As you drive on the motorway south from Granada towards the coast, the road carves through the pass, and a little brown road sign near Otura is the only prosaic and mundane testimony to its existence. Running parallel to the main road is a smaller artery that sports an equally woebegone little monument – a curious cement cube, complete with a small pyramidal roof that attests to the Moor's sigh and the altitude of its exhalation, some 865 metres (2,800 feet).

Salman Rushdie, the Booker Prize-winning Anglo-Indian novelist, took this mythical point in history as the title for his 1995 work, *The Moor's Last Sigh*. Only the first and last parts of the novel take place in Spain. The central character and narrator of the text, Moraes Zogoiby, has Boabdil's nickname, 'the Unlucky', as a surname. Most of the work centres on Cochin and Bombay and the machinations of Moraes's dubious family of spice merchants.

The 'Moor', as he is known, has the misfortune of ageing at twice the rate expected. At the end of the book, a worn-down Zogoiby flies to Andalucia to reclaim his mother's stolen paintings. In the Benengeli fortress home of Vasco Miranda, the Moor writes down his story. The interwoven plot, touches of magic realism and historical allusions in Rushdie's novel are very difficult to classify. In many ways, the narrator is Boabdil and Bombay the lost multicultural paradise that Granada could also have been.

The Lebanese-born French writer Amin Maalouf also delved into the world of cultural exile by focusing on the life of traveller and writer Hasan al-Wazzan in his work, *Leo the African* (*Léon l'Africain*). The novel, first published in Britain in 1988, is split into 'books', with the first detailing the Granada of 1488–94. The lawyer Ildefonso Falcones, who found fame in 2006 with his evocation of medieval Barcelona in the *Cathedral of the Sea* (*La catedral del mar*), is another writer to use this monumental epoch. *The Hand of Fatima* (*La mano de Fátima*) deals with the Moorish revolt in 1564 through the lives of Hernando, an Arab with a Christian father, and Fátima, his beloved. Hernando's plan is to find common ground between the two faiths.

One author very well versed in the fictionalisation of historical Muslim culture is the British Pakistani writer and political campaigner Tariq Ali. In 2010, the city of Granada awarded him the Granadillo Prize in honour of his Islam Quintet. In our previous literary guide to Sicily, we looked at *A Sultan in Palermo*, which forms part of the series. The first in the quintet is *Shadows of the Pomegranate Tree*, a family saga that relates the struggles of Muslims living in post-conquest Granada. The novel starts with the infamous book-burning conducted by Cardinal Cisneros. The tolerance of his predecessor had not been enough for an insistent Catholic Church, intent on converting Muslims. Ximenes de Cisernos was a zealot, more than happy to sweep away the centuries of learning that had put Moorish culture scientifically and philosophically far in advance of Christian Spain. Ali gives us this chilling portrait of a real-life event, which brings home the maxim that, if you burn books, people are never far behind:

Rare manuscripts vital to the entire architecture of intellectual life in al-Andalus, were crammed in makeshift bundles on the backs of soldiers.

Throughout the day the soldiers constructed a rampart of hundreds of thousands of manuscripts. The collective wisdom of the entire peninsula lay in the old silk market below the Bab al-Ramla.

Some effort was made to save medical texts, which were transported to the Cardinal's central Spanish library. The more enlightened soldiers enlisted to carry out this dreadful task, remembering the Moorish tales of their childhoods, would slyly remove a tome from the pile and slip it in front of an Arab doorway, where it would be scooped up by a robed figure and locked away.

The poet Lorca was aware of the tragedy this kind of barbarism implied, calling the fall of Muslim Granada a 'disastrous event'. In an interview a few months before his death, Lorca also expounded upon the unique science and sensitivity that were part of this lost world. These comments, flying in the face of right-wing opinion on the success of Christian Spain, together with his denigration of the Granadine bourgeoisie, cannot have helped his precarious situation when the Civil War broke out.

Fuente Vaqueros

Before we tell the story of Lorca's death, to fully understand him as a man and a poet, we need to start with the place of his birth. Fuente Vaqueros is a 30-minute car journey to the west of Granada and is a quintessential town of the Vega. The flat approach betrays little of significance until you pass a half-constructed building wearing an impressive piece of street art that represents the unmistakable features of Lorca. The official monuments start at the southern end of the main square, which, according to

Gibson, differs greatly from the poet's day when it was a meadow, the fertile loam of which would have run through the young Lorca's fingers.

Lorca was born at 4 Calle de la Trinidad. Opposite the entrance to this street, at the northern end of the square is a monument constructed by Cayetano Aníbal, entitled *Pueblo a Garcia Lorca*. This homage from the people shows a naked poet emerging from the folds of the stone slab that sits atop a fountain of cooling water. A second slab next to the figure depicts two birds against an abstract background.

The terraced house in Calle de la Trinidad is a cut above many in the town; its solid two-storey façade presents a comfortable face to the world. Now a museum, it even includes the poet's cot and some first editions of his works. Lorca's father went on to become a considerable landowner in the surrounding area. His increasing wealth saw him purchase the summer residence at the Huerta de San Vicente that we have already visited. Unlike many of his landowning brethren, Federico Senior treated his workers with decency and paid them a fair wage, a cause of resentment amongst his fellow landowners in later years.

Another key player in Lorca's life is also remembered in Fuente Vaqueros. A rather serious-looking bearded bust sits in a hedged rose garden behind the central roundabout. The features depicted belong to Fernando de los Ríos, a prime mover in the Spanish Socialist Party (PSOE) and one-time teacher at the University of Granada, where he became firm friends with Lorca. De los Ríos also accompanied the poet on his journey to New York, and went on to become the minster of justice in 1931 for Spain's Second Republic, and it was this association that tainted Lorca in the minds of the Nationalists. When the troops came to the Huerta in search of the family's caretaker, Gibson tells us, Lorca intervened to prevent a beating, only to be verbally abused as de los Ríos's queer little friend.

Víznar

We can see from the family's liberal tendencies, in addition to Lorca's friendships and allegiances, that he was becoming a target for the supporters of Franco. The writer's fame was increasing worldwide, but the Falange had little respect for the world of letters. Lorca knew he had no choice but to go into hiding. He could have chosen the house of Manuel de Falla, whose protection seemed assured. One other option was to flee to the safety of the Republican front. He chose, instead, to stay in the house of fellow poet and nominal supporter of the Falange, Luis Rosales. In fact, it was the house of Rosales's father; yet, despite the family's right-wing credentials, he was discovered and dragged to the civil government building.

Petitions were made on the poet's behalf by the Rosales brothers, but to no avail. Unsure about what to do with the famous Granadine, the civil governor, José Valdés, contacted General Queipo de Llano in Seville, who infamously retorted, 'Give him lots of coffee', his cold-blooded code for assassination. Accordingly, Lorca was driven to Víznar, a short journey north of Granada and the chosen location for the political murder of hundreds of victims, largely perpetrated by the Black Squad fanatics of the Nationalist cause who were more than happy to volunteer for such a grim role. In all our journeys in the footsteps of literary figures, the three hours we spent retracing Lorca's last moments have been the most affecting. In many ways, the figure of Lorca distilled the fate of so many in the bitter fratricidal conflict of the Spanish Civil War, bringing its true horrors home to anyone willing to take the road to Víznar.

The killings did not actually take place within the town itself, but along the road to neighbouring Alfacar. At a sharp bend, running alongside a water channel, is the Barranco de Víznar, most easily identified by a yellow information sign some 50 metres (55 yards) beyond the curve. The sign directs the visitor to a path that leads back into the Barranco, or ravine. This is not actually the site of Lorca's death but it was the place of execution for hundreds who followed him later on in the war during the months after August 1936. The gully is now covered in trees which were hastily planted to hide the fact that the area is a site of mass graves. Under the green canopy, rough-hewn marble slabs carrying plaques to the dead bear witness to the atrocities.

There is one part of the gully forming a natural dip that provided the assassins with a ready-made burial site. Many bodies were thrown from the heights to the bottom of this pit. In memorial, a large makeshift cross has been laid out using stones from the surrounding woodland. At the head of the cross is a plinth with the inscription 'Lorca eran todos' ('They were all Lorca'). To find the poet's grave, it is necessary to return to the Alfacar road and continue for a few minutes more until you see, on the right-hand side, the Parque Federico García Lorca. An entrance gate sits atop a small flight of brick steps.

The Hispanophile writer Jason Webster also retraced this journey in his book *¡Guerra!*. Webster, who has previously written on flamenco and the modern-day Moors in Spain, chose, in this book, to focus on the legacy of the Civil War. In so doing, he took a taxi to the Parque and was disappointed by what he saw. He found it a barren space reminiscent of gardens in a newly developed town. Webster clearly thinks it is not worthy of Lorca or the others who died with him.

In many ways, the park can be divided into two areas. There is the formal area that was not to Webster's taste, with its inlaid pebbles and poetic quotes on the surrounding walls. Whatever opinion the park provokes, it has at least put a stop to any further development that could have encased the poet's remains in concrete. The most poignant area is away from the monumental zone and consists of an olive tree and a commemorative stone. This is commonly held to be the site of Lorca's shooting, along with the three others who were held with him – the crippled schoolteacher Galindo González and the two anarchist bullfighters, Joaquín Arcollas and Francisco Galadí.

Amid controversy over the exhumation of Civil War remains, Jason Webster went to visit one of the physical anthropologists at Granada University who has responsibility for identifying victims. The complication in Lorca's case continues to be the fact that the poet is buried with the three others mentioned above. All families of the deceased must be in agreement and it would seem that, according to the anthropologist, the Lorca family would like him to remain undisturbed. To this day, the four are thought to lie under the sun-baked earth in the vicinity of the gnarled olive that witnessed their last moments.

The tree overlooks perhaps the most fitting place to remember Lorca. A few hundred metres from the entrance to the park is the Fuente Grande, known as Ainadamar (The Fountain of Tears) by the Muslims. The teardrop-shaped pool is fed by a spring that constantly bubbles to the surface, creating ripples that gently break

12   *Ainadamar (The Fountain of Tears), near Alfacar*

free, infinitely weeping. The fountain still, to this day, feeds Lorca's Granada with its life-giving water.

One of the first writers to go in search of the poet's final journey was Gerald Brenan, whom we last met in Churriana near Málaga. In a conversation with his driver, reported in *The Face of Spain*, Brenan discovered that the chauffeur had fought for Franco but was prepared to admit that atrocities were committed by both sides and that everyone had lost their minds. Brenan was all too familiar with the horrors of war; his own Spanish story had started with a need to escape the bitter experiences of conflict in the First World War, and the place he found to do just that was Yegen in the Alpujarras.

Las Alpujarras

The Alpujarras are reached from Granada by taking the motorway south and turning to Órgiva and Lanjarón, famous for its spring water. Richard Ford was sufficiently struck with the area's beauty to call the valleys 'the Switzerland of Spain' – an epithet you could occasionally apply to the countryside, if not the architecture. The region was the last stronghold of Moorish influence after the fall of Granada. James Howell's wonderful little pamphlet, *Instructions for Forreine Travell*, first published in 1642, even has this gem of information: 'In the Mountaines of Granada (Alpuxarras) they speake *Morisco*, that last part of *Spaine* that was inhabited by the *Moores*, who had possessed it above seven hundred yeares.'

Yegen in the eastern Alpujarras was, fittingly enough, a Berber village. In his acclaimed account *South from Granada*, Brenan describes the place as impoverished but with a certain fertile, organic beauty:

It was a poor village, standing high above the sea, with an immense view in front of it. With its grey box-shaped houses of a battered Corbusier style, all running down the hill and fusing into one another, and its flat clay roofs and small smoking chimneys, it suggested something that had been made out of the earth by insects. It had too an abundance of water, flowing along the mountain-side in irrigation channels.

He rented a house from the local *cacique* (man of power and influence) and was happy to spend his time reading for hours on end in an effort to replace the university education he never had. Initially, money was tight, but a somewhat reduced inheritance enabled him to prolong his Spanish sojourn which, with the exception of relatively short absences, would turn into a lifelong affinity as a resident of Spain.

Brenan's books, *The Face of Spain*, *The Literature of the Spanish People*, *The Spanish Labyrinth* and, of course, the aforementioned *South from Granada*, have become classics of Hispanophile literature and have led to Brenan being considered the high priest of British Hispanicism. *South from Granada* is the account of his life in the Alpujarras during the years 1920 to 1934, albeit an interrupted stay. The book is peppered with sharp insight on issues as diverse as politics, ritual, romance and religion. In 1974, Brenan permitted a Spanish translation, a decision he would come to regret.

As he pointed out in more than one interview, the book was never intended for a Spanish audience and, although many of the people he wrote about could not have read the text – even if they had still been alive – there was no doubt their families could. Some of the portraits, despite being affectionate, were nonetheless far from flattering. Perhaps because of this impact, Brenan spent his later years in Alhaurín, mostly avoiding Yegen. A further reason also loomed large from his past.

To find details on this story, we can turn to two sources that come from the writer's own perspective. Firstly, the filmmaker Fernando Colomo created a movie, released in 2003, based on Brenan's time in the Alpujarras, using the same title as his book. In the film, Brenan, played by Matthew Goode, has a relationship with a village girl, which results in her pregnancy. As we can see from Brenan's *Personal Record*, the basic facts were, indeed, true; the writer did have a relationship with a local girl. In fact, he elaborates significantly on the start of their affair in his autobiography.

Juliana, the 15-year-old in question, was actually employed by the writer as a maid, and it seems that he became completely infatuated with her, eventually slipping into her bed whilst she pretended to be asleep. Brenan tells us that their love was deep and passionate and that it lasted for a good few years. There is no reason to suspect, given the available evidence, that this was not true; however, everything changed when Juliana gave birth. Her side of the story is told in Antonio Ramos Espejo's well-researched book, *Ciega en Granada* (*Blind in Granada*), first published in 1990.

Their daughter was born in 1931, in the very same year that the Englishman married the American poet Gamel Woolsey in Rome. Brenan admitted that he came to feel much affection for his wife but did not marry her out of any great love or passion. Therefore, when Brenan returned to Yegen, he did so as a married man who was interested in taking complete control of his young daughter's life and education. Perhaps seeing no other option in the face of such a gulf in future prospects, Juliana gave her baby to Brenan and Gamel, even seeing her name changed from Elena to Miranda Helen.

The saddest outcome of the whole story was Brenan's reluctance to allow Juliana access to her child – a child she would continuously look for amongst the tourist throng in Granada. As the years went by, the only thing that prevented the ageing mother from vainly trying to spot Miranda on the unlikely chance of their paths crossing – especially given that she had married a doctor in Paris – was Juliana's increasing blindness, which gives Ramos Espejo's book its poignant title.

During the happier Yegen years, and if we are to believe Colomo's film, when Juliana and Brenan were already in a relationship, Brenan's Bloomsbury friend Ralph Partridge arrived for a visit with the painter Dora Carrington and the newly famous writer Lytton Strachey. This impossible ménage brought its own complicated brand of relationship. Carrington, as she was always known, was obsessed with the homosexual Strachey, who, in turn, found her boyish figure and artistic talent platonically attractive. At the time, Partridge was living with Carrington with a view to marriage. To further complicate matters, Brenan was more than enamoured with Carrington.

The painter's fascination with Strachey is apparent from Brenan's account in *South from Granada*. He even tells us in his *Personal Record* that the pair later holidayed together in Wales, sleeping in the same bed 'ineffectively'. Some of Carrington's art from the Yegen visit betrays her state of mind – soft hills with skin-like textures form sensual outlines, their suggestive intimacy and touches of surrealism giving a glimpse of her desires.

The trip from Granada to Yegen must have been a comical sight, with the aesthete Strachey reluctant to ford the Rio Grande, which would have saved much time. To top it all, it seemed that Partridge and Carrington were in the middle of an argument. Strachey felt unable to connect with the world at large, to the extent that he would ask others to communicate his wishes to servants and, if on his own, would go without.

Brenan admits that the end of the visit was something of a relief; although he knew he would miss Carrington and Partridge, he was happy to forgo the tiresome task of ensuring that the food was suitable for Strachey's troublesome digestion. The last remark in the chapter on Strachey in *South from Granada* tells us that the author of *Eminent Victorians* strongly advised Leonard and Virginia Woolf to skip a visit to Brenan in the Alpujarras. Fortunately, they ignored this advice and, in 1923, made the trip.

Virginia was central to the Bloomsbury group – the shifting association of intellectuals and writers that dazzled literary London. Her greatest work was yet to come, with the publication of *To the Lighthouse* in 1927 and *Orlando* in 1928. Prone to bouts of mental instability as she was, it might have been better if she had heeded Strachey's advice, given the tone of her writing on the 1923 journey:

> This wrinkled red and white screen [the Sierra Nevada] is found to consist of stones, olive trees, goats, asphodels, irises, bushes, ridges, shelves, clumps, tufts, and hollows innumerable, indescribable, unthinkable. The mind's contents break into short sentences. It is hot; the old man; the frying pan; it is hot; the image of the Virgin; the bottle of wine; it is time for lunch; it is only half-past twelve; it is hot.

Once in Yegen, the Woolfs did enjoy their stay, although Virginia was rather flippant in her descriptions of Brenan, who she said was, 'slightly blurred' and bore 'some phantasmagorical resemblance to Shelley', sitting reading and eating grapes for much of the day. Jan Morris, in the 1993 book she edited, *Travels with Virginia Woolf*, notes that Brenan respected Virginia's genius but felt her to be blinded by the Bloomsburys.

Another key figure in this literary set, Vita Sackville-West, who would have a tempestuous lesbian relationship with Virginia Woolf, also had Andalucian connections. In fact, Vita's grandmother was Josefa Vargas, a half-Gypsy dancer from Málaga who married Lionel Sackville-West, the one-time diplomat and future peer. Vita tells this fascinating familial story in her 1937 work, *Pepita*, and, in the same decade, uses a further Spanish backdrop in her book *Family History* – a tale of love across the social divide that has the protagonist, Evelyn, lingering in a 'hot and scented' Granada after leaving the aristocratic Miles.

The Bloomsbury set, with all its brilliance and insecurity, was destined to be tinged with tragedy. After Lytton Strachey's death from cancer at the age of 51, a distraught Carrington took her own life. Virginia Woolf also found suicide to be the only way out; filling her coat pockets with stones, she walked into the river Ouse in the English county of Sussex. Gerald Brenan, as we know, lived a long and generally happy life, dying at the age of 92 in 1987.

It would be impossible to leave the Alpujarras without mentioning that other British writer and resident, Chris Stewart. Chris has become something of a phenomenon, having written four books about El Valero, the farm he owns south of Órgiva. He describes the latest in the series, *The Last Days of the Bus Club*, as the fourth in the *Driving Over Lemons* trilogy. His adventure started in 1988 when he left Órgiva, the neat little Alpujarran market town which has attracted its fair share of those in search of alternative lifestyles.

Accompanied by a property agent named Georgina, Stewart tried to negotiate his vehicle around the copious lemons strewn across the road. The agent told him to drive over them, and so was born the unforgettable title of his first book. Much has been made of Chris's early appearance as the drummer in the rock band Genesis – no doubt flamed by his publishers. However, as Stewart rather disarmingly points out in an interview at the end of *The Almond Blossom Appreciation Society*, he only played on two songs on the first album.

Chris's writing is full of enthusiasm and anecdotal charm. It is, in part, thanks to the success of his books that he no longer has to travel to the dark recesses of northern Sweden to earn money as a sheep-shearer, although he still turns his hand to the trade when neighbouring farmers need a spot of help. Not revelling in a rock-star lifestyle, his continuing connection to the land leads him to undertake exploits that make for enjoyable reading.

Unlike Brenan's works, the Spanish translations of Chris's books have been well received by the neighbours. He took the precaution of giving people the option of anonymity and changing some names. One of the central figures, his good friend 'Domingo', who appears under this pseudonym, is now something of a sculptor and has chosen, much to Chris's delight, to use this as his artistic nom de guerre. The Spanish, in general, appear to have taken to his affectionate portrait of rural life, although, as he admits, most urban Andalucians think he is a little mad to live the hard life of a farmer.

Almuñécar

South from Chris Stewart's farm and westwards along the coast is Almuñécar, the Castillo of Laurie Lee. Lee spent two periods of time in the town – once just before the Civil War, as documented in *As I Walked Out One Midsummer Morning*, and the second in his postwar retracing of previous foststeps, recounted in *A Rose for Winter*. During his first stay, Lee managed to talk his way into some accommodation at the Hotel Mediterráneo in exchange for odd jobs and entertaining the guests with his violin. The hotel no longer exists but was located on the Paseo del Atillo, then closer to the beachfront than it is today.

Lee shared a room with a Jewish lad called Jacob who hailed from Cologne and, despite his tubby appearance, was something of a hit with the ladies, particularly the guests of a certain age. The Bauhaus design of the Mediterráneo was not in keeping with the rest of the town's architecture, which Laurie describes in the following terms: 'Almuñécar itself, built of stone steps from the delta, was grey, almost gloomily Welsh. The streets were steep, roughly paved, and crossed by crude little arches, while the square was like a cobbled farmyard.'

The description is almost unrecognisable today, the grey façades now whitewashed and development extending into the hills, but the steep lanes cannot deny their gradients. The town has escaped the worst excesses so prevalent closer to Málaga, even if Lee's evocative images are hard to place in the modern context. In the account of his second visit Lee, for political reasons, disguised Almuñécar as 'Castillo of the Sugar Canes'.

Accompanied by his wife, Kathy, he stayed in the same hotel, now empty and decaying. A generation had been decimated by the war and those who remained scratched a living from fishing. One figure who seemed to have survived with wealth intact was Don Paco, who bestrode the streets of the town like a rotund potentate. People owing him money were forced to duck behind pillars at his approach. These power-wielding landlords were feared by the populace and, when he questioned the locals in the bars, Lee noticed how the people shrank at the mention of certain names.

Today, the local population makes much of its money from tourism. Lee returned often enough in later years to see the changes. Behind the town, on a track up into the mountains, lived the artist Michael Still, who became friendly with the Lees, inviting them to stay at his very own *castillo*, and it was at Still's suggestion that the BBC made a follow-up film to its 1987 dramatisation of *As I Walked Out One Midsummer Morning*. Its release gave Lee the opportunity to give local TV and radio interviews in his still more than passable Spanish.

In 1988, the town decided to honour the writer with a monument, which can also be found along the Paseo del Atillo, right next to the blue-and-white depiction of a Phoenician mariner and opposite the six-storey seafront apartments. Lee's tribute is a simple white dovecote with the following words in Spanish: 'The people of Almuñécar, in recognition of the great writer, Laurie Lee, who lived in our town in the years 1935–36 and 1951–52 and immortalised it under the pseudonym of Castillo in his works *As I Walked Out One Midsummer Morning* and *A Rose for Winter*.'

Guadix

Our final literary stop in Granada Province is the unique town of Gaudix, over two hours' journey by car from Almuñécar or 45 minutes to the east of Granada. Guadix is principally renowned for its cave dwellings, particularly those located in what is now called the Barriada de las Cuevas. For those who are in search of more detail, there is a visitor centre in the Plaza Padre Poveda. The caves that are still inhabited are not the hovels they were in previous centuries, often now equipped with mod cons, freshly painted doors and chimneys that jut through the undulating moonscape of the parched plain. It is not uncommon to see television aerials and the occasional satellite dish pointing skywards from these troglodytic dwellings.

To the north of the town is the Cuevas Pedro Antonio de Alarcón, an apartment hotel remarkable not only because it allows you to stay in underground accommodation, but also because it bears the name of the town's favourite literary son. Alarcón was born in Guadix in 1833. His writing is most associated with realism, particularly the *costumbrismo* style linked to the likes of Fernán Caballero in Cádiz, but his characters also show touches of Romanticism. His skill in observing customs, landscapes and folklore lent itself to travel literature, a subject which Alarcón tackled to most effect in the text *La Alpujarra*, the account of his journey on horseback through what would become Brenan's mountains.

The English-speaking world knows him best for his story *The Three-Cornered Hat* (*El sombrero de tres picos*), later interpreted musically by Manuel de Falla. The three-cornered hat in question is a physical representation of power, which is happily satirised by the author. The story concerns a miller, his beautiful wife and the local magistrate (*corregidor*), the original wearer of the black *sombrero*, who is rather taken with the miller's spouse. There is much deceitful switching of attire and humorous physicality, wonderfully reminiscent of Cervantes, and all neatly wrapped up in a moralistic ending for the characters involved. In this speech by the *corregidor*'s wife, we are given the full image of the pompous law-enforcer:

[M]y husband, the Corregidor of the City, reached this his house two hours ago, with his three-cornered hat, his scarlet cloak, his knightly sword, and his staff of office. The servants and alguacils who are now listening to me, got up and greeted him as he came through the door; mounted the stairs and went into the reception room.

The inflexible magistrate meets an undignified end in prison under the martial rule of the French. Alarcón prefaced his work with an explanation that the tale would be recognisable to most Spaniards, even admitting he had first heard a similar account from a local goatherd.

Sixty-seven years after the death of Alarcón, the town finally erected a statue to its illustrious son, in the park that runs parallel to the Avenida Medina Olmos. On the occasion of its unveiling, an 84-year-old priest, Miguel, the son of Alarcón, wrote to the local council stating that, although his father's 'literary activity and other circumstances obliged him to live apart from his birthplace, his heart was always there, imbued with the memories of the environment of his early childhood'.

7

CÓRDOBA PROVINCE

A Twist of Faith

Let not my jealous foes
Exult in my disgrace,
For Fortune comes and goes
Nor tarries in one place.
(Ibn Hazm, *Mutability*, 994–1063)

Córdoba

There is really only one good way to approach Córdoba: via the Roman bridge that spans the Guadalquivir, although drivers will have to use the modern one to the left. The Torre de Calahorra guards the south-eastern entrance to the many-arched structure, beyond which a view opens to the city skyline dominated by the famous Mezquita. Although a significant Roman settlement, owing to victories against the Carthaginians, it is for the Muslim caliphate that Córdoba owes its place in history.

Most visitors approaching from this direction head straight for the Mezquita, less than 100 metres from the north-western end of the bridge. The outside of this mosque-cathedral reveals the Moorish origins of the structure, with its rounded doorways now dedicated to Christian saints. Calle Torrijos leads to the first open gateway, the Postigo de la Leche; however, many enter through the more spectacular Puerta del Perdón, its intricately carved arch

13   The Mezquita from Calle Torrijos, Córdoba

also leading to the Orange Tree Court. This patio was originally constructed with runnels and fountains that were used for ritual ablution before prayer in the mosque.

Jason Webster, a former student of Arabic, was well placed to write about the Moorish legacy in his book, *Andalus,* first published in 2004. He joined up with Zine, an illegal immigrant from Morocco who had been lured to Spain with the promise of a non-existent job. Instead, when Webster found him, he was facing intolerable conditions on a fruit farm. The two of them toured the sites of Moorish import throughout the region. In Córdoba, Zine was somewhat shocked by what he saw in the patio:

I found Zine in the Orange Tree Court that served as a sort of ante-chamber to the indoor section of the mosque. Tourists sat on low walls in the shade of the trees, writing postcards, changing the film in their cameras, or, as one German was doing with a certain irreligious devotion, simply picking his nose while his girlfriend spoke to a friend back home on her mobile phone.

Jason tells us of his friend's rather extreme reaction – Zine wanted to leave immediately, finding the place 'dirty'. In his eyes, the mosque had been profaned by so many casual visitors; to him it was still the religious institution it had originally been. The Islamic Council of Spain has even approached the Vatican with a request for permission to formally pray within the building. To date, the answer continues to be negative.

During Friday prayers, at the height of Abd al-Rahman's rule in the tenth century, many doors would have been flung open onto the courtyard. Today, the visitor filters into the main building through an entrance to the right of the patio. Nothing quite prepares the senses for what appears next. After welcoming the coolness of the air, it takes a few seconds to appreciate the glade of graceful arches that fill the space. Smooth, elegantly narrow pillars hold aloft the red-striped double curves that continue in a seemingly infinite march into the distance.

Few writers have described the scene more evocatively than the Victorian novelist and traveller Matilda Betham-Edwards. Although a specialist on France and of Huguenot descent, she also spent time in Spain with the proto-feminist Barbara Bodichon in the late nineteenth century. The account of her travels in the peninsula was written up in the book *Through Spain to the Sahara*. The Mezquita was clearly a defining moment:

To have seen the Mosque of Cordova forms an era in one's life. It is so vast, so solemn, so beautiful. You seem to be wandering at sunset time in a large and dusky forest, intersected by regular alleys of tall, stately palms. No matter in what direction you turn your face, northward, southward, eastward, westward, the same beautiful perspective meets your eye, file after file of marble and jasper columns supporting the double horse-shoe arch.

The inconvenience of other tourists aside, there is only one jarring note that rudely interrupts the notion that you have travelled back in time to the caliphate. As you approach the centre of the building, you become aware that a bizarre grafting has occurred, a strange experiment akin to splicing the head of a bull onto the body of a gazelle. In fact, it took three centuries for the Christian authorities to insist on the building of this cathedral choir within the heart of the mosque.

The year 1523 saw the decision to go ahead with the Churrigueresque choir stalls and organ in the full face of opposition from the more enlightened town council. A distant King Carlos V rather nonchalantly sanctioned the addition. When he eventually decided to visit the city, he was appalled by his own decision: 'You have built what you or others might have built anywhere, but you have destroyed something that was unique in the world.'

Destroyed seems too strong a word, as the building still exists, preserved for posterity. Close observation of the dark mahogany carvings, completed by Pedro Duque Cornejo, shows them to be of great skill but completely out of context. It is this jarring juxtaposition that visually relates the more conflictive side of Andalucia's history better than any other single location. Moorish architecture clashes full-on with the New World mahogany brought home by Christian conquistadors.

The original mosque reached its full extent under Caliph Hisham II at the turn of the eleventh century, although the real power at this time was wielded by Almanzor, as the young Hisham ascended to the caliphate at the tender age of 11. Almanzor was something of a Machiavellian character; whilst the young ruler idled away his time, the hajib (chancellor) built extensively and kept the army occupied in battle against the Kingdom of León. The first ruler to adopt the title of caliph was Abd al-Rahman III, an audacious move, given that the name implied a political and religious succession that could be traced back to the Prophet Muhammad.

Abd al-Rahman obviously felt himself to be sufficiently powerful and wealthy to deserve the honour. He came from the Ummayad dynasty and he had previously been known as the emir. The Ummayads originated from the Middle East with a power base in Syria; however, Abd al-Rahman's ancestry was somewhat mixed. Northern Spanish genes from his mother and grandmother resulted in blue eyes and the reddish hair that it was said he had to dye black. From his lofty position, he was able to patronise the arts liberally and to encourage Córdoba's reputation as one of the primary intellectual centres in Western Europe.

It was a tradition continued by his son, al-Hakam II, who expanded further the library started by his father. The eleventh-century writer and polymath Ibn Hazm, quoted at the head of this chapter, tells us that the library had 44 volumes of 50 folios apiece. Ibn Hazm was born in Córdoba in 994, 18 years after the end of al-Hakam's reign. In fact, he was to witness the sack of Córdoba by Berbers from North Africa and to see the end of the caliphate. Richard Fletcher, an academic with the gift of writing for a wider public, tells us, in his eminently readable account, *Moorish Spain*, that the 19-year-old Ibn Hazm was shocked to see the barbarity with which scholars were executed and the library dispersed.

The puppet caliphs finally came to an end in 1031, giving rise to smaller mini-states known as *taifas*. Ibn Hazm became akin to a wandering scholar, unattached to any specific authority. Fletcher calls him 'an independent author' who detached himself from politics after the Ummayad defeat. He wrote works of theology, law and philosophy but is best remembered for his text on love, which some modern scholars have called the masterpiece of Arab Andalusi literature. It is translated into English as *The Dove's Neck-Ring*.

The extensive work has 30 chapters and was split into four sections: the foundations of love, the essence of love, the dangers of love and the dishonour or continence of love. This quote, known as 'Slander', falls into the essence section:

> They chide at me, and say
> My love is sickly slender;
> But I will not obey
> The sly reproofs they tender.
> Will not the bough whereon
> The sun is ever shining
> Be very apt anon
> To whither and be pining?

Another writer who was to witness the disintegration of caliphal Córdoba was Ibn Zaydun, born in 1003. He is most famous for his relationship with the Ummayad princess and poet Wallada, and for the poetry that flowed from this doomed liaison. For a short period of time, Zaydun's passions were reciprocated by the princess but she soon tired of the attentions of a commoner. The lovelorn poet poured his anguish into the stanzas of 'Ode in the Letter Nun', a tribute to Wallada with rhymes based on the ending –nā:

How many nights did we spend, drinking finest wine,
Until the hand of morning started writing in the sky,
And the morning-stars began to beat upon the dark,
Chasing away the night-stars and defeating night itself?
But we had stolen greedily the sweetest of delights,
Without a false note intruding, of worry or of care.
If only those nights had lasted longer, so would my happiness –
But nights of love are destined not to last.

The collapse of the relationship and political machinations involving Ibn Zaydun meant that the poet found himself gaoled in Córdoba for the best part of two years. He spent the time composing further poetry, including 'The Satirical Letter', a derisory portrait of Ibn Abdus, Wallada's new suitor. Fortunately, he eventually found his feet in Seville after fleeing the city of the Ummayads.

Not every Moorish poet was concerned with the more idealistic aspects of love. Ibn Quzman, writing in the twelfth century, is one such example: a son of a noble Cordoban family, he was tall, blond and blue-eyed, with a more than passing interest in the fashions of the day. This dandified peacock did not, however, have the looks to match. His marriage failed and he was a rather bawdy drunkard. In the small text *20 Great Works by Andalusi Authors*, his list of sins is impressively wicked: an impious, adulterous, squanderous, sodomising rapist – that is, if you are to believe the hype of a writer who aggrandised his own mischief. This example of one of his compositions illustrates a comic, light-hearted observation of the corporeal. It has the splendid title, 'The Radish':

> The radish is a good
> And doubtless wholesome food,
> But proves, to vex the eater,
> A powerful repeater.

From the baser works of Ibn Quzman, we proceed to raise the tone and focus on the philosophies of two greats of medieval Córdoba: Ibn Rushd, better known as Averroes, and Moshe ben Maimon, known as Maimonides. In Calle de Cairuán, in front of the city walls, is the statue of Averroes. Seated, wearing flowing robes, he has a book propped up on his knee, appropriate enough for this sage who produced a veritable mountain of written works. Among these were treatises on medicine, owing to his position as a physician, works on the law and insights into Muslim theology. To the Christian world, he is best known for his comments on the works of Aristotle, the Greek philosopher.

Like so many scholars before him, he fell foul of courtly intrigue, when those surrounding the leader, Abu Yaqub Yusuf, looked unfavourably on Averroes and his works. In the latter half of the twelfth century he was banished from the city. This was a fate he shared with Maimonides, who also has a statue in Córdoba. Maimonides, another writer, philosopher and physician, belonged to the Jewish faith; his statue heralds the entrance to the Judería (Jewish Quarter). Plaza Maimonides is a very short walk away to the west of the Mezquita. The whitewashed, cobbled square houses the bullfighting museum, next to which a little alley meanders into the narrow backstreets, past Plaza de Tiberiades.

This little square is home to the bronze image of Maimonides, seated in a similar position to his twelfth-century contemporary, Averroes, also wearing the flowing robes, turban and slippers of the day. The pointed ends to his footwear are shiny from the touch of thousands of tourists who rub his toes, whether for luck or in a vain attempt to imbue themselves with some of his wisdom. Moshe ben Maimon was, and is to this day, one of the most influential philosophers in Jewish history.

His two significant contributions revolved around his quest for clarity in Jewish law and his desire to enliven Jewish religious consciousness. He also looked into Aristotelian philosophy, comparing and contrasting it with Jewish theology in his *Guide for the Perplexed*, a text that seeks to clarify aspects of the Torah. This is how Maimonides explains the rationale behind the title of his book:

> It seeks to explain certain obscure figures which occur in the Prophets, and are not distinctly characterised as being figures. Ignorant and superficial readers take them in a literal, not in a figurative sense. Even well informed persons are bewildered if they understand these passages in their literal signification, but they are entirely relieved of their perplexity when we explain the figure, or merely suggest that these terms are figurative.

The forward-looking philosophy of the Cordoban was not matched in the political sphere. The Berber Almohad invasion saw the Jews have their *dhimmi* status withdrawn, which meant loss of protected rights for their community. This change would have been felt deeply in the synagogue that neighbours the Plaza de Tiberiades.

On the corner of nearby Calle Averroes, where it intersects with Calle Judíos, is the Casa de Sefarad, a museum that tells the story of Jews in Andalucia. The house has a sound archive and library with texts from some of the well-known Judeo-Spanish writers. Samuel ha-Levi ben Joseph ibn Nagrela, also called Samuel Ha-Nagid, was one such writer, born in Córdoba in 993. Like his later compatriot, Maimonides, he was forced into exile, albeit within Spain. Supposedly, his expertise as an Arabic calligraphist led to his appointment as a secretary to the Granadine vizier, a position he assumed on the vizier's death. He wrote poetry on a variety of subjects, ranging from the military to the laudatory, in addition to that staple of Andalusi pleasure – wine. In the face of the turbulent upheavals experienced in medieval Andalucia, which affected so many talented men of letters, it is encouraging to see that Ha-Nagid praised the power of the pen above most other weapons:

> Man's wisdom is at the tip of his pen,
> His intelligence is in his writing.
> His pen can raise a man to the rank
> That the sceptre affords to a king.

A telling insight into Christian attitudes towards the Jewish story in Spain comes from George Borrow. In his *Bible in Spain*, he gives an interesting account of a meeting with an old priest in the city, who had convinced himself that Borrow was no Lutheran as surely no Protestant could possibly speak Latin and Spanish as well as Borrow. The priest goes on to describe his attitude to Judaism, reminiscent of the worst excesses of the Inquisition in the centuries prior to their meeting in the 1830s:

Nothing gave so much trouble to the Santa Casa as this same Judaism. Its shoots and ramifications are numerous, not only in these parts but in all Spain; and it is singular enough, that, even among the priesthood, instances of Judaism of both kinds were continually coming to our knowledge, which it was of course our duty to punish.

From the Jewish Quarter, after a pleasant 400-metre stroll down to the river, you will reach the grandiosely titled Alcázar de los Reyes Cristianos. Like so many buildings in Córdoba, it has a multilayered history. First Visigothic, then rebuilt by the Ummayads, it fell to the Christian kings and, as the name suggests, was occasionally home to the monarchs, Isabella and Ferdinand, who turned it into a seat of the Inquisition. Paul Gwynne, whom we last saw following the Guadalquivir in Seville, also tracked the river's path through the city of the Ummayads. He found the *alcázar* of 1912 in a rather lamentable state, far from the restored tourist attraction that it is today. Nonetheless, he paints a convincing portrait of its chequered progress through the years:

> On the slope of a hill which looks down upon the river on the west is all that is left of the once magnificent Alcazar. It must have been immense, for it stood upon the foundations now occupied by the episcopal palace, what are called the new and the old Alcazar, the gardens of the Alcazar, and the stables. In Roman times it was here that the principal fortress stood. The Goths erected a palace to Theodofred, father of King Rodrigo, on the same spot. At length, the khalifs of the house of Meruan here installed themselves. The learned Aben Baxkuald tells us that he found here examples of every stage and type of civilisation that Andalucía had passed through.

Gwynne goes on to tell us that the new *alcázar* was a gaol, continuing the nefarious tradition of the Inquisition. Today, the gardens and interior offer a far more agreeable way to spend a few

14 The Gardens of the Alcázar de los Reyes Cristianos, Córdoba

hours. The gardens have been beautifully reconstructed, providing a haven of water-filled tranquillity from the heat of a Cordoban summer. Avenues of water stretch into the distance, softened by gentle fountains and colourful planting. Rows of regimented trees give way to the imposingly weathered figures of the imperious Catholic Monarchs, frozen in time before a supplicant Christopher Columbus in search of his destiny.

Inside, the castle is segmented into a series of rooms that can be visited. The most eye-catching features are the Roman mosaics that were found in the city. Displayed on the walls, they depict scenes from legend and mythology; the most remarkable is a second-century image of Polyphemus and Galatea. The one-eyed Sicilian Cyclops is seated on a rock beside the object of his desire, Galatea, semi-naked and wreathed by a serpent-like figure. It would have been wonderful to imagine the baroque poet Luis de Góngora standing in front of the tessellated image, finding inspiration for his *Fable of Polyphemus and Galatea* (*La Fábula de Polifemo y Galatea*).

Sadly, the mosaic was still hidden during the seventeenth century, when he penned the poem.

Góngora was born in the city in 1561 to prosperous parents. The son of a lawyer, he followed in his father's footsteps and studied law at Salamanca University, where he seems to have spent most of his time gambling. When not whiling away the hours at cards, he started to write his early verses. The promise of an inheritance from an uncle led him to a career in the Church, although his real vocation was letters. It was the aforementioned *Fable* and his *Solitudes* (*Soledades*), both written in Córdoba, that brought his work to a wider audience.

Even during his lifetime, Góngora divided opinion. His verses are laden with the kind of innovation that infuriated some and delighted others. A master of many forms, he liberally sprinkled his works with allusion, Latinisms, mythology and baroque elaboration. Famously, other poets of the Golden Age were antipathetic towards his poetry, particularly Francisco de Quevedo, who often attacked him in print with very sharp barbs, equally piercingly returned. Owing to the number of poets who followed Góngora's considerable lead, the Gongoresque style fell out of favour, as can be seen in this snippet referring to the *Solitudes* from Frederick Bouterwek's 1847 *History of Spanish Literature*: 'This work, like all Gongora's productions in the same style, is merely an insipid fiction, full of pompous mythological images, described in a strain of the most fantastic bombast.'

As we know, it was left to the Generation of '27 – Lorca, Alberti et al. – to resurrect the reputation of the city's finest Renaissance poet. Today, his life is celebrated in Calle Cabezas, where you can find the Casa Góngora, a typical seventeenth-century dwelling with its grilled windows, smartly outlined in red. The interior patio has a small fountain set in cobbles and is framed by an arched colonnade. The house boasts an exhibition centre and is home to studies into the author's poetic output.

The other dedication to the writer-cleric can be found to the left of the Puerta del Puente as you cross the Roman bridge. A plaque embedded into the city wall looks down onto a small mosaic. The black escutcheon atop the plaque commemorates the three-hundredth anniversary of Góngora's death, and the words etched into the marble are taken from his tribute 'To Córdoba':

> Exalted walls, battlements crowned
> with honour, courage, majesty!
> Great river! Great King of Andalusia,
> of noble if not golden sands!
>
> O fertile plains, O high sierras
> which heaven favours and day gilds!
> O my hometown forever glorious
> with pen no less than with the sword!

Edmondo De Amicis, who wrote so well of Seville, was equally fascinated with Córdoba. On entering Calle Góngora, the Italian lets rip at Góngora the poet, 'the Marini of Spain, not less gifted intellectually, but perhaps a greater corrupter of his literature than Marini has been of ours, because he spoiled, maimed, and degraded the language in a thousand ways'. It is harsh, but said with friendly wit, and De Amicis goes on to tell us that the great Lope de Vega claimed that Góngora did not even understand his own work. Yet, as De Amicis points out, Lope de Vega could not escape the influence of Gongorism.

De Amicis acknowledges that the city is very free with its praise for its illustrious sons and this following advice is something we would whole-heartedly reiterate:

Instead of taking a drive in the environs of Cordova, I gave myself up to wandering here and there, and to indulging in fancies about the name of the streets, which in my opinion, is one of the greatest pleasures a man can enjoy in an unknown city. Cordova, *alma ingeniorum parens*, might write at every corner of her streets the name of an artist or illustrious sarvant born within her walls; and, let it be said to her honour, she has remembered them all with maternal gratitude. You will find there the little square of Seneca, and there, perhaps, is the house in which he was born.

The Plaza de Séneca still exists, although the locals refer to it as the Square of the Headless Man (Plaza del Descabezado), owing to the decapitated statute of a Roman in a toga that can be found there. The Stoic philosopher was born in the city and maintained estates in the vicinity, albeit from a distance, throughout his life. His grisly end came in Rome in 65 CE when the Emperor Nero ordered him to commit suicide. Having slit his wrists, he had to cut the veins in his leg as well, finally resorting to poison before he eventually expired.

From Plaza de Séneca, it is a short walk to the Plaza del Potro. From Calle San Fernando, enter a street named after that other Cordoban of Roman fame, the poet Lucan. This Calle Lucano takes you to the Plaza del Potro and our destination. The plaza is significant because of its association with Miguel de Cervantes. The author of *Don Quixote* had many associations with the city, not least of which was the fact that his father was born there. The Plaza del Potro is, indeed, mentioned in his masterwork, once with regard to its sewers and once in the story of a local lunatic: 'In Cordova there was another madman, whose way it was to carry a piece of marble slab or a stone, not of the lightest, on his head, and when he came upon any unwary dog he used to draw close to him and let the weight fall right on top of him.' It may just be coincidence, be we noticed a distinct lack of canines in the city.

In the same district is Calle Ambrosio de Morales, home to the Antonio Gala Foundation. Gala is a dramatist, novelist, poet, essayist and a self-declared Cordoban who grew up in the city although he was born in Castile-La Mancha. He is a well-known figure in the Spanish press and on television. He took to novel writing later in life with notable success. *El manuscrito carmesí* (*The Crimson Manuscript*), an evocation of the life of Boabdil, last sultan of Granada, won the Planeta Prize in 1990. He was one of the first presidents of the Spanish–Arab Friendship Association and, as such, would have been in the right position to turn his literary attention to this rich era in history. Sadly, he has not yet fictionalised the rise and fall of Córdoba's equivalent to the Alhambra, Medina Azahara.

Medina Azahara

You may well see Medina Azahara appearing under various guises owing to its transliteration from the original Arabic. We have adopted the commonly used Spanish spelling which is likely to be seen on signposts; however, a little reading around the subject is bound to produce the following: Medinat az-Zahra, Madinat al-Zahra or any combination thereof. The archaeological ruins at Medina are approximately ten kilometres (six miles) directly west of central Córdoba. Since its disappearance just a few short decades after its spectacular construction, the palace complex at Medina has had a rather mythical reputation. From the early 1910s, Abd al-Rahman III's citadel started to emerge from the hidden layers of the Cordoban plain.

The original building work started in 936 when the Caliph wanted a suitable location to match his new title. He chose this plot on an incline above the Guadalquivir to place the complex that would root his power in the soil of al-Andalus. Even the name of the palace is shrouded in legend. Various versions of the story exist but they all revolve around a central theme. A concubine of Abd al-Rahman had died, leaving him a colossal sum of money which was intended as ransom payment in exchange for prisoners held in Christian lands. Unable to find said prisoners, Abd al-Rahman decided to build the town in question and name it after Zahra, who was either the concubine who had died or the favourite who had taken her place.

When Paul Gwynne followed his romantic Guadalquivir, Medina was only just emerging from its hidden grave. In 1912, the excavations were beginning and, if Paul is to be believed, were being carried out 'very unskilfully, and with rigorous secrecy', the relics taken from the earth being 'flung into heaps'. Fortunately for Medina and similar sites around the world, archaeological practice has vastly improved, although estimates say that a mere 10 per cent of the entire location has been excavated. The ruins are interspersed with careful planting and trimmed hedging, occasionally punctuated with studied reconstruction. Despite the evidence before your eyes, your imagination will need to take flight to reproduce the true magnificence of Abd al-Rahman's creation.

One of the finest chroniclers of Medina Azahara is Ahmed Mohammed al-Maqqari, an Algerian historian of the seventeenth century who read widely from the texts of the period and wrote up his studies in *Mohammedan Dynasties in Spain*. He gives us a clear picture of the sheer expense and monumental task: 'Another well informed writer says that the cost of every block of marble brought to Cordova, either from the Khalif's dominions in Andalus as well as in Africa, or from various distant countries in the hands of the infidels, was ten gold dinárs each.'

Al-Maqqari is at his best when describing the 'wonders' of Azahara. His evocation of the fountains gives us an idea of the utter opulence of the complex:

> However, all agree in saying that such were the taste of the designs on these fountains, and the magnificence of the materials, as to make their value almost beyond estimation. The smaller one, above all appears to have been a real wonder of art [...] When the Khalif received it he ordered it to be placed in the dormitory of the eastern hall called *Al-múnis*, and he fixed on it twelve figures made of red gold, and set with pearls and other precious stones.

Indeed, many writers seem to be captivated by the actions of this Andalucian satrap, who was determined to spare no expense in the pursuit of his fantasy. In his weighty tome, *Iberia*, the twentieth-century American novelist and travel writer James A. Michener was rather more grounded in his evaluation, being sceptical of the figures banded around by his guide – notable among which were the supposed 3,700 Slavonian eunuchs. He also points out that perceiving in the ruins the magnificence attributed by so many requires 'faith'. He is prepared to suspend a certain degree of modern cynicism, but cannot let go entirely of his incredulity.

No such issue was encountered by Nikos Kazantzakis. The Cretan Nikos Kazantzakis, born in 1883 in Heraklion and indelibly linked with his magnum opus, *Zorba the Greek*, was no stranger to controversy surrounding his writing. His *Last Temptation* caused a furore which ended in his excommunication from the Greek Orthodox Church. Surprisingly, Kazantzakis's Spanish travels, in translation simply entitled *Spain*, also attracted criticism. This stems from the fact that the book is split into two halves – before and during the Civil War. Nikos, a left-leaning sympathiser, chose to observe the war from the perspective of Franco's Nationalist troops in an attempt to present an honest and impartial portrait. Needless to say, this decision attracted much disapproval.

The first half of the book is far less contentious, if somewhat rose-tinted. Standing on a parched hillock, gazing towards Azahara, Kazantzakis's mind wanders to the splendours created by the Caliph: 'In the blue twilight, I was trying to make out the blessed peak where the illustrious Sultan Abd-er-Rahman had built his magic palace Medina az-Zahara, to please the woman whom he loved.' He goes on to enumerate the inhabitants of this 'earthly paradise' without a hint of Michener's scepticism, losing himself in the 'endless garden' of his imagination, populated with a team of warriors, poets and women.

Edmondo De Amicis did not even have the benefit of the archaeological discoveries of the early twentieth century to excite his mind's eye. Enthralled by the idea of such an endeavour in homage to a lover, his prose reaches for the heights: 'There were exotics from Syria, fantastic jets for the very high fountains, rivulets lined by palms, and immense basins filled with mercury, which gleamed in the sun like lakes of fire.' The Italian, who also knew the Arab-Norman past glories of Sicily, clearly loved the romance of Oriental Europe. He laments the short-lived erotic–exotic nature of Medina Azahara which 'was invaded, sacked, and burned by a barbarous horde seventy-four years after its first stones had been laid'.

De Amicis was almost as enamoured of Cordoban women as the distant Caliph. Whilst settling down for lunch at a *casa de huespedes* (guesthouse), he was delighted to find himself before the 'most beautiful of all beautiful Andalusian women'. At this point he was obviously constructing palaces for her in his mind: 'She was an overwhelming sort of girl, who would make one take flight or commit any kind of a devilry.'

Much flirting ensued, leaving De Amicis convinced that 'she looked like one of the Arabian virgins of the Usras tribe, who made people die from love.' She, in turn, described him as 'fiery', yet his flames were swiftly dampened by the entrance of a *torero* who was clearly her betrothed. It seems Córdoba has incited both religious and earthier fervours. Passions of a different kind, corporeal and political, were enflamed in the provincial town of Fuente Obejuna.

Fuente Obejuna

The small town of Fuente Obejuna, some 90 kilometres (55 miles) to the north-west of Córdoba, was immortalised in the play *Fuente Ovejuna* by the great Spanish playwright Lope de Vega. De Vega, born in Madrid in 1562, was the most prodigious and well-respected dramatist of the Spanish Golden Age. His long and turbulent life included a considerable amount of womanising, some of which landed him in trouble at court.

Even after taking holy orders later in life, he managed to continue his amorous adventures. Sadly, his old age was a long, bitter reflection on the years that saw the majority of his 12 children dead. Maybe as a penance for his wayward nature, he used to flagellate himself with a whip, evidence of which was found at his death when bloodstains could be seen splattered on the walls. It was a simple chill, though, that finally ended his life at the age of 72.

By 1604, he had already composed 230 plays comprising three acts apiece. De Vega is credited with taking much of the earlier theatre and moulding it into something more national in character; he was quite happy to throw out the rule book, as he tells us himself. Every popular genre is included in his output, notably the historical, religious and romantic. His works are still avidly performed today throughout Spain and at such august institutions as Britain's Royal National Theatre.

Perhaps his best-known work is the aforementioned *Fuente Ovejuna*, which is based on events that actually took place in the town in 1476. De Vega obtained his source material from a text known as the *Crónica de las tres Ordenes Militares* (*Chronicle of the Three Military Orders*). The play details a popular revolt against a feudal ruler, Don Fernán, in the name of the Catholic Monarchs, Ferdinand and Isabella. Critics say that *Fuente Ovejuna* is the best of his plays that extol the virtues of the people against the aristocracy. At the heart of the text is a deep-seated sense of collective honour, which is most offended when Don Fernán, the *comendador*, attempts by *droit du seigneur* to have his wicked way with Laurencia, a local girl. Fernán meets his end at the point of a spear by the hands of the populace, prompting the phrase, which entered common parlance, 'Fuente Ovejuna did it.' The exhortation of Esteban, Laurencia's father, is one of the play's most palpable realisations of this wounded honour:

> A man whose graying beard is bathed in tears
> Asks you, my honest farmers, how our folk
> Should mourn the death of honor in this land.
> What use to mourn our vanished honor now,
> If there is not a man among us who
> Is not degraded by this evil fiend?

In a very sixteenth-century 'all's well that ends well', the townsfolk are pardoned by the Catholic Monarchs when they hear the truth of their story.

It will come as no surprise to learn that there is a Plaza Lope de Vega in modern-day Fuente Obejuna. Its whitewashed walls and gentle steps look down on a square that once witnessed the real-life events in a distant 1476. Federico García Lorca could pay Lope de Vega no greater compliment than to restage his famous play in the town itself when he toured the regions of Spain with La Barraca, the student theatre company he directed in the years before the Civil War.

 **8**

Jaén Province

Army of Olives

Andalusians of Jaén,
proud olive pickers,
tell me from your soul: who,
who raised up the olive trees?
(Miguel Hernández, 'Olive Pickers', 1937)

Jaén

Sitting under the bastion of Santa Catalina, built in 1246 after the Christian reconquest of the city, the provincial capital is encircled by the life-giving olive which is so synonymous with the province. Jaén is often overlooked by the visitor to Andalucia, a fact that is embedded in the very name of the settlement; it is the Spanish representation of the Arabic, *khayyan*, meaning a crossroads on the caravan route to elsewhere.

Although not possessing the plethora of monuments and romantic associations of other more famous Andalucian cities, Jaén still manages to maintain the activity and bustle of a regional hub. Two thoroughfares, the Avenida de Madrid and the Paseo de la Estación, cut to the heart of town, ending at the Plaza de la Constitución – a short walk from the impressive cathedral, largely remodelled by the area's Renaissance architect par excellence, Andrés de Vandelvira.

Théophile Gautier, wandering far from his favoured Alhambra, was awed by the sheer size of the cathedral, 'which seems from a distance, to be larger than the town itself [...] like an artificial mountain by the side of the natural one'. The sprawl of the modern city has redressed this balance but, finding oneself in the square before the edifice, it is easy to appreciate his sentiments. Gautier also mentions the building's renowned relic, a 'true handkerchief in which Saint Veronica took the impression of our Saviour's face'. To this day, the icon housing said handkerchief is removed from its position behind the altar every Friday in order to allow the faithful to kiss the glass. The surface is wiped between kisses by an altogether less venerable piece of cloth.

Walking away from the cathedral, Théophile was amazed to find that a playbill was advertising a work by his friend Bouchardy – something he considered remarkable in a 'barbarous town, where the inhabitants never go out without a poniard'. Such was the unfortunate reputation of nineteenth-century Jaén: a city where the carrying of daggers was commonplace and poverty rife. Gautier actually witnessed a debacle in the *parador* (then a simple inn) over the staleness of the bread being served by the owner, a quarrel which escalated when another guest was certain that the food had been reheated. The truth of the matter was revealed by Gautier when he discovered that the meal in question was intended for another party; it had never reached its destination, having been kidnapped by brigands in the high Sierras on its way from La Mancha.

The modern city has fortunately lost its reputation for violence and the inhabitants enjoy a convivial nightlife in the many tapas bars that surround the Plaza de la Constitución. Nothing unusual will strike the casual observer about their appearance or behaviour today, yet the same could not be said about the Jienenses of Gautier's era. Going against the stereotype of the flamboyant Andaluz, our ostentatious Frenchman found he had to break through the 'icy reserve' of the people to discover their 'charming sweetness'.

However, their initial cool exterior did not extend to their mode of attire. Théophile paints this vivid portrait of the locals' clothing:

> It was at Jaen that I saw more national and picturesque costumes than anywhere else. The men were attired, for the most part, in blue velvet breeches, adorned with silver filigrane buttons, and Ronda gaiters embellished with aiglets and stitching, and worked with arabesques on leather of a darker colour [...] Wide sashes of red or yellow silk, jackets of brown cloth variously trimmed, blue or maroon cloaks, pointed hats with slouched brims, ornamented with bands of velvet and silk tassels, complete the costume, which is very similar to the ancient dress of Italian brigands.

One can only wonder at the practicality of such dress in the 40-degree heat of a northern Andalucian summer, especially when today's residents are commonly seen in the far more suitable shorts and T-shirts.

The interesting preference for heavy clothing in torrid heat was not lost on the Frenchman, who felt the climate and look of the citizens gave the town an African air, especially when accompanied with the 'dazzling whiteness of the houses, which are all whitewashed in the Arabian fashion, the tawny colour of the ground, and the unchanging azure of the sky'. Much of Jaén has lost this typical feel, swept away in a rush to modernise. The Avenida de Madrid is lined with storeyed apartment blocks and commercial premises whose sad concrete is prey to the effects of pollution. One of the most striking aspects of the city's architecture is the juxtaposition of the crafted ancient and the prosaic modern.

Remarkably, in 1955, over 100 years after Gautier visited, H. V. Morton commented on the very same topics. As detailed in *A Stranger in Spain*, Morton approached the town through the serried ranks of its surrounding olives and also headed for the cathedral, where he too was pointed in the direction of the *Santa Faz*, St Veronica's handkerchief. Morton sat for a good while in the hallowed stillness, not out of religious contemplation but rather as an escape from the punishing heat outside.

Eventually rested enough to head out into the 'whiteness', he made his way to a local restaurant, where he was also amazed at the attire of the men gathered there. It was not so much their outlandish dress which perplexed him, but their tendency to remain fully jacketed and complete with tie in a town 'shimmering in the heat'. In an amusing aside, he compares these Jienense gourmands to the soldiers of Hernán Cortés who conquered the tropical Americas in quilted armour.

His table in the restaurant faced a tiled shrine to La Macarena, the Virgin favoured by bullfighters. Whilst musing on the image, he began to notice how the diners treated each other with a restrained courtesy, a little bow and a '*buen provecho*' that he was sure derived from Gautier's dagger-wielding days. After all, Morton assures us, when a man carries a blade, there is a fair chance that impolite arrogance will result in the ill-mannered oaf feeling the cold steel against his skin.

Fortunately, Morton was not the recipient of any indecorous behaviour – quite the contrary. He tells his readers that another suited local asked to share his table. He was a stereotypically fleshy, jovial miller and, what else would he be milling in Jaén, but the eternal olive? He was the owner of a pressing-mill and was only too happy to produce a business card for Morton and invite him to see the golden oil flowing from his presses the following spring. This image of bucolic abundance, however, hides a harsher reality for some – especially in the not so very distant past.

In 1937, Jaén formed part of the southern front where Republicans were trying to stop the Nationalist advance. The poet Miguel Hernández, a fervent supporter of the Republic and member of the Communist Party, was sent to the city in his capacity as both soldier and literary combatant. Hernández was not born in Andalucia, but Orihuela in Alicante Province. Nevertheless, he had a clear understanding of the struggles faced by itinerant agricultural workers in Andalucia, having spent time as a goatherd and farm worker. As a result, he was known in Spanish literary circles as the *poeta pastor* (shepherd poet); although he was not completely self-taught, Hernández had educated himself in literature and writing.

It was to Jaén that Hernández took his new wife, Josefina Manresa, to spend their honeymoon in the far from salubrious residential quarters of the Altavoz del Frente, the propaganda broadcaster he had come to help. It was also in the city that Hernández was able to study, at close quarters, the economic conditions of the olive estates. His poem, 'The Olive Pickers' ('Aceituneros'), is a *cri de coeur* for the plight of the underpaid and overworked pickers throughout Jaén Province:

> Andalusians of Jaén,
> proud olive pickers,
> tell me in your soul: who
> suckled the olive trees?
> Your blood, your life,
> not that of the exploiter
> who grew rich on the
> generous wound of sweat.
> Not that of the landowner
> who buried you in poverty,
> who trod on your brow,
> who made you bow your head.

It is clear from this stanza that the poet believed passionately in fairness, a facet of life sadly lacking for the majority of the rural workforce. Unlike many of the literary supporters of the Republic, Hernández truly added actions to his words, and had already seen the horrors of war when fighting further north. In this regional capital, he was also to use his considerable literary talents, collaborating in the first edition of the wartime newspaper *Frente Sur* (*Southern Front*).

Although Hernández's deeply held political convictions were somewhat shaken when he subsequently spent a month, viewing at first hand the realities of Communist Russia, he never lost his faith in the Republic and the pueblo. As the war drew to its inexorable conclusion and the government fell, Miguel felt he had no other option than to try and cross the Portuguese border. It was here that his reputation as a Red and a poet came to light, having been recognised by someone in the border authority who hailed from his part of Spain. Throughout the brutal interrogation and transfers from gaol to gaol, and despite pleas from the occasional influential friend, he never wavered from his political faith or agreed to accept the new regime. The penal system cannot have helped his already delicate health and he eventually died from tuberculosis in 1942.

Even in the days of our now-familiar English traveller, Richard Ford, or perhaps because of these days and former eras when land was parcelled out to the King's faithful, Jaén has always suffered from the classic *latifundia* system of ownership. Ford was well aware of the drawbacks this entailed, condemning the city with this lofty sobriquet: 'a poor place in the midst of plenty'. Jaén has lost these chronic aspects of urban poverty and now presents a brighter face to the world. Life in the countryside remains far from rosy for some, but wider horizons and greater opportunities have helped. Morton's jolly miller could be said to represent the beginning of a new era.

Andújar and the Olive Country

From anywhere within the city that has a clear view, sentries of olive trees can be seen disappearing into the horizon. It was towards this seemingly infinite crop that H. V. Morton drove his miller friend upon realising he had no transport of his own back to the farm, and time to kill before the bus arrived. The pair reached an unnamed village – a village that could be representative of any in the province, its steep main street struggling through the blankets of grey-green.

Morton refers to his new acquaintance as a small businessman and, indeed, he is a world away from the lofty landowners berated by Hernández. He was not without position in his local community, however, as is apparent from the characters who came to greet the pair when their car pulled up in the whitewashed little square. From the local bar, the writer was then taken to the site of harvests past. He was shown a massive grindstone that would be turned by a blindfolded mule, a practice that appears cruel but the miller assured Morton that the eyepatches were used to help the mule avoid giddiness.

It was still a time when the first-pressed extra-virgin oil was syphoned away into terracotta jars, the size of which could comfortably hold a fully grown man. Even the crushed pulp and stones did not go to waste, being used as fuel for the braziers found in so many rural homes. What the Englishman witnessed was a centuries-old tradition handed down from father to son until more industrial practices were introduced. Carol Drinkwater, the British actor and author who keeps her own olive farm in the south of France, travelled to see olive cultivation further afield in her 2008 book, *The Olive Tree*. When she reached these southern climes, she went in search of *flor del aceite* (flower of the oil) – a further tradition steeped in the kind of mystique more akin to the wine trade.

She managed to track down two brothers who were selling their oil in the United States, no doubt for champagnesque prices. The production method owes much to the techniques witnessed by Morton. The olives are hand-gathered from the trees and ground on the same day between granite stones. Rather than it being a hasty process, the pulverised olive is left for a period of days to produce its liquid slowly. This method increases the amount of fruit needed to produce a single litre of oil, hence the tasty price. In complete contrast, Drinkwater also witnessed the production from a *cooperativa*, an institution gaining ground in olive country, where local farmers gather together to produce an end product.

The kind of plant she toured was very much at the other end of the spectrum, with automated belts and chutes awaiting the harvest from multiple farm vans.

One of the major agricultural hubs of the area is Andújar, a 40-minute drive to the north-west of Jaén. The town is skirted by the Guadalquivir River and is famed for its earthenware jars. Like so much of the province, especially following the collapse of Spain's economic boom and the world financial crisis starting in 2007, the workforce has once again turned its attention to olive cultivation, in addition to the production of sunflower oil, in order to gain a living. Inevitably, the kind of mechanisation witnessed by Carol Drinkwater has meant fewer jobs and more unemployment.

If Andújar acts as the centre for surrounding produce, it has also been at the heart of more than one historical battle. After the town was surrendered to King Fernando III in 1225, it became the base for the Christian armies of reconquest who were fighting to the south of the Sierra Morena. Little remains of the town's Moorish past, although it is a good bet that the bell tower of the Church of Santa María la Mayor in the Plaza de España was based on a minaret. Surprisingly, this provincial church also contains an El Greco painting. Between 1597 and 1607, Doménikos Theotokópoulos, more well-known for his works in Toledo, produced *Christ in the Garden of Olives*, with its characteristic elongated figures and primacy of colour.

Fortunately, the worst excesses of the Civil War did not destroy the church or the painting. The core of the action took place in the Santuario de Nuestra Señora de la Cabeza, where a certain Nationalist Captain Cortés took refuge, later being accused of shielding himself from the enemy by staying amongst the women and children of Republican families. The taking of the sanctuary was covered by Miguel Hernández's *Frente Sur*, with the poet writing of the death of Cortés, a captain whom he considered guilty for the loss of young life: 'Because of him many men lie groaning in Andújar's hospital.'

Insults and accusations flew between the two sides, with the Nationalists accusing the Republicans of the summary execution of people in religious orders. When Franco's soldiers eventually captured the town, it became a regional base that saw many returning troops. One such combatant was Juan Castro Pérez, the central character of Juan Eslava Galán's novel, *The Mule* (*La mula*), published in its original Spanish in 2003. Eslava Galán, a native Jienense, uses humour to point out the absurdities of war. Juan Castro Pérez is a simple muleteer who, despite his humble position in society, has chosen to fight for the Nationalists. One day, he comes across an extra mule that does not form part of his troop. Given the fine fettle of the animal, he decides to adopt her, christening her Valentina, with the intention of taking her home after the conflict is over. Subsequently, finding himself in no man's land when he tries to rescue the wandering beast, Juan meets several desperate Republicans who are looking for a way out of the conflict, which is nearing its conclusion.

The opposition soldiers persuade the reluctant muleteer to take them prisoner, allowing the hapless bunch to find refuge as prisoners of war. Word spreads of Juan's supposed deeds in battle, leading to newspaper headlines, which the soldier candidly denies to his superior. Irrespective of the truth and owing to the need for propaganda, Juan is sent to pick up an award from the Caudillo, none other than Francisco Franco.

Through thick and thin, including the loss of his friend fighting for the Republicans, Juan keeps Valentina by his side. In a bitter twist, when the troops are finally discharged in Linares, just to the east of Andújar, a pencil-pushing stickler in the army offices points out that there is one mule extra who will have to make the trip to the Canaries with the army division from the islands. The heartbroken Juan goes back to his former life empty-handed, through the groves of unkempt olives, left untended during the hard years of war.

Tending and harvesting olives the old-fashioned way is no easy matter, as the writer Michael Jacobs was to find out.

Frailes

Frailes is a small town which, if it were not for Michael Jacobs, would not have found its way onto the literary map of Andalucia. It is some 15 kilometres (nine miles) from the regional hub of Alcalá la Real, which is an hour's drive to the south of Jaén. Frailes climbs a hill from the Rio de las Cuevas and its surrounding streams, sadly depleted through periods of drought. We know Jacobs to be an erudite recorder of Spanish life and literature through his book *Between Hopes and Memories* (1994), lauded by Ian Gibson as 'excellent on literary associations'. On a more personal level, Jacobs recalls in *The Factory of Light* how Frailes became his spiritual home through a series of happy accidents.

In 1997, Jacobs found himself on a train between Prague and Budapest. At a visa stop on the border with Slovakia, he fell into conversation with an elderly Australian couple who broached the subject of Andalucia. To the author's surprise, despite the fact that he had lived in Seville, the couple were intent on telling him their experience of Jaén Province. Their story unfolded in a most unexpected way. By the circuitous route of a Spanish faith-healer who had settled in Sydney, they looked to the small town of Frailes in a desperate search to cure their son of his degenerative illness. They had been told that Santo Custodio, a healer of note, might be able to help. With a strong belief, the couple headed off on their journey, arriving in town by donkey. It seems that, to Jacobs's sceptical surprise, their son was cured.

A couple of years down the line, the name Frailes was once again to enter his life when an accommodation officer in Seville suggested that he and his friends stay in a property just outside the town. A little voice inside his head told him, rather rashly, to accept the rental. He spent the next few weeks reading about the area; sadly, he was able to find little in either history books or travelogues, apart from the fact that the settlement had been a charcoal-burning centre, evidenced by Calle Carboneras, a street that runs parallel to the river.

Initially happy just to find a quiet location where he could fulfil his commission to translate a play by Lope de Vega, Jacobs found himself inextricably drawn into the life of the town. After the summer rental had finished, he returned for an extended stay, beguiled by the overwhelming warmth of the people, the atmosphere conducive to writing and his interest in the esoteric aspects surrounding Santo Custodio. A habitué of the bar La Cueva, and living above the Discoteca Oh!, Jacobs was taken into the hearts of the locals, forming, in particular, something of a double act with the man nicknamed El Sereno – an autodidact and lover of life who was an avid collector of books and an acquaintance of Juan Eslava Galán, the author of *The Mule*.

El Sereno, apart from being a charismatic figure, was a guru on olive production. Despite his small oil harvest, Jacobs's friend was committed to organic farming, cultivating the trees without the use of chemicals. After an initial morning in Sereno's fields and a liquid lunch at La Cueva, Jacobs still remained unconvinced of the difficulties involved in the harvest. He was soon to change his mind. A weekend spent gathering saw the middle-aged writer hitting the trees with a pole in order to drop the olives into a waiting net and then carrying sacks of fruit back to the van like a beast of burden. He compared the physical experience to labour in a Siberian prison camp.

Jacobs's role in the community really came into its own when the subject of the local cinema became the topic of conversation. During his time in the town, the building was still standing but had not been used for some considerable time. Nevertheless, on seeing inside, the writer was awed by the art deco appearance and the dress circle seating that put him in mind of a choir stall in a sixteenth-century church. Remarkably, he was more stunned by this humble jewel than by the magnificence of the Alhambra – maybe owing to his Italian mother's roots in the theatre. Along with his Sancho Panza, El Sereno, he decided to restore the building for one night only, in order to show the town's favourite postwar risqué musical, *El último cuplé* – a *cuplé* being a bawdy variety song.

The pair even went as far as to invite the now ageing but still well-known starring actress, Sara Montiel, who, incredibly, found time in her busy schedule to turn up for the event. One can only imagine the excitement this generated in the little town, especially for those who remembered the original showings when, at a more innocent time, this fairly innocuous film inflamed passions. The success of the evening prompted a stream of television reporters to seek out Jacobs and El Sereno for an interview or soundbite.

Today, the cinema presents a sprightly whitewashed façade to the world. At the Mesón Hostal La Posa, Calle Tejar leads into Calle Cruz which bends uphill. A few metres beyond the Hostal, the green sign 'Cinema España', reinstated by the owner for the big day, proclaims the building's heritage. The equally vivid green doors, shutters and eaves still reflect a degree of care and pride. La Posa would have done a roaring trade that evening and is still a good spot to stop for a drink and a tapa, although, as happened on Jacobs's first visit to the town, do not be surprised if all faces turn to greet the foreigner.

Baeza

In complete contrast to little Frailes, Baeza boasts World Heritage status in recognition of the stature and charm of its Renaissance architecture. Surprisingly, perhaps due to its northerly location 50 kilometres (30 miles) to the north-east of Jaén, it remains little visited by those from outside Spain. In turns Roman, Visigothic and Moorish, before it was a hothouse for warring aristocrats, the town owes its magnificence to the settlement of such factional fighting, which favoured the victorious nobility with estates, money from agriculture and the wherewithal to produce the monumental architecture present today.

The majority of notable buildings centre on the Paseo de la Constitución, the porticoed hub of the town. At the south-western end of the Paseo, the elegantly cobbled square known as the Plaza de los Leones houses the former offices of the city's scribes and the Jaén Gate, dedicated to a visit by King Charles V. Through the gate and turning to the left, a suitably atmospheric street with whitewashed two-storey houses frames the corner tower of the old university which had its charter revoked in 1824, becoming a school in 1875. To one side of the central patio, adjoining a sixteenth-century lecture theatre, Antonio Machado, the Sevillian poet, carried out his day job as a schoolmaster. Where they once interpreted Ovid and Virgil to the level of graduate and doctor, Machado, born on the same date as the inauguration of the school, now taught French to secondary school students.

Machado was from a long line of scholarly characters with a liberal frame of mind. His early years in Seville were shortened when the family moved to Madrid due to his grandfather's position at the university there. The family sent him to be schooled at the Institución Libre de Enseñanza, an educational establishment that was to have a profound effect on his thought and his attitudes to education. The institution advocated tuition free from academic dogma or the perceived political and religious strictures of the day.

After leaving school, he eventually acquired a degree. One of his early literary contracts in 1899 was to work on a French–Spanish dictionary in Paris, where he met the likes of Jean Moréas, Paul Verlaine and Rubén Darío. It was this trip and the cataclysmic events of 1898, when Spain lost Cuba, Puerto Rico and the Philippines in a brief war with the United States, that persuaded Machado to devote himself more fully to poetry. However, like so many literary figures before and after, he needed a steadier form of income. Unsurprisingly for one so grounded in academia, he turned to teaching – although he realised he had no vocation in this field.

Having scored respectably enough in the *oposiciones*, the state exams required to enter the profession, he was posted to Soria in Castille, where he met and married Leonor Izquierdo in 1909. There was a considerable age gap between the two but it was clear that the

34-year-old Antonio adored his young wife. He was to have too few years by her side as Leonor was soon diagnosed with tuberculosis, dying in 1912.

It was a heartbroken Machado who relocated to Baeza. Fanny Rubio starts the first chapter of her recently published and excellent account of Machado's time in the town, *Baeza de Machado* (*Machado's Baeza*), with this startling revelation from the poet to his friend, Juan Ramón Jiménez: 'When I lost my wife I thought of shooting myself. The success of my book saved me and, God knows, not through vanity! But because I thought, if there was a useful force within me, I had no right to extinguish it.' The creative force he spoke of had just produced one of his masterworks, *The Castilian Country* (*Campos de Castilla*).

The second edition of the text included the poems written after his arrival in Baeza, notably those which poignantly evoke his time with Leonor, exemplified by this snippet from 'Caminos' ('Paths'):

> The little white paths
> cross and diverge,
> searching out the scattered hamlets
> in the valley and sierra.
> Country paths …
> Oh, I can no longer walk with her!

These are precisely the thoughts that must have passed through his grieving mind as he sat in his classroom. Rubio constantly refers to Machado as the 'poeta tristón', which can be translated as the downhearted or melancholic poet; although she does point out that Machado tried to immerse himself in delivering the kind of education favoured by the Institución Libre.

The old university building, which commemorates the poet with a plaque on its honey-coloured outer wall, is centred on the aforementioned patio, the upper arched storeys of which are glassed over, whilst the lower floor maintains something of a monastic air. Machado's classroom has been recreated as accurately as possible with rows of school desks, complete with inkwells, facing towards the maestro's raised table placed directly underneath the blackboard. On one side of the table is a shelf holding a briefcase and on the other is a hatstand with a carefully hung umbrella. It is as if Machado and his students have just departed for a break and will soon be filing in once again to resume class.

The walls are decorated with maps and botanical drawings. A book cabinet at the back of the classroom holds a selection of academic tomes, although, on careful perusal, none appears to be French. The museum aspect of the schoolroom is fulfilled by a central wooden cabinet housing newspaper articles and letters, including an application from Machado to the rector of Granada University. Amongst the cuttings are some articles on progressive educational theory and descriptions of his time in Baeza. Machado peers down on the cabinet from an oil painting on the wall, his benign, enigmatic expression and characteristic receding hairline leaving no doubt as to his identity.

Across the street from the former school is the Palacio Jabalquinto, among the most beautiful buildings in the town. Two central pillars flank a loggia underneath which the Gothic and Moorish collide in a series of stone bands and studded reliefs that appear as true diamonds when the glaring Andalucian sun provides stark shadow. The whole façade can be categorised by the architectural term Isabelline. Once home to the aristocratic Benavides family, the building is now a seat of the Universidad Internacional de Andalucia, appropriately given the name Sede Antonio Machado. The casual visitor can wander the central patio, which is adorned with a cooling fountain, and take a coffee in the gardens – which celebrate the poet with a bronze bust and an inscription of his work underneath the quintessential olive. One of the poems he wrote whilst working at the school is simply entitled 'The Olive Trees' ('Los Olivos') and is included in Alan S. Trueblood's 1982 translations of Machado's *Selected Poems*:

Parched old olive trees
standing full in the sun,
powdery with dust
from the Andalusian earth.
Land of Andalusia combed
by hot midsummer suns,
ruled into lines of olives
stretching from hill to hill.
They bask in the sun,
these lands,
broad hills and far-off ranges
fretted with olive groves.
A thousand trails.

The solitary poet used to enjoy walking through the town and the surrounding countryside. A favourite of his was a path through stones and trees around the perimeter of Baeza, starting from the lion fountain; the route today is known as the Paseo de Antonio Machado.

Although not full of the joys of life, he still joined that very Spanish institution, the *tertulia*; in fact, he participated in two of these convivial gatherings of like-minded souls. One was held in the back room of a pharmacy in Calle San Francisco, a street that leads to the top end of the Plaza de la Constitución. The other, being more political, took place in the Casino de Artesanos, a club for local artisans and workmen.

Machado was also not without visits from literary friends and acolytes. He was visited twice by a young Federico García Lorca, once in 1916 and again the following year. Lorca and his group listened to the renowned poet give a lecture on 'The Castilian Country', followed by a recitation of its verses. As Ian Gibson points out, Lorca was a profound admirer of the older man's poetry – so much so that he annotated his own copy of Machado's *Complete Works* with a laudatory verse. In the Casino de Artesanos, Lorca repaid the pleasure of hearing the maestro's verses by playing a piece by Manuel de Falla on the piano.

The young man from Granada was much taken by Baeza, although he also saw a quiet melancholy, where 'Everything is vaguely soporific … as if ancient shadows walk the sad, silent streets that will weep at midnight'. These *Sketches of Spain* come to their apogee when he talks of the Cathedral Square, just beyond Calle Obispo Romero Mengíbar:

> The overbearing cathedral perfumes the square with incense and wax that filter through its walls as a reminder of its sanctity.
>
> In the distance, houses of golden stone with age-old inscriptions commemorating heroic deeds faded by too much sun, and windows flaking behind rusty, rickety grilles.
>
> The square is painfully, privately silent …

15   The Cathedral of Santa María, Baeza

Some of these words are carved into a plaque as you look upwards towards the cathedral. What really exercised Lorca during his visit to Machado was the discovery of a proposal to urbanise the square by planting an English garden where the cobbles of centuries lay. Fortunately for all concerned, this idea never materialised.

Unlike Lorca, Machado is less known to a general English-speaking audience, and his works tend not to sit alongside the Granadine or Pablo Neruda in the poetry sections of bookshops in the Anglo-Saxon world. Yet his reputation as one of the great poets of his generation is now firmly rooted in the Spanish world of letters. Many translations do exist, but his champions have been less vociferous. One early advocate was John Dos Passos, the American novelist and writer of Portuguese extraction.

Dos Passos's most commercial work was the 1925 *Manhattan Transfer*, a novel of life in New York, charting the city up until the dawn of the Jazz Age. Three years previously and a considerable time before his involvement in the Spanish Civil War along with Hemingway, the American published *Rosinante to the Road Again*. The title plays with references to Don Quixote's horse and peripatetically idiosyncratic visions of Spain, in this case, the author's own.

Dos Passos was too late to meet Machado in Baeza, but the Sevillian's poetry had clearly started to claim a wider audience and was the reason for Dos Passos's pilgrimage to Segovia, where Machado had relocated to be near his brother and fellow poet, Manuel. In the American's eyes:

Antonio Machado's verse is taken up with places. It is obsessed with the old Spanish towns where he has lived, with the mellow sadness of tortuous streets and of old houses that have soaked up the lives of generations upon generation of men, crumbling in the flaming silence of summer noons or in the icy blast off the mountains in winter.

Placing the poet at the vanguard of Hispanic literature, Dos Passos hails the 'restraint and terseness of phrase' in Machado's *The Castilian Country* as marking 'an epoch in Spanish poetry'. He goes on to translate some of the verses himself, including a small segment of the following, set down here more fully by Alan Trueblood. The text in this 'One Day's Poem' ('Poema de un día') captures Machado's feelings on being the rural schoolmaster in Baeza:

> So here I am,
> a modern language teacher
> (lately master in *gai-saber*,
> apprentice to a nightingale)
> in a cold, damp town,
> sprawling and sombre,
> part Andalusian, part in La Mancha.
> Winter. A fire going.
> Outside drizzle falling,
> thinning sometimes into mist,
> sometimes turning to sleet.
> Picturing myself a farmer,
> I think of the planted fields.

It is easy to forget that Andalucia has a winter too and this verse embodies the melancholic mood of the recently arrived teacher, chilled, lonely and faced with a town turning inwards towards the hearth.

As one would expect from a liberally minded intellectual, Machado was a fervent supporter of the Spanish Republic, actively working during the Civil War for publications like *Hora de España* and for the Servicio Español de Información. As the Republican government moved from city to city as the Nationalists closed in, so Machado followed its members. Eventually arriving in Barcelona, the poet had no other option than to attempt the tricky route through the Pyrenean foothills and then via Portbou to France and

16 Statue of Antonio Machado, Calle San Pablo, Baeza

political exile. He made it to the town of Collioure, but the journey and his ill-health took their toll. A few short weeks after his entry to France, the poet died, just days before his aged mother, who had made the journey with him.

More than one image of Machado remains in Baeza, but if you want to sit awhile, there is a space next to him on the bench in Calle San Pablo, where you'll see him pensively reading, his bronze hat placed by his side and his cane resting against the arm of the seat. His carefully groomed hair and high forehead are tilted gently forwards as he rests his chin on his hand.

Úbeda

Fond of walking, Antonio Machado would often leave the confines of Baeza and make for Úbeda, a good two-hour walk to the east, albeit a short trip in a car. Úbeda forms part of the same World Heritage Site as its sister town and is the larger of the two settlements. The historical centre is focused on the Plaza de Vázquez Molina, a gem of late sixteenth-century architecture. A statue in the square commemorates Andrés de Vandelvira, the architect responsible for the majority of the buildings that can be seen.

The Palacio de las Cadenas, on the northern side of the square, was originally named for the chains that used to link the pillars of the forecourt. Now a municipal building, the palace was built for the secretary of Felipe II, the aforementioned Vázquez Molina. Another of the architect's works is the Sacra Capilla del Salvador, the chapel at the end of the square that lies to one side of the *parador*. Universally recognised as a masterwork of the Spanish Renaissance, the building's original design was by Diego de Siloé, the man responsible for Granada Cathedral, and Vandelvira added to his plans.

Such religious grandeur delighted Penelope Chetwode, who had set out on horseback in the summer of 1961 to explore Jaén Province. Chetwode had married the poet John Betjeman in 1933 but, by the early 1950s, the pair had gone their separate ways. A Roman Catholic convert, Chetwode punctuated her journey by attending Masses at every opportunity. In the foreword to Chetwode's book, *Two Middle-Aged Ladies in Andalusia*, her daughter, the writer Candida Lycett-Green, tells us that her mother was in seventh heaven, indulging her passion for religion, food, horses and architecture.

It was the horse component of that list which preoccupied Chetwode on arriving in Úbeda, desperate as she was to find stabling and food for her mare, La Marquesa. She even tried throwing herself on the mercy of the Civil Guard but eventually found a stable and a bed with a local family. It was to the *parador* in this central square that she turned to indulge her palate, partaking of what she described as Úbeda's version of the Bath bun. Her real reason for visiting the town, though, was to participate in the liturgical feast of the poet and mystic St John of the Cross, who had died here in 1591 – a celebration she labelled more highbrow than popular.

Details of Plaza Vázquez Molina and many other locations within Úbeda are hidden in the works of Antonio Muñoz Molina, a native of the town who started his writing career as a journalist in Madrid. Now a prize-winning author, member of the Real Academia Española and former director of the Cervantes Institute in New York, Muñoz Molina's first novel, *A Manuscript of Ashes* (*Beatus ille*), published in 1986, is set in Mágina, a distorted and disguised version of Úbeda. He took the name from the surrounding Sierra and, magpie-like, selected nuggets of geography and life from his hometown.

Finding the locations from the oblique references in his texts is akin to a treasure hunt. *A Manuscript of Ashes* is a multilayered novel split between the dying years of Franco's dictatorship in the late 1960s and the Civil War. The central character, Minaya, returns to Mágina after being gaoled during a student protest in Madrid. He has decided to seek refuge with his Uncle Manuel in order to write up a thesis on his uncle's friend, the poet Jacinto Solana. As the novel progresses, secrets from the past come to light, including the fact that Solana and Manuel were in love with the same woman, Mariana, a beguiling artist's model. Engaged to Minaya's uncle, Mariana was shot through an open window in Manuel's house by a supposed stray bullet on her wedding night.

Solana, later gaoled for his Communist activities, spent ten years in detention before returning to the house in Mágina and dying in mysterious circumstances. The poet's papers were burned and his masterwork, *Beatus ille* (which gives the original Spanish version of Muñoz Molina's book its title) went missing. Minaya resolves to find the errant novel and, in doing so, restore the reputation of Jacinto Solana. The text weaves between the two eras as multiple characters add their voices to a complex plot, slowly revealing, not only the denouement, but the hidden corners of the town.

The first chapter contains some elusive yet evocative descriptions of Manuel's grandiose house, with its closed balconies and illuminated corners that throw a diffuse light on the neighbouring street without revealing the plaza in front. The shadowy lane discloses a hint of whitewashed wall and a grating belonging to a church whose high niche holds a decapitated St Peter. A careful inspection of the Plaza de Vázquez Molina reveals two decapitated statues in the front-facing niches of Santa María de los Reales Alcázares. Muñoz Molina tells his readers that the statue was vandalised by the rage of previous years, perhaps by the more fervent anti-clerical Republicans, details of which Penelope Chetwode heard, chapter and verse, from the local priests.

The fictional church, though, gives the surrounding square its name, which obviously does not apply to the Santa María. However, as Muñoz Molina has admitted in interviews, he changes Mágina as he pleases by caprice or whim. If we were to look for a Plaza San Pedro matching the name of the butchered statue, we would indeed find it a short walk to the north-west of Vandelvira's Renaissance heart. According to Muñoz Molina's description, it receives no traffic, is fronted by a shuttered palace that looks onto a fountain and borders a church. The gargoyles on the ecclesiastical façade could even represent those that gush with water on rainy days leaving stains of mould in their tracks.

We can be more certain of other specific locations. When the writer was awarded the Príncipe de Asturias literary prize in 2013, one of the country's most prestigious, Úbeda celebrated by temporarily renaming with signs those sites specifically recognised in his Mágina-based novels, including *A Manuscript of Ashes* as well as the yet-to-be-translated *El jinete polaco* (*The Polish Horseman*) and *El viento de la luna* (*The Wind of the Moon*). Using the old names identified with the author, the Plaza de Andalucía with its monument to General Saro became the Plaza del General

Orduña and the Antiguas Carnicerías once again took over the police commissioner's offices.

There is one final destination for the Muñoz Molina aficionado in Úbeda – his family home. A green ceramic plaque inscribed with the date of his prize has been attached to the relatively humble building where he grew up. The white house with its grilled balconies sits opposite the Casa de las Torres off Plaza San Lorenzo. Via the town hall's cultural offices, occasional guided walks are available in the footsteps of the author's characters, taking the participants through the veiled realities of Muñoz Molina's imagination.

Sierra Morena

Above Úbeda, the wild, beautiful, yet harsh Sierra Morena forms the natural border between La Mancha and Andalucia. The reputation of the Sierra preceded it as Sancho Panza and Don Quixote entered the high passes. They wanted to proceed swiftly through the wild country, avoiding the possibility of bandits. Instead, they encountered an unhappy madman, Cardenio, who had fled from a thwarted love. Incredibly, and much to Sancho's dismay, 'in such an out-of-the-way place as this', Quixote decides to imitate his hero, Amadis, 'playing the victim of despair, the madman, the maniac', so that his faithful squire can pass on the details of this penance to his fictionalised lady-love, Dulcinea del Toboso. The famous pair wandered across the mountains, entering the Despeñaperros Pass where Quixote chooses the spot where he is to remain and perform his atonement:

> Thus talking they reached the foot of a high mountain which stood like an isolated peak among the others that surrounded it. Past its base there flowed a gentle brook, all around it spread a meadow so green and luxuriant that it was a delight to the eyes to look upon it, and forest trees in abundance, and shrubs and flowers, added to

the charms of the spot. Upon this place the Knight of the Rueful Countenance fixed his choice for the performance of his penance.

Nikos Kazantzakis knew the story of *Don Quixote* well and punctuates the two halves of his Spanish travelogue with a poem in homage to Cervantes's creation. The Greek's verses start with this evocation of the wandering knight caught in the vastness of the Sierra Morena:

> His mind fumed and all boundaries grew dim,
> imagination licked the world about him
> and roaring, rearing fires clothed him round.
> Then, like a salamander, Fate drew near
> and licked her lips amid the cooling flames;
> his mind leapt high in the barren wilderness.

Another adventurer synonymous with love is Giacomo Casanova, who died at the end of the eighteenth century. His considerable, multi-volume autobiography, *History of My Life* (*Histoire de ma vie*), contains this pearl of egotistical advancement; it seems that the Italian philanderer had designs on becoming governor of the Sierra Morena. Curiously, in a bid to populate the Sierra and make it a safer place for travellers, German and Swiss settlers were invited to make their homes in the area. Casanova had taken a particular interest in these plans and, on noting that the Swiss families were not thriving, he suggested that it would be a far better idea if Spaniards replaced them.

Casanova put pen to paper, expounding his theories on making the colonies prosper, and he claims that they were valued, not only by the government minister, Grimaldo, but also by the Venetian Ambassador, who, no doubt, could foresee the benefits of placing a fellow Venetian at the head of a governorship in such a Spanish domain. Much to Casanova's disappointment, he was not successful in obtaining the desired post.

The story of the German speakers in the Sierra Morena is recounted by Joseph Townsend in his 1791 account, *Journey through Spain*. Townsend was a vicar but also a geologist and doctor who had the dubious reputation of presaging Thomas Malthus's arguments against public welfare. His comments on the incomers are equally blunt: 'One Turrigel, of Bavaria contracted for sixth thousand husbandmen; but, instead of men trained to agriculture, he brought only vagabonds who all either died or were dispersed, without advancing the work for which, at an immense expense, they had been brought.'

Townsend tells us that the settlers each received a plot of land, a house, two cows, one ass, five sheep, five goats, six hens, a plough and a pickaxe. The experiment was clearly not to the Englishman's liking as 'these new settlements swarm with half naked beggars'. The towns were dotted throughout the Sierra but, most notably, around La Carolina. When Hans Christian Andersen passed through in the 1860s, he tells us that 'for many years past the German language had died out.'

The area is still remote but now has a less fearsome reputation. In 1953 it was to become the solitary world of Marcos Rodríguez Pantoja, who at the age of seven was abandoned in the mountains with the task of attending a herd of goats. He lost all contact with the outside world, and his adopted family became the wildlife that surrounded him. He was eventually captured 12 years later by the Civil Guard and forced to reintegrate with human society. His story, *Marcos: Wild Child of the Sierra Morena*, was written up by the Mallorcan novelist, educator and anthropologist, Gabriel Janer Manila.

Fortunately for Janer Manila, the wild boy of the Sierra had already acquired a rudimentary level of language, which, although rusty and limited in vocabulary, was enough to recount his life experiences. Janer Manila was able to investigate the essence of humanity and the connection between nature and nuture. Marcos, before being abandoned, had managed to gain a few survival skills by watching an old shepherd; however, everything he learned in the wild environment derived from the close observation of the natural world around him. Incredibly, he was able to form symbiotic relationships with certain animals. Subsisting on goats' milk and the rabbits he had learned to trap, he would often feed the milk or meat to any approaching creature.

On one occasion he found a snake which he realised was hungry. After Marcos had fed it with milk, the snake curled up beside him and seldom left, becoming his protector in the face of more dangerous animals. This fellow-feeling for wildlife enabled the boy to create a type of community which he greatly missed when the creatures were not in the vicinity. During these lonely hours, he felt compelled to howl for lack of company, resulting in reciprocal calls and even visits from his favourites.

When faced with a dilemma, Marcos would think it through and adapt a solution. One such example was the fording of a river to collect plants to eat. Initially, he created a flax rope to pull himself across, but realised that his animal friends would not be able to accompany him. His next move was to fashion a boat,

> so the fox, the snake and a few animals who came with me could get across. The boat was a big piece of cork tied with a string, which I looped around the roots of a tree. The whole family I had got on the boat. Sometimes a few birds came too. The birds could fly but they liked to ride there.

The interesting word here is 'family'. The abandoned Marcos never tried to return to so-called civilisation, owing to his previous experience of maltreatment. He knew he was not wanted in the human world, and the mountains represented freedom. Instead, he created a new family with the animals. Janer Manila goes on to say that the significance of the boy's boat was his identification with the creatures. When the raft capsized one day, Marcos reported that 'all of us animals dried off', revealing his feeling of kinship.

His reintroduction to society and subsequent move to Mallorca provided a very rude awakening. He was easy prey for those who wished to take advantage of his naivety and incredible ability to work hard, particularly in the hospitality industry. It is no surprise that Marcos later came to the conclusion that life with animals was preferable to life with humans. His fascinating history was turned into a film by Gerardo Olivares in 2010. Marcos makes a guest appearance at the very end of *Entrelobos* (*Among Wolves*).

This amazing tale of the human capacity to adapt as a wild child in the even wilder mountains of Jaén would not be out of place in Jan Potocki's fantastical *Manuscript Found in Saragossa* (*Manuscrit trouvé à Saragosse*), completed in 1814. Potocki's tale, though, wanders much further from this truly inspirational story of survival into the realms of the gothic and picaresque imagination. Potocki was a Polish aristocrat educated in French-speaking Switzerland. Something of an adventurer and wandering scholar, he was fascinated by studies into the historical origins of the Slavs and was also a devotee of the esoteric, including secret societies and aspects of the supernatural. He travelled widely, one of his favourite destinations being Spain.

It was a depressed Potocki who returned to his native Poland in early 1812 and set about finishing the *Manuscript*, written in his preferred French. The work is largely set in the mountains and valleys of the Sierra Morena and is split into vignettes or interwoven segments that contain a plethora of bizarre and diverse characters – everyone from cabbalists and outlaws to bewitching Moorish princesses and solitary hermits.

The book starts with a description of how the supposed manuscript was found in a house searched by French troops during the 1809 sack of Zaragoza and then translated into French. Divided into days, the narrator takes the reader through his adventures via the divergent life stories of the characters involved. Day one sets the scene at a time when the foothills were yet to be populated with the aforementioned new Teutonic settlements and 'travellers who ventured into that wild country found themselves assailed, it was said, by countless terrors which would make even the stoutest of hearts tremble'.

Journeying out from Andújar, our storyteller, Alphonse van Worden, a member of the Walloon Guards, insists he has to take the shortest route to Madrid, rather than the safer diversion through Extremadura. He eventually finds himself at the doors of a hostelry called the Venta Quemada, a less than auspicious name which could translate as the Burning or Burned-Out Inn but was actually named after the Marqués de Peña Quemada. Emerging from a valley to reach the *venta*, he notices a sign imploring visitors to carry on without stopping for the night.

Foolishly, the young guard ignores the advice. The inn, a former Moorish fort, is apparently deserted, prompting Alphonse to search for his own food. A bell and two black female servants interrupt his exploration. This is the tip of Potocki's chillingly inexplicable iceberg, as two nubile Arabian princesses make an appearance, tempting him with food and dance. Emina and Zubeida turn out to be daughters of Gasir Gomelez, the Dey of Tunis. The inseparable pair had agreed they would marry the same man and thus now implore the guard to convert and marry them both. Unable to make the transition to Islam, Alphonse is invited to 'consort with us in your dreams' – an invitation that needs no repetition, but the downing of a magic potion.

Potocki alludes to a dream-filled night of harems and 'wanton fancies'. The morning brings a shock. Awoken by sunlight, Alphonse is lying beneath a gibbet he had seen in the neighbouring settlement of Los Hermanos. Instead of hanging from it, the two dead bandits despatched by the gallows are now his unearthly open-air bedfellows. Covered in rotting cloth, flesh and rope, Alphonse makes a bolt for the banks of a tributary of the Guadalquivir, where he encounters a meal of chocolate, wine, sponge cake, eggs and bread left by two passing travellers.

From this peculiar start, Potocki's stories rove across this fictionalised Sierra landscape, becoming increasingly strange and rooted in themes of disguise and conspiracy, suitable subjects for an eighteenth-century occultist. The Pole's final moments are alleged to have been even weirder. At home in Uładówka, Potocki's state of mind was declining into progressive instability. It was reported that he had become convinced of his own lycanthropy. The most likely explanation of his death focuses on this fear. Persuaded of his werewolf tendencies, he created a silver bullet, asked his castle chaplain to bless the object and then shot himself through the head.

❀ 9 ❀

ALMERÍA PROVINCE

Heat and Dust

Almería river
(God guard thy gleaming sward),
Viewing thee, I shiver
Like an Indian sword.

(Ibn Safar, *Almería*, twelfth century)

Almería

As the above verse from the Moorish poet Ibn Safar suggests, the province of Almería is even more prone to drought and scarcity of water than most other areas of Andalucia. The 'gleaming sward' he speaks of is all too often a desiccated trickle. This dry landscape approaching the provincial capital was well described by Gerald Brenan in *South from Granada*: 'One bumped in a cloud of dust across the great stony plain, hugged the yellow cliffs where they dropped to the sea, and suddenly saw the white city spread out before one like an illustration in a book of Eastern travel.'

Sadly, we have to disillusion the reader at this point. The approach to the city of Almería from the west – the direction of Brenan's travel – is now plagued with high-rise buildings poking through a sea of plastic. Tourist towns such as El Ejido and Almerimar are literally surrounded by what is known locally as *plasticultura*, the forced growth of cash crops under enormous greenhouse-like sheets of condensation-creating polythene. The tomatoes, peppers and berries are fed by a system of drip irrigation that produces the fruit and vegetables that fill northern European supermarkets. These are also the conditions under which certain less-scrupulous businessmen have exploited the likes of Zine, Jason Webster's friend.

This type of agriculture has made quick money for some in what was, and to some extent still is, an impoverished region; although the number of empty polytunnels is testament to the fact that not everyone has made the anticipated profit. It is actually a relief to see the stilted motorway tip downwards towards the outskirts of the city, where there is at least a sense of the Almería that Brenan once described. The pre-war capital was the nearest urban settlement of any great size to Yegen, where Brenan had set up home. He admits that it was his escape when he wanted a change from village life and says it was easy to reach – if one could call a nine-hour trudge easy.

His most lively account concerns his first visit in 1920 when he went to buy furniture but was wonderfully side-tracked by a certain Agustín Pardo. Brenan describes him as a man in declining health with a wrinkled face and eye bags that Pardo claimed were gained in the pursuit of 'vice'. This native of the city was a small-scale trader who bought produce from the boats without asking too many questions. He also had a side-line in guiding sailors to the local brothels. Brenan accepted the invitation to visit some of the local establishments, assuring us that is was purely in the interest of research.

The pair headed for the Plaza Vieja, now known as the Plaza de la Constitución, 'a small arcaded square, whitewashed and planted with trees, and during most of the day deserted and empty'. The square still resembles this description, although it has been considerably spruced up with the addition of a luxurious spa hotel, continuing in the Arab bath tradition. From this secular cloister, they headed upwards towards the Alcazaba along a road of single-storeyed houses which were home to the brothels. Brenan did not feel threatened by the atmosphere, considering it squalid rather than menacing.

Pardo guided him to one house after another, where Brenan would be introduced as an onlooker rather than a participant, taking a glass of wine and chatting to the attendant women. The madams were universally overweight, lending them a certain presence that Pardo claimed earned respect but also gave them a motherly air. In one of the low-slung houses belonging to a madam named Teresa, the pair met a policeman who took a perverse pride in telling them that Almería was called the 'culo de España' which Brenan translates as 'bum' but could also be the 'arse-end of Spain' – an epithet that would have been difficult to deny in the 1920s, given the poverty, illiteracy, exploitation and migration in this province.

Keen to show his debauched credentials, Pardo is quick with self-deprecatory quips about his own louche behaviour and is equally verbose when telling stories about others, especially the tale of a baker who died *in flagrante* when celebrating a lottery win, neither of which his wife would have known about had he not died in such circumstances. Initially, the locals boycotted the bakery but returned when his daughters took over serving. Their perfumed presence was much appreciated after having endured the deceased's bad breath. It also ended well for the widow, who enjoyed the unspent lottery winnings.

There is a final vignette to the Agustín Pardo saga. One following afternoon, the owner of Brenan's guesthouse saw the erstwhile Lothario meeting the writer and enquired about their friendship. It seems that Pardo had succumbed to alcoholism and, contrary to his own words, had a wife but no children. Brenan asked why this might be and received a reply intimating that the self-styled Don Juan was most probably impotent. The story is reminiscent of a cut-price version of Vitaliano Brancati's *Beautiful Antonio*.

Thirty years later, the Catalan writer Juan Goytisolo found himself in Almería. Born in 1931 to a family who had become rich from slave-produced sugar cane in Cuba, Goytisolo rebelled against his Jesuit education, reading much contemporary French literature, notably Gide and Camus. This love of left-wing French ideals and a desire to escape Spain took him to Paris. In his book *La Chanca*, named after the district of Almería he writes about, Goytisolo tells the reader what brought him back to Spain and this area in particular.

In spite of his initial feelings, Goytisolo used to scan French newspapers for mentions of home. He would also fall into conversation with fellow expats and, on one occasion, started talking to an Almeriense who had relatives in La Chanca. The man, Vitorino, was bitter about the poverty and injustice that existed there. In that moment, Goytisolo resolved to see for himself. The following morning he scanned the papers; with no mention of home and Parisian grey skies, he ventured out into the street, where it seemed no one understood his French. Enough was enough. He packed his bags and headed south.

Having arrived in Almería, he was overcome with a tranquillity that is not often associated with the district neighbouring the Alcazaba that his imaginary visitor could see from its walls:

> The La Chanca neighbourhood crouches at his feet, luminous and white like an invention of the senses. At the far end of the hollow, the houses look like dice capriciously flung down. The geological violence, the nakedness of the landscape are astonishing. Tiny and box-like, the shacks mount the declivity, embedded in the jagged surface of the mountain like cut garnets.

Traditionally a fishermen's quarter and home to many of Gypsy origin, the area stretches down to the harbour-front road. In the twenty-first century, La Chanca has undergone a degree of regeneration – many of its houses have been brightly painted, giving it the appearance of a Mondrian canvas. The addition of fragmentary mosaic tiling on some façades completes the bohemian picture, especially when accompanied by flamenco played at full volume in the backstreets. Not for nothing is La Chanca home to some of the best flamenco artists in this part of Spain.

17   La Chanca and the Alcazaba, Almería

The realities, especially in the 1950s when Goytisolo visited, are less picturesque. He walked across the Plaza Pavía where some young boys watched carefully for distracted market stallholders so that they could steal bread, fruit or even dried lentils to fill their empty stomachs. Handing round his French cigarettes in a bar on the square, he was regaled with stories of migration to France and Barcelona. This triggered the memory of his expat friend in Paris who had asked him to look up a relative.

Goytisolo headed further into La Chanca territory and had the sense that he was entering another world – a world without running water, electricity, doctors or medical supplies. Ricocheting from street to street in search of the elusive relative, Goytisolo covered much of the barrio; seemingly the higher he climbed, the worse the poverty became until the inhabitants were virtual cave dwellers, resigned to their fate. Laundry lay baking on the cracked rocks as the sun beat down – 'obstinate, lewd, arrogant as the ace of diamonds, the sun is a stifling reverberation, whitening everything, lord and master of La Chanca.'

When the Catalan eventually encountered his friend's family, he was greeted with wary suspicion and had to prove his connection to the said Vitorino by producing the handwritten card on which he had scribbled the address. Having verified the handwriting, the family invited him inside and told him that Antonio, the relative, had been taken away by what we can only presume to be the police. He was not the first to resort to stealing to make ends meet; proud men were forced to renounce their integrity in the face of hunger.

Goytisolo still maintains his connection with Almería and the surrounding countryside. After years living in Paris with his wife, Monique Lange, the cousin of Marcel Proust, he felt compelled to move to Marrakech after her death. He continues to follow the story of La Chanca from North Africa and has championed the work, both literary and regenerative, of the recently deceased poet José Ángel Valente. Valente's house in Almería, close to the Plaza de la Catedral and situated in the street they have named after him, is now a museum. Visitors to the poet's home are shown a documentary of his life that contains warm words from Goytisolo.

Valente was originally from Galicia and another in the long list of authors who studied law, never to practise. He changed courses to finally graduate in Romance language philology, a programme of study that enabled him to take up a position in Oxford University's Department of Spanish. No lover of Francoist Spain, he was content to continue his self-imposed exile in Geneva and Paris as a translator for international organisations of repute, including UNESCO. It was only in 1986, 14 years after being tried in absentia by a military tribunal for supposed derogatory remarks about the army, that Valente returned to Spain, settling in his adopted home of Almería.

He died in 2000 at the age of 71, leaving behind a significant body of poetry and a plethora of translations from the greats of world literature, among which feature Dylan Thomas, Eugenio Montale, Constantino Cavafis, Paul Celan and John Keats. Despite the court martial, his poetry is not overtly social in terms of commentary, tending more towards the metaphysical. He described his own verse as a process of self-discovery and it seems to lend itself to pictorial representation. He also made this striking comparison between the two genres: 'A poem is an invisible or voiced painting, and painting is a visible poem or one without words.' The walls of his house, recently opened to the public, are adorned with images that mirror the words – side by side. A timeline of his works demonstrates Valente's fascination with art and his output includes more than one essay on the subject.

The *casa-museo* – his house and museum – preserves the beautiful whitewashed cellar with its arched alcoves and original stone sink. As is to be expected, the bookshelves in his study reflect his breadth of reading in the major European languages. Information boards recount his life; one of the most interesting describes his attraction to the city of Almería and its surroundings. His move south was primarily an answer to 'the inescapable call of the light'. He may have drawn inspiration from the area, but he was keen to be more than a passive onlooker. Valente became involved in organisations designed to preserve the urban landscape of La Chanca and the fragile environment of the Cabo de Gata.

Inevitably, his environs soaked into his verse. This poem from *The Singer Does Not Awaken* (*No amanece el cantor*), part of the anthology in translation, *Landscape with Yellow Birds*, demonstrates how the light forced its way into his interior mindscape: 'The patience of the south. Its huge lizards set forth. The dark carapace of night bitten by salt. The question fails to become a sign. Asking, "Why?" Who will answer out of the fullness of the light without destroying us?' After his death, the aforementioned documentary was made, focusing on his deep connection to the province; it was appropriately titled *El lugar del poeta* (*The Poet's Place*).

The piercing, stark light of Almería that burns shadows into the desert wilderness prompted further evocative verse from an altogether more unexpected quarter. In 1929, a young Aldous Huxley, who would soon become renowned for his portrait of dystopian London, *Brave New World*, set out on a tour of Spain with his first wife. Driving down the coast through Valencia and Murcia, they arrived at Almería. The brightness of the skies must have helped Huxley, who was refused entry to the army in the First World War due to an inflamed cornea that seriously impaired the vision in one eye.

On arriving, he found a beauty in the dry, hostile land around the city and, in a letter to the academic Arturo Medina some years later, he described the moment when the poetry of the environment struck him. He was driving southwards through a ferocious gust and a burning sun into the desolate lands of 'wind and fire'. The inspirational moment led to a sonnet in the classic form, simply entitled 'Almería', which was published in the collection *The Cicadas and Other Poems*. It ends with these lines:

> You have the light for lover. Fortunate Earth!
> Conceive the fruit of his divine desire.
> But the dry dust is all she brings to birth,
> That child of clay by even celestial fire.
> Then come, soft rain and tender clouds, abate
> This shining love that has the force of hate.

Huxley told Medina that he was searching for a pure intellectuality and spirituality which he found in the pure skies and barren earth of this corner of south-eastern Spain, so different from the maternal lands of Valencia.

Níjar and the Cabo de Gata

In his Spanish journey, *Between Hopes and Memories*, Michael Jacobs deliberately sought out the prosaic and the problematic. He was drawn to the province of Almería because an acquaintance, born in the area, had described it to him as 'a shithole' – another overly harsh label we can add to the one given by Gerald Brenan's police officer. Jacobs is driven by curiosity and a desire to understand the issues involved. He cites Brenan's observation about poverty and the pleasure in the contrasts it offered – an uncomfortable remark at the best of times, especially coming from someone who could escape its clutches.

Jacobs continues his investigation by referring to Goytisolo, who approached the subject from a different angle. Like *La Chanca*, Goytisolo's fictional *Juan the Landless* trilogy took much from his travels in the province. His real *cri de coeur*, however, is found in the travelogue *The Countryside of Níjar* (*Campos de Níjar*). The town in the title is situated 30 minutes to the east of the capital if travelling by car. It lies between the rugged Tabernas Desert and the protected coastal strip of the Cabo de Gata. The book sees Goytisolo walking the byways or travelling by bus between the sea and the Sierra de Alhamilla.

Much of the country surrounding Níjar used to be mining territory, and the closure of the lead and manganese mines hit the local workforce hard. As he met men and women from these towns, he was regaled with tales of hardship and emigration; even the seemingly noble profession of potter carried with it the whiff of exploitation. Goytisolo entered Níjar via the lonely Paseo, with its sparse one-storey houses, and headed for the ceramics quarter in the side streets. The town had, and still has, a justified reputation for the creation of quality pottery.

In the 1950s, the potters were still using foot pedals to turn their wheels and producing wares that enriched the shop owners and middle-men who sold the goods in Barcelona and Madrid for prices that would have shocked the artisans. Goytisolo hinted at the fact that some were beginning to realise that working for themselves would bring greater rewards in what was then the juddering beginnings of a tourist industry. In any case, one of the men brought everything into perspective when he told Goytisolo that his job was infinitely preferable to working underground in the crippling conditions endured by the miners.

Níjar is much changed in the twenty-first century and the alterations are due to the unstoppable juggernaut of tourism. The once-meagre main street, Calle el Parque, is now lined with stores selling cotton shirts and tie-dye skirts, alongside incense and lanterns, all designed to attract tourists. The *barrio alfarero*, or potters' district, is reachable via Calle Almería, and the locals now have their own shops attached to the studios where they can still be observed working at the wheel. In spite of this, the number of premises makes it hard to imagine that they are all receiving the remuneration they dreamed of in the 1950s.

Before leaving Níjar, there is one further literary association that has to be mentioned. We must return to the summer of 1928 and take a cursory glance through the press of the time. The name of the town and its surroundings were then inextricably linked to a crime that caused something of a scandal. A few hours before her marriage, a young woman had decided to run off with her cousin, who was later found dead. The Civil Guards, who investigated the case, were initially told that a masked man had killed her unfortunate relative.

Under further questioning, the would-be bride eventually told the truth – it was in fact her sister's husband who had discovered the elopement and had told his brother, the bridegroom. The young woman laid the blame for the actual murder on her putative husband. However, the truth came out in a statement given by the brother-in-law, who admitted he had pulled the trigger. These events may sound remarkably familiar to anyone acquainted with the theatre of Federico García Lorca as they form the basis for his play *Blood Wedding* (*Bodas de sangre*).

There is no need to speculate on these links – Lorca admitted after the premiere that he had based the play on the reports he had read four years before in the newspapers. It is clear he took a good deal of poetic licence with the realities of the story, changing details to suit his needs and to give the tale a touch of operatic tragedy absent from the squalid crime, although the backdrop captures the sense of desolation in the landscape. In the second act, a stage setting encapsulates the poverty of the terrain, with its massed prickly pears, sombre, silvery tones and panoramas of biscuit-coloured hues, hardened like the local ceramics.

Conditions may have dramatically improved, but the economy is still mired in over-reliance on one sector and in some areas even such tourism is relatively thin on the ground – Rodalquilar is just one such example. The entrance to the town, a further 30 minutes south-east of Níjar, displays its history clearly: a black silhouette of a man by the roadside, wearing a hard hat, stands proudly shouldering a pickaxe. Rodalquilar once boasted the only goldmine in Spain; today the ruins of times past are still visible, as they were to Goytisolo. Faded pastels on bricked-up storerooms crouch behind fences and denuded trees. Goytisolo had this vision:

> The silence is overwhelming. I contemplate the bare brown hills. Here and there yellowish patches mark the mouths of the mine. In the valley you can see the ruins of houses and a round, abandoned warehouse. The road hugs the hillside and as it turns through a curve it rises above the washeries and the town of Rodalquilar [...] It is a small town, asymmetric and apparently with no center of gravity.

In the town's inn, he spotted two young women dressed in city clothes. Rather than visitors, they turned out to be teachers who were obliged to work in the villages before having the chance to apply for a position in the capital. The man in the bar, seated next to Goytisolo, explained that the richer women avoided this perceived ignominy by paying others to take their place. The local admitted that the country folk did not dare engage the teachers in conversation, thereby condemning them, unwittingly, to an excruciatingly lonely existence. This snapshot of mid-twentieth-century life seems centuries older still; the town now does its best to capture passing tourist traffic on the way to the beaches of the

Cabo de Gata. It also has a growing reputation as a base for those committed to artisanal artistic endeavour.

The beaches are a few scant kilometres to the south. One of the most popular is San José, a town that boasts a horseshoe of sand and the requisite spread of beach-side restaurants and bars. The twenty-first-century development is low key and low level, but a world away from the place Goytisolo visited. He found a settlement destroyed by the slump in mining and yet to make a new identity for itself. To him, it was 'a sad, wind-swept town, half its houses roofless, the other half standing on cracked walls [...] The traveler who walks its streets feels a distressing sense of fatalism and abandonment.' Goytisolo escaped to take a swim in the cove of Cala Figuera, with its decayed watchtower built to guard the coast. It remains today, its crumbling walls providing a romantic backdrop to the blue of the bay. Just as Goytisolo observed, this stretch of the coast is exposed to the winds; an insistent tug at the hem of poverty in the 1950s but now a dream for the seasoned surfer.

Goytisolo's travels in the region largely focused on the countryside to the south and east of Níjar. His writings seldom touch on the even more distinctive landscape that stretches beyond the Sierra Alhamilla to the north of Almería. It is one of the driest parts of Spain and its desertscapes are said to resemble the runnels of the moon.

The Tabernas Desert

The town of Tabernas has one historical claim to fame. Its Moorish castle, balanced high on the hill above the town, provided a suitable stopover for the Catholic Monarchs Ferdinand and Isabella whilst siege was being laid to the city of Almería. A walk up to the ruins is perhaps ill-advised in the piercing summer heat that has contributed to the desertification of the land that stretches out in all directions. Careful observation of building façades in the town will reveal more than one incongruous silhouette – black figures in

Stetsons, wearing low-slung holsters, ready to draw. The cowboy is not a native of these parts but an Italian import, for this is Spaghetti Western territory.

Some critics have actually dubbed the area 'Paella Western Country', although that is equally inaccurate as paella is a dish that originates from the very different region of Valencia. The reference to Italian food is really a reference to the fact that the director of several of the films in question was the Roman Sergio Leone. His epics are now classics of the genre: *A Fistful of Dollars*, *For a Few Dollars More* and *The Good, the Bad and the Ugly*. The land was a remarkable stand-in for the American Wild West, with its gulches and monumental natural architecture.

The road that branches off to Tabernas from the main highway into Granada Province is bordered by two former film sets – Mini Hollywood and Fort Bravo. These rather kitsch tourist attractions, complete with Wild West mock shootouts in high season, were once home to more serious endeavours. Mini Hollywood was built by the designer Carlo Simi as a representation of El Paso in the second film to have *Dollars* in the title. One of the English-speaking world's most knowledgeable writers on the subject is Christopher Frayling, an academic, Fellow of Churchill College, Cambridge, and a specialist in popular culture.

Frayling has written several works about these films including *Spaghetti Westerns: Cowboys and Europeans from Karl May to Sergio Leone* and *Once Upon a Time in Italy: The Westerns of Sergio Leone*, both recently updated and reissued. He is also the director's biographer. In the first of these books he describes the inauguration of Calle Sergio Leone in Almería in the year 2000, an occasion that once more allowed him to meet Leone's widow, Carla, who credits Frayling as the first critic to take her husband's work seriously.

Up until the publication of *Spaghetti Westerns*, Leone was convinced of the pejorative use of this moniker for his films. Frayling tells us that it was the influence of his book that persuaded the director to embrace the term as something more than a simple put-

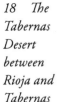

18 The Tabernas Desert between Rioja and Tabernas

down or reference to nationality. The author also poses the question of Spanish influence in a genre fully identified with this filmmaker. As he points out, many of the movies were Spanish co-productions, reliant on these desert locations for their atmosphere and character. It was a time that those involved in the film industry now remember with affection: an era when Almería saw the likes of Clint Eastwood and Eli Wallach, in addition to the whole host of technical workers needed to make a film happen.

In many ways, it is easier to evoke the atmosphere of the best of these Westerns by wandering through the dusty terrain than it is to visit the adapted film sets that leave the visitor entertained but not necessarily infused with the spirit of the original productions. Sorbas is a location that has little parallel in the rest of Europe; its houses overhang a gorge and its surrounding terrain of gullies and crags perfectly mimic the vision of America populating the dreams of Sergio Leone. At twilight, during the height of summer, when the sparse vegetation is bleached of colour, the landscape puts on a spectacular geological display of shifting hues caught in the declining sun. The metallic shadows of lunar quality mirror Lorca's silvery tones.

Mojácar

The town of Mojácar, or rather the *towns* of Mojácar, lie 80 kilometres (50 miles) to the north-east of Almería. In many ways, Mojácar Pueblo and Mojácar Playa are a microcosm reflecting the road that much of twentieth-century Andalucia has travelled. The swathe of beach and its translucent sea are now backed by a rash of concrete cubes, spilling their visitors towards an extensive strip of bars, clubs and restaurants. The place has capitalised on its best assets – a balmy climate and an inviting coast. Northern Europeans, starved of light, descend on the town as either holidaymakers or with a view to making it a more permanent home.

The parched countryside is now laced with green; manicured landscaping mirrors the crisp lines of modern development. Five golf courses in the vicinity suck precious water from other needs. Some of the locals are well aware that the goose who laid the golden egg has taken flight, leaving her offspring to fend for themselves in an increasingly competitive society. As development spawns development, ecologists have come face to face with those responsible for planning. Juan Goytisolo even wrote an article in

2014 that appeared in the national daily, *El País*. He laments the agglutinate development lacking any charm, calling it 'stodgy', and hits his target with this stark statement: 'We were poor, we dreamed ourselves rich and, on waking, we discovered ourselves poor again.'

Thirty minutes' walk away from the neon and hedonism is the hilltown of Mojácar Pueblo, a settlement that can trace its roots back to prehistory. The Roman polymath Pliny mentioned it as a place of importance in Baetica, the name by which the Romans knew the administrative region. Guidebooks will tell you that, 50 years ago, the local women, wearing headscarves, would wash the family clothes in the main fountain and it was not until the 1960s that reliable electricity and water supplies reached the town. The local council celebrates the strong Moorish connection that saw a feisty mayor demand a short-lived autonomy from the Catholic Monarchs centuries previously, by inscribing *Puerta de la Ciudad* in both Spanish and Arabic above the settlement's entrance gate.

Next to the Church of Santa María stands the Mojaqueras statue commemorating the pseudo-Moorish dress of a water-carrier, gripping a shawl between her teeth to keep it over the lower half of her face, whilst simultaneously balancing a pitcher on her head. From this square, narrow alleyways filter all human traffic towards the inevitable precipice. Both the *miradores* (viewing points) of the Plaza Nueva and the Castillo have vertiginous views over the flatlands to the coast.

In the late 1970s, the critic and diarist Kenneth Tynan found Mojácar to be a suitable place for some summer rest and recuperation. In many ways, Tynan is more associated with the likes of Ronda, owing to his passion for the *corrida*, which he demonstrated in the book *Bull Fever*. As reviewers have noted, he makes an attempt at intellectualising the spectacle, likening Shakespeare's Othello to the *toro* and Iago to the matador. He is certain that any self-respecting playwright or novelist should find parallels in the bullfight. We suspect this is more to do with

Tynan's exhibitionist temperament than a wider affinity between the world of letters and the world of *tauromaquia*.

His diaries, as the cover to the published edition states, are 'irreverent, indiscreet, wildly funny, sad, shocking and inspiring' and one would expect nothing less from the impresario who created *Oh! Calcutta!*, once infamous for its nudity and sexual references. Tynan calls Mojácar an 'obscure south-eastern corner of Spain', and it was in 1978 that he decided to make the trip, accompanied by Nicole, with whom he enjoyed something of a sado-masochistic relationship that he had not found with his wife, Kathleen.

Their villa was a scant 100 metres from the sea at a time when the town could boast of a sparsely populated coastline. In suitably graphic detail, he describes a particularly energetic bout of lust with Nicole that left him and his member in agony – a problem that cast a shadow over their holiday. The difficulties were further exacerbated when he woke to find Nicole at the beach and his camera, pen, 1,000 dollars' worth of pesetas and her handbag all stolen. To his absolute horror, a neighbour told him that he had escaped lightly because a similar victim of a recent burglary had woken to find the intruders in her bedroom and had been knee-capped by gunshot.

In a desperate bid to recoup his losses, he reported it all to the necessary authorities but found he could not get a workable phone line unless he travelled 12 kilometres (seven miles) to another village. American Express also wanted him to make the trek to Granada to report the theft in person at their offices in the city. To compound the farce, a lorry scraped the side of his Jaguar on one of the narrow mountain roads of the region and he had a coughing fit which led to a hernia. In a final twist, Tynan recovered his finances and managed to have his stolen American visa reissued, only to realise on landing in Los Angeles from Spain that his manuscript about Mel Brooks, which he had written in Mojácar, had gone astray in a missing piece of luggage.

*

Tynan's misadventure was wonderful fodder for a diary and, maybe, for a travelogue that was never written. It seems to us that Andalucia has attracted more than its fair share of idiosyncratic visitors. We need only think of Richard Ford and George Borrow, who brought their own baggage to their descriptions of people and place. Many of those who travelled in the nineteenth century were pushing an agenda, although they may not have realised it at the time. They portrayed an Andalucia that has become entrenched in the popular imagination ever since. Washington Irving, Théophile Gautier, Prosper Mérimée and many others conjured the romantic illusion of a passionate race, living with a hedonistic *carpe diem* attitude.

History tells us another story, of a region where there was little romance in poverty; those with the money and time to indulge fanciful notions often had scant inclination to improve the lives of those less fortunate. This well-spring of disaffection would eventually bubble to the surface and erupt in the fratricidal chaos of the Spanish Civil War – a legacy that took decades to unravel. Rivers of ink have flowed in the pursuit of explanation, justification and understanding that makes for necessary reading in order to juxtapose these grim realities with the frivolity of the romantic myth-makers.

However, we have glimpsed the grains of truth filtering through the imaginative lens of the Victorian travel writer. Climate plays no small part in dictating a lifestyle that seemed so alien to earnest visitors from the north. A searing summer has much of its everyday ritual played out in the coolness of night. And if there is a certain indolence about Andalucia, it has nothing to do with the perceived and infamous *mañana* attitude. As more than one Spaniard has pointed out to your authors, a Scandinavian working through the heat of a southern summer would more than likely prove less productive than your average local.

Occasionally, though, it needs an outsider to gain the kind of insight that is often impossible for a local, whose roots tap deeper waters. Hispanophiles such as Michael Jacobs, Gerald Brenan and Ian Gibson have seen the region at one remove, being both adopted by the place and separate from it. It is very difficult to imagine a Spaniard in the postwar years writing about Lorca's grave in the way that Brenan achieved and Gibson built upon. Not without controversy, their books have brought light to corners that censorship and restriction would once have preferred remained in the dark. Even Borrow, in his characteristic and not always complimentary way, gave a voice to the Gypsy community that to this day remains on the fringes of mainstream society.

If foreign authors have usually tended towards the exotic, then natives to the region and the peninsula as a whole have, understandably, had other focuses. The likes of Eduardo de Ory in Cádiz sought to strengthen the literary ties between Andalucia and the Spanish-speaking Americas, whilst Benito Pérez Galdós wanted to paint the spectacular sweep of his country's history through the realistic fictional protagonists of his stories. Goytisolo and Miguel Hernández were more concerned with the injustices of society, their poetry and prose a cry from the heart.

Perhaps more than any other writer, Federico García Lorca symbolises Andalucia as a whole and all its personalities. In his works we find a flavour of that passion beloved of the Romantics coupled with concerns for his society, the position of women and the marginalised, all laced with tragedy and death. In the 80 years since his shocking assassination, much of Andalucia has changed beyond recognition. The coastal developments of the Costa del Sol would have been alien to his generation and have given livelihoods to many families that had previously scratched a poor living from barren soils. However, it has all come at a price, not least to the environment.

Try as they might, stereotypes and development have not reduced Andalucia to the homogenous 'stodge' referred to by Goytisolo. It remains an incredibly diverse region, from the glories of Arabic Granada and Córdoba eulogised by its poets, to the wilds of the

Coto Doñana and the high mountains of the Sierra Nevada. It still allows the likes of Chris Stewart to create his own rural idyll whilst permitting Somerset Maugham to prowl the streets of Seville in search of experience.

We will give the last word to Lorca, a man whose poetic voice was so prematurely silenced. This passage, taken from *Sketches of Spain (Impresiones y paisajes),* was written about Granada's Albaicín, but could so easily refer to the corners of many a lane, be it in the heart of provincial Baeza or amongst the rural whitewash of Frailes:

> When walking these streets you sense the mystical is battling against the voluptuous. Numbed by the alarming succession of shadows and slopes, you glimpse the gentle colours of the silvery valley, melancholic and iridescent.

AUTHOR PROFILES

Pedro de Alarcón (1833–91)
Born in Guadix near Granada. In 1874 he wrote *The Three-Cornered Hat*, his most well-known work, which draws heavily on Andalucian traditions. He also worked as a journalist, founding a paper in the port city of Cádiz, and penned a travelogue about the Alpujarra mountains.

Rafael Alberti (1902–99)
A Spanish poet and artist from Puerto de Santa María near Cádiz of Italian extraction. Part of the Generation of '27, Alberti moved in avant-garde literary circles. His Marxist ideology led to his exile during the Civil War and he did not return to Spain until 1977.

Tariq Ali (1943–)
British Pakistani novelist and political campaigner. He is the author of the Islam Quintet – the first of which is *Shadows of the Pomegranate Tree*. It is a fictional account of a family's struggle to deal with the collapse of Moorish Granada in the face of the Christian reconquest.

Manuel Altolaguirre (1905–59)
Poet and publisher from Málaga who established the renowned Imprenta Sur, a press that published work from the Generation of '27. Whilst in England on a study grant from the Spanish government, he established *1616*, the magazine intended to strengthen literary ties between the two countries.

Edmondo De Amicis (1846–1908)
Italian novelist, journalist and traveller. After a military career, De Amicis settled into a writer's life. His post as a newspaper correspondent proved fertile ground for his travel writings. In 1873, he published *Spain*, having travelled extensively in the country, especially throughout Andalucia.

Martin Amis (1949–)

English novelist whose first book, *The Rachel Papers*, won the Somerset Maugham Award. Twice nominated for the Booker Prize, he spent much time in Spain when his mother moved there and settled with the writer Alastair Boyd. Amis has also lived in Uruguay and worked at Manchester University.

Hans Christian Andersen (1805–75)

Prolific Danish writer famed for his fairy tales. He also wrote plays, novels, poems and travelogues, including *In Spain*. His works have been translated into more than 100 languages and have become classics. From a relatively poor background, he rose to mix with the upper echelons of Danish society.

Averroes (1126–98)

Ibn Rushd, otherwise known as Averroes, was a Cordoban thinker, writer and physician who wrote on many subjects. He defended the philosophy of Aristotle in the face of theological opposition from fellow Muslims and has been dubbed the founder of secular thought in Western Europe.

J. G. Ballard (1930–2009)

English novelist and short-story writer who grew up in Shanghai. He is known for works with a dystopian vision of modernity. He took up writing full time in 1960. Film adaptations have been made of his works, including *Crash* and *Empire of the Sun*. His novel on the Costa del Sol, *Cocaine Nights*, is his take on a dysfunctional expat community.

Gustavo Adolfo Bécquer (1836–70)

Sevillian poet and writer who was moderately well known in his lifetime. Most of his works were published posthumously, including the complete *Rhymes* and the *Legends*, composed from many sources. He is now recognised as a key figure in Spanish literary history.

Luis Berenguer (1923–79)

Galician writer and one-time frigate captain who relocated to San Fernando near Cádiz. The most famous of his six novels, *El mundo de Juan Lobón*, was turned into a Spanish television series. He was the winner of two prestigious literary prizes in the later years of his career.

Matilda Betham-Edwards (1836–1919)

Novelist, travel writer and poet. Her extensive travels took her across the Iberian Peninsula, all the way down to the sands of Africa. Her account, *Through Spain to the Sahara,* shows she was not afraid of stepping outside her comfort zone. She also maintained significant correspondence with Victorian literati.

Vicente Blasco Ibáñez (1867–1928)

Novelist, journalist and politician from Valencia. Blasco Ibáñez firmly established himself as a writer whose works lent themselves to cinematic representation. His novels *The Four Horsemen of the Apocalypse* and *Blood and Sand* proved a suitable vehicle for the young Rudolph Valentino. He was a committed Republican.

Jorge Luis Borges (1899–1986)

Argentinian writer famed for his short-story compilations. In 1919, he spent an extended period of time in Andalucia, visiting Granada and Córdoba, then settling in Seville, where he mixed with a group of young poets at the vanguard of Spanish ideas. He also had a long-lasting friendship with Fernando Quiñones, the writer from Cádiz.

George Borrow (1803–81)

English polyglot, writer and specialist on Gypsy culture. He is best known for *The Bible in Spain,* his tales of time spent selling Bibles along the by-roads of the peninsula. It has become a travel classic. He also wrote *The Zincali,* an account of Gypsies in Spain, many of whom lived in Andalucia.

Alastair Boyd (1927–2009)

Hispanist and travel writer, who became Baron Kilmarnock. Boyd lived much of his life in Ronda, reflected in his work *The Road from Ronda.* He married the ex-wife of Kingsley Amis. Boyd also wrote *Travels in the Mountains of Andalusia.* From 1983 to 1986 he was Chief Whip for the Social Democratic Party in the House of Lords.

Gerald Brenan (1894–1987)

English writer, associated with the Bloomsbury set, who settled in the Alpujarra mountains near Granada. His works include *The Spanish Labyrinth,* an account of the Civil War and its origins; *South from Granada,* his life in the village of Yegen; and the educational tract, *The Literature of the Spanish People*. He married the American author Gamel Woolsey.

Lord Byron, George Gordon (1788–1824)
British Romantic poet. Famously called 'mad, bad and dangerous to know', he left England for an extended tour of Europe in 1809, returning home in 1811. His autobiographical poem, *Childe Harold*, features Seville and Cádiz, as do his letters. He also wrote the epic *Don Juan*. He was eventually exiled from Britain in 1816 owing to a marriage scandal.

Fernán Caballero (1796–1877)
The pen name of Cecilia Francisca Josefa Böhl de Faber. Although born in Switzerland, she spent a great deal of her later life in Cádiz. Her best-known book is *The Seagull*. Many of her stories focus on local customs and she was happy to discuss them with Washington Irving.

José Manuel Caballero Bonald (1926–)
Spanish author from Jerez de la Frontera. His first poetic works immediately gained acclaim and, for a period of four years, he moved to Bogotá, Colombia. In 1998, the Fundación Caballero Bonald was inaugurated in his hometown of Jerez. He was awarded the prestigious Premio Cervantes in 2012.

Albert F. Calvert (1872–1946)
Author, traveller and engineer born in Middlesex, England. He published extensively on Spain; among his works are the 1912 book *Sculpture in Spain* and his text on the Arab period, *Moorish Remains in Spain*. He was awarded two honours by the Spanish royal family and became a knight of the Orders of Alfonso XII and of Isabella the Catholic.

Giacomo Casanova (1725–98)
Venetian whose name has become synonymous with sexual conquest. Exiled from his native city, he travelled all over Europe, often adopting aristocratic pseudonyms. His memoirs detail the complex social lives and structures of eighteenth-century Europe and contain enlightening elements of his life in Spain.

Luis Cernuda (1902–63)
Andalucian poet, part of the Generation of '27. He left Spain during the Civil War, initially staying in the UK. Cernuda grew up in Seville and,

whilst at the university there, attended some lectures given by the poet Pedro Salinas. His works were initially influenced by the Spanish Golden Age but show many changes in style.

Miguel de Cervantes (1547–1616)
Spanish author of *Don Quixote* and *The Exemplary Novels*. After fighting in the Battle of Lepanto, he spent six months recuperating from his injuries. He then focused seriously on his writing. Andalucia makes an appearance in *Don Quixote* and the *Novels*, particularly the tale of the Sevillian underworld, 'Rinconete and Cortadillo'.

Abel Chapman (1851–1929)
An English hunter-turned-naturalist and writer, Chapman took an active part in conserving parts of the Coto Doñana. He teamed up with Walter J. Buck to write two books on Spanish wildlife that contain much information on the Coto. Chapman also became a member of the Society for the Preservation of the Wild Fauna of the Empire.

François-René de Chateaubriand (1768–1848)
French writer and politician. In recognition of his defence of Christianity at a time when intellectuals were turning against religion, the Russian Tsarina made him a man of means, allowing him to travel without financial restraints. His visits to Spain led to two works that contributed to his fame – *The Martyrs* and *The Adventures of the Last Abencerrages*.

Penelope Chetwode (1910–86)
Daughter of a baron and wife of the poet laureate, John Betjamin. Chetwode wrote an account of her journey around north-eastern Andalucia by horse, whimsically titled *Two Middle-Aged Ladies in Andalusia*. It is full of gentle anecdote, affection for the landscape and the equine culture of the region.

Rubén Darío (1867–1916)
Poet from Nicaragua at the forefront of the Modernist movement. He had a tremendous influence on the world of Spanish letters. He travelled widely in Europe, with extended stays in Spain and Paris, including a period as the Nicaraguan ambassador in Madrid. His struggles with alcohol plagued his last years.

John Dos Passos (1896–1970)

American author of Portuguese ancestry. His most famous work is *Manhattan Transfer*, a novel of urban life in New York. He was widely travelled and wrote of Andalucia in his 1922 book, *Rosinante to the Road Again*. He returned to the country during the Civil War, during which time his friendship with Hemingway ended over political disagreements.

Carol Drinkwater (1948–)

English actress and author famed for her television role as the wife of fictional vet, James Heriot. Her Olive Farm books have made her a bestselling author. One in the series, *The Olive Tree,* took her away from her base in southern France in search of olive cultivation throughout the Mediterranean.

Robert Dundas Murray (1818–56)

Youngest son of Lord Elibank, Dundas Murray was considered an expert on Andalucia in his day. In addition to *The Cities and Wilds of Andalucia*, he also wrote a short story, 'The Lonja of Seville' and an essay, 'The Spanish Gypsy: The History of a European Obsession'.

Javier Egea (1952–99)

Egea was born in Granada and was considered one of the most important poets of the 1980s, receiving the Juan Ramón Jiménez Premio Hispanoamericano for his masterwork, *Paseo de los tristes*, named after the street that runs at the foot of the Alhambra Palace. He committed suicide in 1999. He was part of the Other Sentimentality poetic movement, along with Luis García Montero.

George Eliot (1819–80)

The pen name of Mary Ann Evans, author of novels, short stories and verse. She used a male pseudonym to escape the stereotypes of female writers and became known for classics such as *Middlemarch*, *Silas Marner* and *Daniel Deronda*. She wrote a long verse work, *The Spanish Gypsy*, inspired by her travels.

Juan Eslava Galán (1948–)

Writer from Jaén who has occasionally used the English pseudonym Nicholas Wilcox. His works have a strong historical influence and range from the Civil War era, through the time of the Templars, to the Carthaginian period.

Ildefonso Falcones (1959–)

Spanish lawyer and writer. His first book, *The Cathedral of the Sea*, was the most read in Spain in 2007. His novel, *The Hand of Fatima*, is a fictionalised account of the Kingdom of Granada almost a century after the last Moorish king left the city. The municipality of Juviles, near to the city, named a street in his honour in recognition of the novel's popularity.

Richard Ford (1796–1858)

The English son of an MP who trained as a lawyer. He spent four years travelling extensively throughout Spain. The fruit of his journeys was the two-volume classic, *Handbook for Travellers in Spain*, spiced with anecdote and peppered with personal opinion. He inspired many to write their own accounts.

Ronald Fraser (1930–2012)

Historian born in Hamburg to a British father and American mother. After a spell as a Reuters correspondent, he moved to Spain in the 1950s, specialising in oral history and interview. His books have chronicled Andalucian village life and the Peninsular War, in addition to the Spanish Civil War and its aftermath.

Solomon Ibn Gabirol (1021–58)

Also known as Avicebron, Ibn Gabirol was a Judeo-Andalucian poet and philosopher. He was one of the first to teach Neoplatonism in Europe and to reconcile it with Jewish philosophy. It was in the eighteenth century that Solomon Munk discovered Ibn Gabirol and Avicebron were the same person, thanks to his study of a translation of *The Fountain of Life*, the philosopher's masterwork.

Antonio Gala (1930–)

Born in Castile-La Mancha, but an adopted Cordoban, Gala has written novels, poetry, plays and essays. His novel *El manuscrito carmesí* deals with the fall of Muslim Granada. He has also been president of the Spanish–Arab Friendship Association.

Benito Pérez Galdós (1843–1920)

Born in the Canary Islands, Galdós was a much-respected literary figure in nineteenth-century Spain. In his 46 *National Episodes* he fictionalised the significant moments of Spanish history. He introduced Dickens to a Hispanic audience by translating *The Pickwick Papers*, but is best known to an English-speaking public for his novel *Fortunata and Jacinta*.

John Galt (1779–1839)

Writer and commentator born in Irvine, Scotland. His travel writing met with moderate success, but he was more fortunate when he turned to biography – producing accounts of Lord Byron and Benjamin West. Among his business ventures was a failed attempt to set up a Gibraltarian trading company.

Ángel Ganivet (1865–98)

Born in Granada, a diplomat and writer of philosophical works. He is best known for his *Granada la bella*, a vision of the city he loved that was being lost by development. His diplomatic career took him to Riga on the Baltic, where, plagued by syphilis, he committed suicide.

Théophile Gautier (1811–72)

French writer of the Romantic movement. He is often credited with portraying many of the images of Andalucia that have become common currency in the popular imagination. His compilation of poems, *España*, covers many aspects of Andalucian culture. He also wrote the travelogue *Wanderings in Spain*.

Ian Gibson (1939–)

Irish-born naturalised Spaniard. His principal fame in Spain, and abroad, is as the biographer of personalities such as Lorca, Dalí and Machado. He spent many years living in Granada and has also produced a guide to the city's sites associated with Lorca. He is also now a novelist and TV presenter.

Luis de Góngora (1561–1627)

Baroque poet from Córdoba. He wrote during Spain's Golden Age, creating a style known as *culteranismo*, full of allusion and allegory. Some of his verses celebrate the landscapes around his hometown. Centuries later, Góngora had a significant influence on the Generation of '27 poets.

Juan Goytisolo (1931–)

Spanish writer born in Barcelona, now resident in Marrakech. After studying law, Goytisolo took up writing in earnest. His renowned trilogy incorporating *Marks of Identity*, *Count Julian* and *Juan the Landless* was banned until the transition to democracy in Spain. The books deal with themes of identity, betrayal and change. *The Countryside of Níjar* and *La Chanca* are his meditations on Almería Province.

Paul Gwynne (1869–1942)

A pseudonym used by Ernest Slater, one-time editor of the *Electrical Times*. He wrote *Along Spain's River of Romance*, which follows the course of the Guadalquivir. His novelistic output includes *The Bandolero*, a tale of long-lost family, bullfighting and banditry.

Samuel Ha-Nagid (993–1056)

Jewish scholar, politician and poet who started his career as a merchant in Córdoba. He rose to become vizier in Granada. He was one of the most famed Hebrew poets of the Middle Ages and is credited with applying certain attributes of Arabic poetry to create new styles.

Nathalie Handal (1969–)

Born in Haiti to a Palestinian family, Handal has lived in North and South America as well as Europe. The author of poetry and plays, Handal's main Spanish-focused work is the poetry collection, *Poet in Andalucía*, named in homage to Lorca. She promotes international literature through her work with Words Without Borders.

Ibn Hazm (994–1064)

Born in Córdoba, Ibn Hazm was a prodigious author of some 400 works, 40 of which survive. His best-known piece is *The Dove's Neck-Ring*, a treatise on love, although he also wrote many works on law, ethics and Muslim theology.

Ernest Hemingway (1899–1961)

An American winner of the Nobel Prize for Literature, Hemingway was a journalist during the Civil War. His experiences led to numerous books set in the peninsula, including *For Whom the Bell Tolls*. He is most remembered in the south for his accounts of bullfighting in *Death in the Afternoon*.

Antonio Hernández (1943–)

Prize-winning Spanish poet and novelist born in Arcos de la Frontera who was given the key to his hometown in 1999 for services to literature. His poetic output is extensive and has culminated in his being awarded the Premio Nacional for Poetry in 2014.

Miguel Hernández (1910–42)

Spanish poet from Orihuela, Valencia. He received little in the way of formal education. Because of his time as a goatherd, he was known as the 'shepherd poet'. A member of the Communist Party, he was based in Jaén for part of the Civil War. After the conflict, he eventually died in prison of tuberculosis.

Gerald Howson (1926–2014)

Born in Cambridgeshire, England, Howson distinguished himself in numerous fields. He used English teaching as an excuse to live in Spain and study flamenco guitar, a period of his life he wrote up in *The Flamencos of Cadiz Bay*. He then moved into photojournalism and eventually took a teaching post in the subject.

Pearse Hutchinson (1927–2012)

Irish poet who was also an accomplished translator. His trip to Andalucia in the 1950s had a profound effect on his work. He subsequently went on to learn Galician and Catalan, spending much time in Barcelona. His first original compilation, *Tongue Without Hands*, took its title from a line found in the Spanish classic, *El Cid*.

Aldous Huxley (1894–1963)

British writer who emigrated to the United States. His dystopian vision of London, *Brave New World*, has become a classic. Huxley moved to California in 1937, working as a screenwriter. He is also renowned for *The Doors of Perception*, his account of psychedelic drug-taking. His 1931 poetry collection, *The Cicadas and Other Poems*, records his Spanish journey.

Henry David Inglis (1795–1835)

A Scottish travel writer and journalist. He visited Spain in 1830 and published the appropriately titled *Spain in 1830*. He went on to contribute articles to numerous publications, including *Colburn's New Monthly Magazine*, for which he wrote 'Rambles in the Footsteps of Don Quixote'.

Washington Irving (1783–1859)

American author, essayist and biographer famous for his stories *The Legend of Sleepy Hollow*, *Rip Van Winkle* and *Tales of the Alhambra*. He served in the United States Legation to Spain and travelled extensively throughout Europe. Much of his work takes a satirical look at society, interlacing fact, fiction and essay.

Michael Jacobs (1952–2014)

Jacobs was born in Genoa and settled in Andalucia. His bestselling work, *The Factory of Light: Tales from my Andalucían Village*, was a mystical memoir set in his adopted village of Frailes. He also travelled around Spain, which led to his book in search of cultural insight, *Between Hopes and Memories*.

Julian Jeffs (1931–)

Cambridge-educated Jeffs fell into a job in the sherry trade in Jerez. Before leaving to become a barrister, he wrote the classic text on Andalucia's famous wine, simply entitled *Sherry*. It details both the methods of production and the structure of bodegas fundamental to the industry.

Juan Ramón Jiménez (1881–1958)

Born in Moguer, near Huelva, Jiménez won the Nobel Prize for Literature in 1956. He celebrated his region in the prose poem *Platero and I*, verses that relate the story of a writer and his donkey. Like many others, he was exiled as a result of the Civil War and eventually died in San Juan, Puerto Rico.

Nikos Kazantzakis (1883–1957)

Cretan writer famed for *Zorba the Greek*. He was nominated nine times for the Nobel Prize for Literature. He returned to worldwide consciousness in 1988 on the release of a film adaptation of his book *The Last Temptation of Christ*. In addition to his novels and plays, he produced many travel books.

Arthur Koestler (1905–83)

Hungarian-born journalist and author, long-time resident of Britain. Pretending to be a Franco sympathiser, he tried to infiltrate the National-ist headquarters in Seville during the Civil War. He was later arrested in the same city and imprisoned. His experiences form the book *A Spanish Testament*.

Laurie Lee (1914–97)

English poet, novelist and screenwriter. He took part in the Spanish Civil War as a member of the International Brigades fighting Franco. His trio of Spanish books, *As I Walked Out One Midsummer Morning*, *A Moment of War* and *A Rose for Winter*, recount his experiences in the region and take in the pre-war, conflict and postwar periods.

Patrick Leigh Fermor (1915–2011)

British author famed for the books he wrote about his epic walk across Europe to Constantinople. He was also a member of the Cretan resistance in the Second World War and an accomplished linguist and translator. His writings on Spain appear in his compilation *Words of Mercury*.

Federico García Lorca (1898–1936)

Spanish poet and dramatist from Fuente Vaqueros, west of Granada. He formed part of the famous Generation of '27, a group of educated poets and writers influenced by avant-garde and baroque forms. His writings are deeply rooted in the Andalucian countryside and Gypsy folklore. He was assassinated for his political beliefs during the Civil War.

Alejandro Luque (1972–)

Journalist and writer who lives in Seville and writes for the *Correo de Andalucía* newspaper. His works include a compilation of short stories, a travelogue, a collection of poetry and a biography of the friendship between Jorge Luis Borges and Fernando Quiñones, *Palabras mayores*.

Antonio Machado (1875–1939)

Poet born in Seville. Machado was part of the literary movement known as the Generation of '98. After moving around Castile and suffering the loss of his wife, he went back to Andalucia, living for a while in Baeza. It was in this town that he mourned his wife through poetry.

Maimonides (1135–1204)

Moshe ben Maimon, or Maimonides, was a Jewish Torah scholar and physician who also wrote on astronomy and philosophy. Born in Córdoba and dying in Egyptian exile, he is now recognised as one of the foremost philosophers in Jewish history.

Julio Mariscal Montes (1922–77)

Poet from Arcos de la Frontera in Cádiz Province. A contributor to many literary journals, his first book was published in 1953. Mariscal Montes was an admirer of flamenco, a dedicated teacher and a poet at the forefront of the grouping, Alcaraván.

José Martínez Ruiz (1873–1967)

Martínez Ruiz wrote under the pseudonym Azorín. Originally from Valencia Province, he produced essays, travelogues and novels. His output reflected his many interests, from political essays on anarchism to *Don Quixote*.

Somerset Maugham (1874–1965)

British novelist and playwright. Originally trained as a doctor, he gave up medicine owing to literary success. In 1897, Maugham left for Seville, where he stayed for many months. His *The Land of the Blessed Virgin* recounts his time spent in Andalucia. Later, he wrote *Don Fernando* – a look at fifteenth- and sixteenth-century Spain via its writers and artists.

Prosper Mérimée (1803–70)

French story-writer, historian and dramatist. Trained as a translator, Mérimée found a great deal of inspiration in Andalucian mystery and folklore. He was made famous by writing *Carmen*, which was subsequently set to music by Bizet. He also published his travel diaries from trips around the region.

James A. Michener (1907–97)

Pulitzer Prize-winning American author known for his factually accurate fiction with a strong locational bias. He also wrote travelogues – the most famous of which is *Iberia*, detailing his journey in Spain and Portugal. His fictional work on Andalucia, *Miracle in Seville*, combines the themes of bullfighting and religion.

Henry Canova Vollam Morton (1892–1979)

Prolific English journalist and travel writer who often wrote under the initials H. V. He famously scooped the opening of Tutankhamun's tomb for the *Daily Express*. Morton travelled extensively throughout Europe and the Middle East. His Spanish travel book, *A Stranger in Spain*, remains popular to this day.

Guy Mountfort (1905–2003)

An advertising executive who pursued his interests as a conservationist. In addition to his book on the Coto Doñana, *Portrait of a Wilderness: The Story of the Coto Doñana Expeditions*, he was recognised as an accomplished field-guide writer. He was an instigator of the World Wide Fund for Nature.

Antonio Muñoz Molina (1956–)

Former director of the Cervantes Institute in New York, Muñoz Molina was born in Úbeda. *The Manuscript of Ashes*, his first novel, is an imaginary recreation of his birthplace. His book *Sefarad*, which details the Sephardic diaspora following the reconquest of Granada, won the PEN Translation Prize for its English version, *Sepharad*, translated by Margaret Sayers Peden.

Eduardo de Ory (1884–1939)

De Ory was first published at the age of 14, writing about his native city, Cádiz. A prodigious creator of literary journals, he also founded the Real Academia Hispano-Americana de Ciencias y Artes, a society designed to forge transatlantic links with the larger Hispanic world. His son, Carlos Edmundo de Ory, went on to become a respected poet and essayist.

Victor Perera (1934–2003)

Guatemalan, born of Jewish ancestry. Perera is best known for his book *The Cross and the Pear Tree*, in which he traces his ancestry from fifteenth-century Spain to the present. He spent many years teaching at the University of California and penned a novel, *The Conversion*, which fictionalised an American searching for his Judeo-Spanish origins.

Rafael Pérez Estrada (1934–2000)

Former law student from the University of Granada, Pérez Estrada went on to become a writer whilst practising as a lawyer. He was a finalist for Spain's Premio Nacional de Literatura on more than one occasion and penned over 40 books, including plays and poetry.

Arturo Pérez-Reverte (1951–)

Former war correspondent who turned to literature. Renowned for his novels about the Golden Age soldier Captain Alatriste, Pérez-Reverte's stories take much inspiration from his country's history, although he is not exclusively a historical novelist. He is a member of the Spanish Royal Academy.

Jan Potocki (1761–1815)
Polish nobleman who dabbled with ethnology, writing and Egyptology. He travelled in three continents, joined more than one secret society and contributed to the beginnings of ethnological study. In terms of writing, he is best known for *The Manuscript Found in Saragossa*. He committed suicide with a silver bullet.

Emilio Prados (1899–1962)
Malagueño poet known for his work fusing elements of the natural world with existential concepts. Problems with his lungs meant a lengthy stay in a Swiss sanatorium, but it led to his decision to focus on writing. He founded the magazine *Litoral* with fellow poet Manuel Altolaguirre.

Fernando Quiñones (1930–98)
Born in Chiclana de la Frontera, Quiñones started his career by writing for newspapers. Closely associated with Cádiz, he used to enjoy a daily stroll along La Caleta Beach. Flamenco is a theme in many of his works, including the lauded *De Cádiz y sus cantes*. His work also covered the genres of poetry, the short story and novels.

Ibn Quzman (1078–1160)
Poet born in Córdoba who was feted as an innovator of form and usage. He wrote *zajals*, a verse style that used rhyme and colloquial language. He was known for his drinking and rowdy behaviour, a way of living occasionally reflected in his poetry.

Rainer Maria Rilke (1875–1926)
Born in Prague, the German-speaking Rilke developed into a renowned poet of mystical verses. After a spell in Paris, Rilke spent an extended period during the early 1910s in Ronda. He is best remembered for the *Duino Elegies*, a verse cycle that he returned to over a ten-year period of composition.

Salman Rushdie (1947–)
Booker Prize-winning Anglo-Indian novelist. Much of his work is set in India and some has famously courted controversy. He used the story of Boabdil, the last Moorish king of Granada, as an allegorical parallel for his story *The Moor's Last Sigh*.

Robert Southey (1774–1843)
Writer labelled as one of the 'Lake Poets' of the Romantic movement. A young radical, he became increasingly more conservative and was lampooned by Lord Byron in his poem *Don Juan*. Southey enjoyed travelling in Spain; his letters from an extended stay there have been published, and he even translated *El Cid* for an English audience.

Walter Starkie (1894–1976)
Irish scholar, author and musician. He was an adept translator of Spanish literature and a fluent speaker of Romani. Like George Borrow, he became acquainted with the Gypsies of Andalucia, writing *Spanish Raggle Taggle* and *Don Gypsy*. He also wrote *Spain: A Musician's Journey Through Time and Space* and even penned a tract comparing Shakespeare and Cervantes.

Chris Stewart (1950–)
A former member of the rock band Genesis, and an itinerant sheep-shearer, Stewart finally settled in the Alpujarra mountains. He has written a series of books about his pastoral life in the Sierras: *Driving Over Lemons*, *A Parrot in the Pepper Tree*, *The Almond Blossom Appreciation Society* and *The Last Days of the Bus Club*.

Henry Swinburne (1743–1803)
English travel writer who spent two years travelling around Spain. His subsequent account, *Travels Through Spain, in the Years 1775 and 1776*, became very popular. Edward Gibbon, in his study of the decline of the Roman Empire, even references Swinburne's book on the country.

Louisa Tenison (1819–82)
Lady Louisa Anson became a Tenison when she married the Anglo-Irish Edward King-Tenison, with whom she travelled the Middle East, a trip that formed the basis of her book *Sketches from the East*. She soon followed this with *Castile and Andalucía*, a text that centres on her residence in Málaga.

Giles Tremlett (1962–)
Madrid-based journalist for the *Guardian* newspaper, he has also reported from the city for *The Economist*. Tremlett is the writer of *Ghosts of Spain* and a biography of Catherine of Aragon. Tremlett also makes occasional appearances as a reporter on Spanish television.

J. B. Trend (1887–1958)

A British academic and professor of Spanish at Cambridge. He was particularly interested in Spanish music, and his book *A Picture of Modern Spain: Men and Music* has whole sections devoted to this passion. He was in regular correspondence with the composer and friend of Lorca, Manuel de Falla.

Mark Twain (1835–1910)

American author with a satirical wit, famous for *The Adventures of Tom Sawyer*. In his travelogue *Innocents Abroad* he cruised down the Andalucian coastline, taking in Gibraltar. His wry observations portray a New World view of Old World propensities.

Kenneth Tynan (1927–1980)

English critic and writer who collaborated with many famous authors and actors. Tynan considered himself 'enslaved' to the Andalucia of bulls and flamenco, writing *Bull Fever* in 1955. His diaries also detail his fascination with Andalucia.

José Ángel Valente (1929–2000)

Poet, translator and essayist from Galicia. Valente settled in Almería after periods spent in Oxford, Geneva and Paris. His translations include the works of Keats, Dylan Thomas and Gerald Manley Hopkins. Almería became a touchstone for the author and features in his poems and essays.

Lope de Vega (1562–1635)

Spanish Golden Age playwright and poet. He was born in Madrid, but his works covered many Andalucian topics. He was a prodigious author who has over 500 plays attributed to him. Despite joining the priesthood in later life, he was prone to many dalliances and had children with several women. His form of theatre revolutionised the Spanish stage and his plays are often performed today.

Jason Webster (1970–)

Born in California, of Anglo-American extraction. After studying Arabic at Oxford, Webster settled in Spain. The country provides the inspiration for his work, his most recent being a series of detective novels. His first book, *Duende*, recounts his journeys in search of the soul of flamenco music.

Andalus is a study of the continuing Moorish influence on the region and immigration from Africa.

Robert Wilson (1957–)

British author specialising in crime fiction. Books in his Javier Falcón detective series have been nominated for the CWA Gold Dagger award. The first book in the series, *The Blind Man of Seville*, features Semana Santa, the city's famous Holy Week procession. The books have been serialised on TV.

Virginia Woolf (1882–1941)

Modernist British writer associated with the Bloomsbury group. Her book *Orlando*, about a nobleman who lives for centuries without noticeably ageing, is a disguised portrait of her one-time lover Vita Sackville-West. Suffering from depression, she committed suicide by walking into a river in East Sussex.

Ibn Zamrak (1333–93)

Poet and politician from Granada. He was court poet to the Nasrid ruler Abu Abd Allah Muhammad V. Some of his verses adorn the walls of the Alhambra, forming part of the decoration. A pawn in the political machinations of rival factions, he was assassinated by Muhammad VII.

Ibn Zaydun (1003–71)

Zaydun divided his time between the cities of Seville and Córdoba. Romantically and literarily, his works are very much linked to Wallada, the poet daughter of the Umayyad caliph of Córdoba. Owing to personal and political intrigue, Zaydun found himself exiled.

CHRONOLOGY OF EVENTS

	Literary and Cultural Events	Political Events
*c.*1100 BC		Foundation of Cádiz (Gades) by the Phoenicians.
*c.*500 BC		Carthaginians attack Tartessos.
*c.*500 BC	The historian Hecataeus of Miletus first uses the term Iberia.	
206–197 BC		Romans establish the 'Andalucian' provinces of Hispania Ulterior and Hispania Baetica.
4 BC	The philosopher Seneca born in Córdoba.	
53		Future emperor Trajan born in Itálica near Seville.
76		Future emperor Hadrian born in Itálica near Seville.
77	Pliny the Elder mentions the Andalucian provinces of Rome in his *Naturalis Historia*.	
409		The Vandals and Suebi enter Hispania.
711		Tariq ibn Ziyad and his army arrive from North Africa to intervene in a Visigothic civil war.
718		Muslims take control of much of the peninsula.

	Literary and Cultural Events	Political Events
756		The Emirate of Córdoba established.
929		The Caliphate of Córdoba established.
994	Birth of the polymath and poet Ibn Hazm.	
1031		The Caliphate breaks into smaller kingdoms.
1135	Birth of the philosopher Maimonides.	
1160	The philosopher Averroes becomes a judge in Seville.	
1236		Córdoba falls to the Christians.
1238		The foundation of Nasrid Granada and the start of the building of the Alhambra.
1361	Ibn Zamrak appointed Nasrid court poet.	
1476	The revolt in Fuente Obejuna which inspired Lope de Vega's later play.	
1479		Dynastic union of the kingdoms of Castile and Aragon.
1492	Antonio de Nebrija, from Seville Province, publishes the first Spanish grammar.	The last Muslim state, Granada, falls to the Christians.
1492		Christopher Columbus first sails west towards the Americas from Palos.
1492		Issue of the Alhambra Decree expelling the Jews.
1503		The Casa de Contratación (House of Trade) established in Seville.

	Literary and Cultural Events	*Political Events*
1516		The Hapsburg Charles V (Charles I of Spain) ascends to the throne.
1568–71		Alpujarra rebellion leading to the expulsion of the Morisco population.
1571	Miguel de Cervantes injured in the Battle of Lepanto.	
1605	Cervantes publishes the first part of *Don Quixote*.	
1612	Góngora publishes his *Fable of Polyphemus and Galatea*.	
1616	Cervantes dies.	
1627	Luis de Góngora dies.	
1641		Conspiracy of Andalucian nobles uncovered, seen by some as a secessionist movement.
1642	James Howell publishes his *Instructions for Forreine Travell*, which includes the Alpujarras.	
1700		Death of the last Spanish Hapsburg leads to the start of the War of the Spanish Succession; ends in 1714.
1713		Gibraltar ceded to the British in the Treaty of Utrecht.
1715		The Bourbon Philip V signs a decree removing the rights and privileges of Spanish regions.
1775–76	Henry Swinburne travels through Spain.	
1797	Goya paints in the Coto Doñana.	

	Literary and Cultural Events	*Political Events*
1808		Start of the War of Spanish Independence (Peninsular War).
1809	Lord Byron arrives in Seville.	
1812	Andalucia features in Byron's *Childe Harold's Pilgrimage*.	The Cádiz Cortes creates the first modern Spanish constitution.
1843	Théophile Gautier publishes *Wanderings in Spain*.	
1845	Richard Ford publishes *Handbook for Travellers in Spain*.	
1873		First Spanish Republic declared, lasting until 1874.
1898	Ángel Ganivet commits suicide in Riga.	Spain loses its last colonies in the Americas.
1912	Antonio Machado moves to Baeza.	
1923–30		The Jerezano Miguel Primo de Rivera establishes a military dictatorship.
1927	A group of poets, including Lorca and Alberti, first become known as the Generation of '27.	
1931		Second Spanish Republic declared, lasting until its fall at the end of the Spanish Civil War.
1936–39		The Spanish Civil War.
1936	Lorca assassinated by Nationalist firing squad.	
1937	Hemingway agrees to report on the Civil War.	
1939		General Franco recognised by the British and French as the Spanish head of state.

	Literary and Cultural Events	*Political Events*
1956	Juan Ramón Jiménez awarded the Nobel Prize for Literature.	
1975		Franco dies and Spain begins its transition to democracy.
1977	Vicente Aleixandre awarded the Nobel Prize for Literature.	
1977	Rafael Alberti returns to Spain from exile.	
1978		The new constitution recognises the country's autonomous communities.
1981		A military *coup d'état* is aborted in the face of opposition from King Juan Carlos, Franco's chosen successor.
1981		The Autonomous Community of Andalucia forms after a referendum.
1982		Spanish Socialist Party (PSOE) leader from Seville, Felipe González, becomes prime minister of Spain.
1986		Spain joins the EEC.
1987	Gerald Brenan dies.	
1987	The BBC dramatises Laurie Lee's *As I Walked Out One Midsummer Morning.*	
1989		The first Spanish elections to the European Parliament.
1996	J. G. Ballard's dystopian view of the Costa del Sol, *Cocaine Nights*, first published.	
1998		After nine years of regional broadcasting Canal Sur opens its second channel.

	Literary and Cultural Events	*Political Events*
2010	Tariq Ali receives the Granadillo Prize for his Islam Quintet.	
2012	José Manuel Caballero Bonald receives Spain's prestigious Miguel de Cervantes Prize.	
2013		Susana Díaz, from the PSOE, elected as president of the Autonomous Andalucian Government.
2014	Arturo Pérez-Reverte's novel set in Cádiz, *The Siege*, receives the CWA International Award	King Juan Carlos abdicates in favour of his son, Felipe.
2014	Michael Jacobs leaves his final work on Velázquez unfinished; *Everything is Happening* is published posthumously.	

SELECT BIBLIOGRAPHY

Alarcón, P. A. de, *The Three-Cornered Hat* (New York: Alfred A. Knopf, 1918).

Alberti, R., *The Lost Grove*, trans. G. Berns (Berkeley: University of California Press, 1976).

—— *Marinero en tierra* (Madrid: Alianza Editorial, 1981).

—— *Concerning the Angels*, trans. C. Sawyer-Lauçanno (San Francisco: City Lights Books, 1995).

—— *Retornos de lo vivo lejano: Ora maritima*, (Madrid: Ediciones Cátedra, 1999).

Ali, T., *Shadows of the Pomegranate Tree* (London: Verso Books, 2006).

Altolaguirre, M., *Poesías completas* (Madrid: Ediciones Cátedra, 2006).

Amicis, E. De, *Spain*, trans. W. W. Cady (New York: G. P. Putnam's Sons, 1886).

Amis, M., *Experience* (London: Vintage, 2001).

Andersen, H. C., *In Spain and A Visit to Portugal* (New York: Hurd and Houghton, 1870).

Ballard, J. G., *Cocaine Nights* (London: Fourth Estate, 2010).

Bécquer, G. A., *Legends, Tales and Poems* (New York: Ginn and Company, 1907).

Berenguer, L., *El mundo de Juan Lobón* (Madrid: Ediciones Cátedra, 2010).

Betham-Edwards, M., *Through Spain to the Sahara* (London: Hurst and Blackett, 1868).

Borges, J. L., *Selected Poems* (London: Penguin, 2000).

Borrow, G., *The Zincali; or, An Account of the Gypsies of Spain* (London: John Murray, 1843).

—— *The Bible in Spain* (London: J. M. Dent & Co., 1906).

Bouterwek, F., *History of Spanish Literature*, trans. T. Ross (London: David Bogue, 1847).

Boyd, A., *The Road from Ronda* (London: Collins, 1969).

Brenan, G., *Personal Record, 1920–72* (London: Jonathan Cape, 1974).

—— *The Literature of the Spanish People* (Cambridge: Cambridge University Press, 1976).

—— *South from Granada* (London: Penguin Classics, 2008).

—— *The Face of Spain* (London, Serif Books, 2010).

—— *The Spanish Labyrinth: An Account of the Social and Political Background of the Spanish Civil War* (Cambridge: Cambridge University Press, 2015).

Byron, Lord (George Gordon), *Poetical Works* (Oxford: Oxford University Press, 1967).

—— *Selected Letters and Journals*, ed. L. A. Marchand (Cambridge, MA: Belknap Press, 1982).

Byron, W., *Cervantes: A Biography* (London: Cassell, 1979).

Caballero, F., *The Seagull*, trans. A. Bethell (London: Richard Bentley, 1867).

Caballero Bonald, J. M., *Andalusian Dances*, trans. C. D. Ley (Barcelona: Editorial Noguer, 1959).

—— *Sevilla en tiempos de Cervantes* (Seville: Fundación José Manuel Lara, 2003).

Calvert, A. F., *Sculpture in Spain* (London: John Lane, 1912).

Carvajal y Robles, R. de, *Poema heróico del asalto y conquista de Antequera* (Málaga: Universidad de Málaga, 2000).

Casanova, G., *History of My Life*, trans. W. R. Trask (New York: Alfred A. Knopf, 2006).

Castelar, E., *Vida de Lord Byron* (Havana: La Propaganda Literaria, 1873).

Cernuda, L., *Ocnos*, trans. A. Dempsey (Madrid: Turner Publicaciones, 2009).

Cervantes, M. de, *The Ingenious Gentleman Don Quixote of La Mancha*, trans. J. Ormsby (London: Smith, Elder & Co, 1885).

—— *The Exemplary Novels*, trans. W. K. Kelly (London: Henry G. Bohn, 1855).

Chapman, A. and Buck, W. J., *Wild Spain* (London: Gurney & Jackson, 1893).

—— *Unexplored Spain* (London: Edward Arnold, 1910).

Chateaubriand, F.-R. de, *The Last of the Abencerrajes*, trans. A. S. Kline (Project Gutenburg, 2011).

Chetwode, P., *Two Middle-Aged Ladies in Andalusia* (London: John Murray, 2002).

Cornwell, B., *Sharpe's Trafalgar* (London: Harper, 2011).

Darío, R., *Selected Writings* (London: Penguin Classics, 2006).

Dos Passos, J., *Rosinante to the Road Again* (Black Hill: Onesuch Press, 2011).

Drinkwater, C., *The Olive Tree* (London: Weidenfeld & Nicolson, 2011).

Dundas Murray, R., *The Cities and Wilds of Andalucia* (London: Richard Bentley, 1853).

Egea, J., *Paseo de los tristes* (Granada: Diputación Provincial de Granada, 1999).

Egea, J. and García Montero, L., *El manifiesto albertista* (Granada: Cuadernos de Vigía, 2003).

Eliot, G., *Daniel Deronda* (Oxford: Oxford University Press, 1998).

—— *The Spanish Gypsy: The Legend of Jubal and Other Poems* (Honolulu: University of the Pacific Press, 2003).

Ellis, P. J., *The Poetry of Emilio Prados* (Cardiff: University of Wales Press, 1981).

Eslava Galán, J., *The Mule* (London: Random House, 2008).

Falcones, I., *The Hand of Fatima* (London: Doubleday, 2011).

Fernández-Armesto, F., *Columbus* (Oxford: Oxford University Press, 1992).

Fielding, X., *Images of Spain* (London: Bounty Books, 2005).

Fletcher, R., *Moorish Spain* (London: Phoenix Press, 2001).

Ford, R., *Handbook for Travellers in Spain: Part 1* (London: John Murray, 1855).

—— *Handbook for Travellers in Spain: Part 2* (London: John Murray, 1855).

—— *The Letters of Richard Ford* (London: John Murray, 1905).

Fraser, R., *Pueblo: A Mountain Village on the Costa del Sol* (London: Allen Lane, 1973).

—— *Blood of Spain: An Oral History of the Spanish Civil War* (London: Random House, 1982).

—— *In Hiding: The Life of Manuel Cortes* (London: Verso, 2010).

Gala, A., *El manuscrito carmesí* (Barcelona: Editorial Planeta, 2001).

Galdós, B. P., *Trafalgar: A Tale*, trans. C. Bell (New York: William S. Gottsberger, 1884).

—— *Cádiz* (Madrid: Bolchiro, 1952).

Galt, J., *Voyages and Travels in the Years 1809, 1810 and 1811* (London: T. Cadell and W. Davies, 1812).

Ganivet, A., *Granada la bella* (Buenos Aires: Editora y Distribuidora del Plata, 1947).

García Montero, L., *A Form of Resistance*, trans. K. King (London: Katie King, 2013).

Gautier, T., *Wanderings in Spain* (London: Ingram, Cooke, and Co., 1853).

Gibson, I., *The Assassination of Federico García Lorca* (London: Penguin, 1983).

—— *Lorca's Granada: A Practical Guide* (London: Faber and Faber, 1992).

—— *Cuatro poetas en Guerra: Antonio Machado, Juan Ramón Jiménez, Federico García Lorca, Miguel Hernández* (Barcelona: Editorial Planeta, 2007).

Góngora, L. de, *Polyphemus and Galatea* (Edinburgh: Edinburgh University Press, 1977).

—— *Selected Shorter Poems* (London: Anvil Press Poetry, 1995).

Gorton, T. J. (ed.), *Andalus: Moorish Songs of Love and Wine* (London: Eland, 2007).

Goytisolo, J., *The Countryside of Níjar and La Chanca*, trans. L. Luccarelli (Plainfield, IN: Alembic Press, 1987).

—— *Juan the Landless*, trans. H. Lane (London: Serpent's Tail, 1990).

Grayling, C., *Once Upon a Time in Italy: The Westerns of Sergio Leone* (New York: Abrams, 2005).

—— *Spaghetti Westerns: Cowboys and Europeans from Karl May to Sergio Leone* (London: I.B.Tauris, 2006).

Grove, V., *The Life and Loves of Laurie Lee* (London: Robinson Press, 2014).

Gwynne, P., *Along Spain's River of Romance: The Guadalquivir* (New York: McBride, Nast and Co., 1912).

Ha-Nagid, S., *Selected Poems* (Princeton: Princeton University Press, 1996).

Handal, N., *Poet in Andalucía* (Pittsburgh: University of Pittsburgh Press, 2012).

Hastings, S., *The Secret Lives of Somerset Maugham* (London: John Murray, 2010).

Hemingway, E., *The Dangerous Summer* (London: Hamish Hamilton, 1985).

—— *Death in the Afternoon* (London: Arrow Books, 1994).

—— *For Whom the Bell Tolls* (London: Arrow Books, 2004).

Hernández, A., *Guía secreta de Cádiz* (Madrid: Sedmay Ediciones, 1979).

—— *El mar es una tarde con campanas* (Málaga: Diputación de Málaga, 2001).

Hernández, M., *Poemas sociales de guerra y de muerte* (Madrid: Alianza Editorial, 1993).

—— 'The Olive Pickers', in *Viento del pueblo* (Madrid: Ediciones Catedra, 1989), translation available online at https://we-celebrate-andalucia-day.wikispaces.com/Miguel+Hernández+Poetry (accessed 15 May 2016).

Hespelt, E. H. and Williams, S. T., 'Two Unpublished Anecdotes by Fernán Caballero Preserved by Washington Irving', *Modern Language Notes*, 49/i (1934), pp. 25–31.

—— *Washington Irving's Notes on Fernán Caballero's Stories* (New York: Modern Language Association, 1934).

Hotchner, A. E., *Papa Hemingway: A Personal Memoir* (London, Scribner, 1999).

Howell, J., *Instructions for Forreine Travell* (London: A. Constable and Co., 1895).

Howson, G., *The Flamencos of Cadiz Bay* (London: Bold Strummer, 1994).

Hutchinson, P., *Tongue Without Hands* (Dublin: Dolmen Press, 1963).

Huxley, A., *The Cicadas and Other Poems* (London: Chatto & Windus, 1931).

Inglis, H. D., *Spain in 1830* (London: Whittaker, Treacher, and Co., 1831).

Irving, W., *The Life and Voyages of Christopher Columbus* (New York: N. and J. White, 1834).

—— *Tales of the Alhambra* (Paris: Baudry's European Library, 1840).

Irwin, R., *The Alhambra* (London: Profile Books, 2005).

Jacobs, M., *Between Hopes and Memories: A Spanish Journey* (London: Picador, 1994).

—— *The Factory of Light: Tales from my Andalucían Village* (London: John Murray, 2004).

—— *Andalucía* (London: Pallas Athene, 2013).

Jeffs, J., *Sherry* (Oxford: Infinite Ideas, 2014).

Jiménez, J. R., *Platero and I*, trans. E. Roach (Austin, TX: University of Texas Press, 1999).

—— *Selected Poems*, trans. S. Ortiz-Carboneres (Oxford: Aris & Phillips, 2006).

Jiménez García, J. L., *Jerez y sus vinos en la obra de Pérez Galdós* (Jerez de la Frontera: Real Academia de San Dionisio de Ciencias, Artes y Letras de Jerez de la Frontera, 2010).

Kazantzakis, N., *Spain*, trans. A. Mims (Berkeley, CA: Creative Arts Book Co., 1983).

Koestler, A., *Spanish Testament* (London: Victor Gollancz, 1937).

Lee, L., *As I Walked Out One Midsummer Morning* (London: Penguin, 1971).

—— *A Rose for Winter* (London: Vintage, 2014).

—— *Selected Poems* (London: Unicorn Press, 2014).

Leigh Fermor, P., *Words of Mercury* (London: John Murray, 2003).

Leigh Fermor, P. and Devonshire, D., *In Tearing Haste* (London: John Murray, 2008).

Lorca, F. G., *The House of Bernarda Alba and Other Plays*, trans. M. Dewell and C. Zapata (London: Penguin Classics, 2001).

—— *Selected Poems* (London: Penguin Modern Classics, 2001).

—— *Sketches of Spain (Impresiones y paisajes, 1918)*, trans. P. Bush (London: Serif, 2013).

Luque, A., *Palabras mayores: Borges–Quiñones. 25 años de amistad* (Cádiz: Fundación Municipal de Cultura del Ayuntamiento de Cádiz, 2004).

Maalouf, A., *Leo the African*, trans. P. Sluglett (London: Abacus, 1994).

Machado, A., *Selected Poems* (Cambridge, MA: Harvard University Press, 1988).

Maimonides, *The Guide for the Perplexed*, trans. M. Friedländer (New York: Barnes and Noble, 2004).

Malahide, T. de, *The Light Literature of Spain; Particularly the Works of Fernan Caballero* (Dublin: Hodges, Foster & Co., 1872).

Manila, J., *Marcos: Wild Child of the Sierra Morena*, trans. D. Bonner (London: Souvenir Press, 1982).

al-Maqqari, A. M., *Mohammedan Dynasties in Spain, Volume 1* (London: W. H. Allen, 1840).

Mariscal Montes, J., *Pasan hombres oscuros* (Madrid: Ediciones Rialp, 1955).

Martínez Ruiz, J. (Azorín), *La ruta de don Quijote* (Madrid: Ediciones Catedra, 1995).

Maugham, W. S., *Don Fernando* (London: Vintage, 2010).

—— *The Land of the Blessed Virgin* (New York: Start Publishing, 2012).

Mérimée, P., *Colomba and Carmen*, trans. M. Loyd (New York: P. F. Collier & Son, 1901).

Michener, J. A., *Iberia: Spanish Travel and Reflections* (London: Secker & Warburg, 1968).

—— *Miracle in Seville* (New York: Dial Press, 2015).

Molina, J., *Doñana: todo era nuevo y salvaje* (Seville: Fundación José Manuel Lara, 2011).

Molina, T. de, *The Trickster of Seville and the Stone Guest* (Oxford: Aris & Phillips, 1986).

Morton, H. V., *A Stranger in Spain* (London: Methuen, 1983).

Mountfort, G., *Portrait of a Wilderness: The Story of the Coto Doñana Expeditions* (London: Hutchinson, 1958).

Muñoz Molina, A., *El jinete polaco* (Barcelona: Editorial Planeta, 2006).

—— *A Manuscript of Ashes*, trans. E. Grossman (Orlando, FL: Harcourt, 2008).

—— *El viento de la luna* (Barcelona: Editorial Planeta, 2008).

O'Reilly, K., *The British on the Costa del Sol: Transnational Identities and Local Communities* (London: Routledge, 2000).

Ortiz Nuevo, J. L., *A Thousand and One Stories of Pericón de Cádiz*, trans. J. Moore (Licking, MO: Inverted-A Press, 2012).

Perera, V., *The Cross and the Pear Tree* (Berkeley, CA: University of California Press, 1996).

Pérez Estrada, R., *Devoured by the Moon*, trans. S. Stewart (New York: Hanging Loose Press, 2004).

Pérez-Reverte, A., *The Queen of the South*, trans. A. Hurley (London: Picador, 2004).

—— *Cabo Trafalgar* (Madrid: Alfaguara, 2008).

—— *The Siege*, trans. F. Wynne (London: Weidenfeld & Nicolson, 2013).

Pliny the Elder, *Natural History*, trans H. Rackham and W. H. S. Jones (Cambridge, MA: Harvard University Press, 1999).

Potocki, J., *The Manuscript Found in Saragossa*, trans. I. Maclean (London: Penguin Classics, 1996).

Quiñones, F., *De Cádiz y sus cantes: llaves de una ciudad y un folklore milenarios* (Seville: Fundación José Manuel Lara, 2005).

Ramos Espejo, A., *Ciega en Granada* (Seville: Centro Andaluz del Libro, 2010).

Read, P., *Forgotten Stories from Spain: The Ambulance Man and the Spanish Civil War* (Granada: Craving Distraction, 2014).

Rilke, R. M., *Poems*, trans. J. Lamont (New York: Start Publishing, 2013).

Rivero Taravillo, A., *Luis Cernuda: Años españoles (1902–1938)* (Barcelona: Tusquets Editores, 2008).

—— *Luis Cernuda: Años de exilio (1938–1963)* (Barcelona: Tusquets Editores, 2011).

Roberts, S. G. H., *The 2012 Galdós Lecture: Galdós and 1812* (Sheffield: University of Sheffield, 2012).

Rubio, F., *Baeza de Machado* (Seville: Fundación José Manuel Lara, 2008).

Rushdie, S., *The Moor's Last Sigh* (London: Vintage, 2006).

Sackville-West, V., *Pepita* (London: Virago, 1986).

—— *Family History* (London: Bello, 2011).

Southey, R., *Poetical Works Complete in One Volume* (London: Longman, Brown, Green, and Longmans, 1850).

—— *The Collected Letters of Robert Southey* (Baltimore, MD: University of Maryland, Romantic Circles, 2011).

Spender, S., *Journals 1939–1983* (London: Faber and Faber, 1992).

Starkie, W., *Don Gypsy: Adventures with a Fiddle in Southern Spain and Barbary* (New York: E. P. Dutton, 1936).

Stewart, C., *Driving Over Lemons: An Optimist in Andalucía* (London: Sort Of Books, 1999).

—— *A Parrot in the Pepper Tree* (London: Sort Of Books, 2002).

—— *The Almond Blossom Appreciation Society* (London: Sort Of Books, 2006).

—— *The Last Days of the Bus Club* (London: Sort Of Books, 2014).

Swinburne, H., *Travels Through Spain, in the Years 1775 and 1776* (London: P. Elmsly, 1787).

Tenison, L., *Castile and Andalucia* (London: Richard Bentley, 1853).

Todd, J., *Dog Days in Andalucía: Tails from Spain* (Edinburgh: Mainstream Publishing Company, 2010).

Townsend, J., *A Journey Through Spain in the Years 1786 and 1787* (London: C. Dilly, 1791).

Tremlett, G., *Ghosts of Spain: Travels Through a Country's Hidden Past* (London: Faber and Faber, 2012).

Trend, J. B., *A Picture of Modern Spain: Men and Music* (Boston, MA: Houghton Mifflin, 1921).

Tubino, F. M. (ed.), *Gibraltar Through the Spanish Eye* (Amazon Media: n.p., 2012).

Twain, M., *The Innocents Abroad* (London: Century, 1988).

Tynan, K., *Bull Fever* (London: Longmans, Green & Co., 1955).

—— *The Diaries of Kenneth Tynan*, ed. J. Lahr (London: Bloomsbury, 2001).

Umbral, F., *Lorca, poeta maldito* (Barcelona: Editorial Planeta, 2012).

Valente, J. A., *Landscape with Yellow Birds*, trans. T. Christensen (New York: Archipelago Books, 2013).

Various, *The Jewish Poets of Spain*, trans. D. Goldstein (London: Penguin Classics, 1971).

Various, *La narrativa de Luis Berenguer: 1923–1979* (Cádiz: Universidad de Cádiz, 1998).

Various, *Almáciga de olvidos: antología parcial de poesía gaditana, sitios XIX y XX* (Cádiz: Universidad de Cádiz, 1999).

Various, *20 Great Works by Andalusi Authors* (Almería: Fundación Ibn Tufayl de Estudios Árabes, 2010).

Various, *Relatos de Don Carnal: 12 historias de Carnaval* (Cádiz: Quorum Editores, 2002).

Various, *Moorish Poetry*, trans. A. J. Arberry (Cambridge: Cambridge University Press, 2010).

Various, *Byron and Latin Culture: Selected Proceedings of the 37th International Byron Society Conference* (Newcastle upon Tyne: Cambridge Scholars Publishing, 2013).

Various, 'Poemario', Café de Levante, Cádiz, 2015. Available at www.cafedelevantecadiz.com (accessed 15 May 2016).

Vega, L. de, *Fuente Ovejuna*, trans. W. E. Colford (Woodbury, NY: Barron's Educational, 1969).

Webster, J., *Duende: A Journey in Search of Flamenco* (London: Black Swan, 2004).

—— *Andalus: Unlocking the Secrets of Moorish Spain* (London: Black Swan, 2005).

—— *¡Guerra!* (London: Black Swan, 2007).

Wilson, R., *The Blind Man of Seville* (London: Harper, 2009).

—— *The Hidden Assassins* (London: Harper, 2009).

—— *The Silent and the Damned* (London: Harper, 2009).

Woods, V., *Jasmine and Lagarto: Pearse Hutchinson's Poetry of Spain* (Logroño: Estudios irlandeses-AEDEI, 2010).

Woolf, V., *Travels with Virginia Woolf*, ed. J. Morris (London: Hogarth Press, 1993).

Woolsey, G., *Malaga Burning* (Reston, VA: Pythia Press, 1998).

INDEX

20 Great Works by Andalusi Authors,
180
1616, 107

Ainadamar (Fountain of Tears), 163
al-Andalus, 159, 188
Alarcón, Pedro Antonio de, 86,
172–3
Alatriste, Captain, 62–3
Albéniz, Isaac, 28
Alberti, Rafael, 77–9, 106, 142, 145,
185
'Álbum de Sanlúcar', 47
Alcalá la Real, 203
Aleixandre, Vicente, 23, 77, 106
Alfacar, 161–3
Alhambra Palace, 4, 12, 138–40,
143, 145–56, 188, 195, 204
Comares Palace, 150
Court of the Lions, 151–2, 154
Court of the Myrtles, 150
Generalife, 138, 155–6
Hall of the Ambassadors, 12, 150
Mexuar, 150
Partal, 138, 154
Puerta del Vino, 149
Water-Garden Courtyard, 156
Alhaurín de la Torre, 115, 165
Ali, Tariq, 158
Alicante Province, 197
'Almeria', 231
Almería, 117–19, 224–31, 235–8
Alcazaba, 225, 227–8
Calle Sergio Leone, 236

Casa-Museo José Ángel Valente,
230
La Chanca, 227–30
Plaza de la Catedral, 229
Plaza de la Constitución, 225
Plaza Pavía, 228
Almerimar, 224
Almohad Dynasty, 182
Abu Yaqub Yusuf, 181
*Almond Blossom Appreciation Society,
The*, 169
Almuñécar, 60, 170–1
Along Spain's River of Romance, 29
Alpujarras, Las, 2, 104, 112, 164–9
Lanjarón, 164
Órgiva, 164, 169
Yegen, 112–13, 164–8, 225
Altavoz del Frente (radio station), 198
Altolaguirre, Manuel, 106–8
*Ambulance Man and the Spanish
Civil War, The*, 118
Amicis, Edmondo De, 7, 37, 186,
190–1
Amis, Martin, 128–9
*Andalus: Unlocking the Secrets of
Moorish Spain*, 175
Andalusian Dances, 94
Andersen, Hans Christian, 96–9,
105, 108–9, 111–12, 219
Andújar, 199, 201–2, 222
Christ in the Garden of Olives, 201
Plaza de España, 201
Santa María la Mayor, Church of,
201

'Angels of Desperation and
   Abandonment', 112
Antequera, 134–7
   Dolmens, 136
   Peña de los Enamorados (Lovers'
      Rock), 134, 136–7
Appian (Roman historian), 35
Arcos de la Frontera, 87–9
   Hotel El Convento, 88
Aristotle (philosopher) 180
*As I Walked Out One Midsummer
   Morning*, 60–1, 93, 170–1
Averroes (Ibn Rushd), 2, 180–2
Azorín (José Martínez Ruiz), 87–9

Baetica, 239
Baeza, 205, 207–14, 243
   Calle Obispo Romero Mengíbar,
      210
   Calle San Pablo, 213
   Palacio Jabalquinto, 208
   Paseo de Antonio Machado, 209
   Paseo de la Constitución, 205
   Plaza de la Constitución, 209
   Plaza de los Leones, 206
   Universidad Internacional de
      Andalucía, 208
Baeza de Machado, 207
Ballard, J. G., 122–4
Bandolero, The, 29
Barcelona, 142, 158, 212, 228, 232
Beautiful Antonio (Il bell'Antonio),
   226
Bécquer, Gustavo Adolfo, 23, 26–8
Berenguer, Luis, 76–7
Betham-Edwards, Matilda, 176
Bethune, Norman, 118–19
Betjeman, John, 214
Between Hopes and Memories, 42,
   203, 231
Bible in Spain, The, 10, 59, 182
Bizet, Georges, 33
Blake Byass, Robert, 92
Blasco Ibáñez, Vicente, 86–7
Blind Man of Seville, The, 31

Blood and Sand (Sangre y arena), 86
*Blood of Spain: An Oral History of the
   Spanish Civil War*, 120
Blood Wedding (Bodas de sangre), 233
Bloomsbury Group, The, 113, 115,
   167–8
Böhl de Faber, Cecilia Francisca
   Josefa *see* Fernán Caballero
Borges, Jorge Luis, 29, 68
Borrow, George, 10–12, 30, 36, 42,
   59, 132, 182, 241–2
Bouterwek, Frederick, 185
Boyd, Alastair, 128–30
Brancati, Vitaliano, 226
Braun, Georg, 6–7
Brenan, Gerald, 3, 104, 112–16,
   131, 164–9, 172, 224–6,
   231–2, 242
British on the Costa del Sol, The, 121
Buck, Walter J., 41, 48–9
Bull Fever, 239
Buñuel, Luis, 57, 77, 142
*Butterfly's Evil Spell, The (El maleficio
   de la mariposa)*, 142
Byron, Lord (George Gordon), 1, 6,
   12–17, 64–6, 85, 93, 107–8,
   156–7
Byron, William, 20, 22, 40

Caballero Bonald, José Manuel, 94
Cabo de Gata, 230–2, 235
   Cala Figuera, 235
   Rodalquilar, 234
   San José, 235
Cabo Trafalgar, 81
Cádiz, 39, 45, 59–77, 80–1, 87, 89,
   93, 100, 172, 242
   Alameda de Apodaca, 71
   Arco de la Rosa, 71
   Café de Levante, 69
   Calle Rosario, 69
   Gran Teatro Falla, 66
   La Caleta, 67, 69
   Oratorio de San Felipe Neri, 64
   Paseo Fernando Quiñones, 67, 69

Plaza España, 64
Plaza Fragela, 66
Plaza Palillero, 66
Plaza San Juan de Díos, 70
Trocadero, 74–5
Cádiz Cortes, 61, 63–4, 75
Calderón de la Barca, Pedro, 18, 73
Calvert, Albert F., 11
Camarón de la Isla (José Monje Cruz), 76
'Caminos', 207
'Campo', 107
Camprubí, Zenobia, 54, 57–8
Cansinos-Asséns, Rafael, 29
cante jondo, 94, 150
Carlos V (Charles V, Holy Roman Emperor), 146, 150, 177
'Carmen', 33
Caro Baroja, Julio, 115
Carrington, Dora, 167–8
Carvajal y Robles, Rodrigo, 136
Casanova, Giacomo, 218
Casas, Bartolomé de las, 52
Castelar, Emilio, 65–6
Castellar de la Frontera, 76
Castile and Andalucia, 109
Castilian Country, The (Campos de Castilla), 207, 212
Cathedral of the Sea (La catedral del mar), 158
Catholic Monarchs (Ferdinand II of Aragon and Isabella I of Castile), 51–2, 138, 184, 192–3, 235, 239
Cernuda, Luis, 23–6, 30, 79, 110
Cervantes, Miguel de, 2–3, 19–23, 28, 39–40, 60, 94, 107, 110, 172, 187, 215, 218
Cervantes Institute, New York, 215
Chapman, Abel, 41, 48–9
Charles II (Carlos II, King of Spain), 83
Chateaubriand, François-René de, 1, 156–7
Chaucer, Geoffrey, 90

Chetwode, Penelope, 214, 216
Chiclana, 63, 67
Childe Harold, 13–14, 66
Cicadas and Other Poems, The, 231
Cider with Rosie, 60, 93
Ciega en Granada, 166
cimetière marin, Le, 105
Cisneros, Cardinal, 151, 158
Cities and Wilds of Andalucia, The, 135
Civitatis Orbis Terrarum, 6
Clay, Henry, 44
Cocaine Nights, 122–3
Coleridge, Samuel Taylor, 15
Collioure, 213
Colomo, Fernando, 165–6
Columbus, 51
Columbus, Christopher, 2, 41, 45, 50–3, 184
Communist Party, 30, 77, 119, 197
Concerning the Angels (Sobre los ángeles), 78–9
Córdoba, 3, 20, 37, 100, 174–88, 191, 242
    Alcázar de los Reyes Cristianos, 183–84
    Antonio Gala Foundation, 187
    Calle Cabezas, 185
    Calle de Cairuán, 180
    Calle Góngora, 186
    Calle Judíos, 182
    Calle Torrijos, 174–5
    Casa de Sefarad, 182
    Casa Góngora, 185
    Judería (Jewish Quarter), 181
    Mezquita, 174–6, 181
    Orange Tree Court, 175–6
    Plaza de Séneca, 187
    Plaza de Tiberiades, 181
    Plaza del Potro, 187
    Plaza Maimonides, 181
    Roman Bridge, 174, 185
    Spanish–Arab Friendship Association, 188
    Torre de Calahorra, 174

Cornwell, Bernard, 82
Correo de Andalucía, El, 68
Cortés, Hernán, 197
Costa del Sol, 96, 116, 119–25, 242
  Frigiliana, 124
  Fuengirola, 119–20, 122
Costa Tropical, 60, 119
Coto Doñana, 2, 45, 47–50, 243
  Acebuche Visitors' Centre, 47
  Matalascañas, 47, 50
  Palacio de las Marismillas, 48
  Santa Olalla, Lagoon of, 47
Countryside of Níjar, The (Campos de Níjar), 232
Crónica de las tres Ordenes Militares, 192
Crónicas de Viaje, 86
Cross and the Pear Tree: A Sephardic Journey, The, 101

Dalí, Salvador, 57–8, 77, 106, 142
Dangerous Summer, The, 115, 128
Daniel Deronda, 133
Darío, Rubén, 71–2, 100, 206
De Cádiz y sus cantes, 68
Dead Babies, 129
Death in the Afternoon, 115, 128
Debussy, Claude, 149
Devoured by the Moon, 112
Dickens, Charles, 63
Dickie, John, 21
Diego, Gerardo, 106
doctor Centeno, El, 92
Dog Days in Andalucía, 124
'Dogs' Colloquy, The' ('Coloquio de Cipión y Berganza'), 21
Dominguín, Luis Miguel, 115, 128
Don Fernando, 18
Don Gypsy: Adventures with a Fiddle in Barbary, Andalusia and La Mancha, 132, 135
Don Juan, 6, 13, 15
Don Quixote, 19, 22–3, 26, 89, 133, 187, 211, 217–18
Done into English, 111

Dos Hermanas, 73
Dos Passos, John, 211, 212
Dove's Neck-Ring, The, 178
Drake, Francis, 59, 89
Drinkwater, Carol, 200–1
Driving Over Lemons, 169
Duino Elegies, 132
Dumas, Alexandre, 16, 62–3
Dundas Murray, Robert, 135

Écija, 37–40, 60
Egea, Javier, 145
El Ejido, 224
El Greco (Doménikos Theotokópoulos), 131, 201
El Puerto de Santa María, 77–9, 89
  Museo Fundación Rafael Alberti, 78
El Puerto del Suspiro del Moro, 157
El Rocío, 45–7
El Torcal, 134
Eliot, George (Mary Ann Evans), 133
Ellis, P. J., 107
Entrelobos, 221
Eslava Galán, Juan, 202, 204
España y América, 71
Estepona, 119, 124
Exemplary Novels, The (Novelas ejemplares), 20–1, 28
Experience, 129

Fable of Polyphemus and Galatea (La Fábula de Polifemo y Galatea), 184–5
Face of Spain, The, 113, 164–5
Factory of Light: Tales from my Andalucían Village, The, 42, 203
Falange, 88, 114, 119, 161
Falcones, Ildefonso, 158
Falla, Manuel de, 66, 70, 106, 148–50, 161, 172, 210
Family History, 168
Felipe II (Philip II, King of Spain), 59, 214

Ferdinand II of Aragon (and Isabella I of Castile) *see* Catholic Monarchs
Ferdinand VII (Fernando VII, King of Spain), 10, 141
Fernán Caballero, 73–4, 86, 172
Fernández-Armesto, Felipe, 51–2
Fernando III (Ferdinand III of Castile), 7, 201
Fielding, Xan, 130–1
Fistful of Dollars, A, 236
Flamencos of Cadiz Bay, The, 70
Fletcher, Richard, 178
Fons Vitae, 103
Fonteyn, Margot, 155–6
For a Few Dollars More, 236
For Whom the Bell Tolls, 115, 126
Ford, Richard, 8–9, 30, 34, 36, 39, 89–90, 92–3, 96–7, 153–5, 164, 167, 199, 241
Form of Resistance, A (Una forma de resistencia), 145
Forreine Travell, 164
Fortunata and Jacinta, 63
Four Horsemen of the Apocalypse, The (Los cuatro jinetes del Apocalipsis), 86
Frailes, 203–5, 243
Franco, Francisco, 24, 53, 71, 76, 78, 88, 114, 116, 119–20, 161, 164, 190, 202, 215
Fraser, Ronald, 120
Frayling, Christopher, 236
Frente Sur, 198, 201
Fuente Obejuna, 191–3
Fuente Ovejuna, 191–2
Fuente Vaqueros, 159–60

Gabirol, Solomon Ibn, 102–3
'Galdós and 1812', 63
Galdós, Benito Pérez, 61, 63–4, 81, 92–3, 242
Galt, John, 84–6
Ganivet, Ángel, 147–9
García Montero, Luis, 145

Garvey, Guillermo, 48
Gautier, Théophile, 4, 9–11, 34, 38–9, 153–4, 156, 195–7, 241
Generation of '27, 23, 77, 105–6, 185
Generation of '98, 88
Ghosts of Spain, 95, 123
Gibraltar, Rock of, 2, 62, 80, 82–7
Gibraltar Through the Spanish Eye, 86
Gibson, Ian, 57, 78–9, 139–40, 143, 160, 203, 209, 242
Goethe, Johann Wolfgang von, 24
Golden Age (Siglo de Oro), 2, 6, 19, 27, 73, 133, 185, 191
Góngora, Luis de, 2, 4, 23, 184–6
Good, the Bad and the Ugly, The, 236
Goode, Matthew, 165
Goya, Francisco, 47–8, 78, 127–8, 131
Goytisolo, Juan, 226–9, 232, 234–5, 238, 242
Granada, 2, 4, 12, 17, 37, 96, 100, 138–59, 161, 164, 166–8, 171, 188, 210, 240, 242–3
  Acera del Darro, 140
  Albaicín, 145, 148–9, 243
  Alhambra, The *see* Alhambra Palace
  Calle Antequeruela Alta, 149
  Calle Real de la Alhambra, 147
  Camino de Ronda, 143
  Cathedral, 214
  Cuesta de Gomérez, 146
  Huerta de San Vicente, 142–3, 160
  Plaza del Campillo, 140
  Plaza Mariana Pineda, 141
  Plaza Nueva, 146
  Puerta de las Granadas, 146
  Restaurante Chikito, 140–1
Granada la bella, 148
Granadillo Prize, 158
Grecia, 29
Greene, Graham, 18

Grove, Valerie, 94
Guadalete, River, 77–8, 87, 89
Guadalquivir, River, 2, 6, 20–1,
    28–9, 33, 45, 48, 174, 183, 188,
    201, 222
Guadix, 171–3
¡Guerra!, 162
Guía secreta de Cádiz, 88
Guide for the Perplexed, 181
Guillén, Jorge, 27, 105–6, 144
Guzmán el Bueno, 17, 83
Gwynne, Paul (Ernest Slater), 29,
    183, 188
Gypsy Ballads, The (*Romancero
    gitano*), 147

Ha-Nagid, Samuel, 103, 182
Haapakoski, Aarne Viktor, 105
Habitación en Arcos, 88
Hadrian, Emperor, 35
Hand of Fatima, The (*La mano de
    Fátima*), 158
Handbook for Travellers in Spain,
    8, 89
Hastings, Selina, 18
Hazm, Ibn, 174, 178
Heart (*Cuore*), 37
Henry IV, Part II, 90
Hernández, Antonio, 87–8
Hernández, Miguel, 194, 197–201,
    242
Herodotus, 2
'Himno al mar', 29
History of My Life (*Histoire de ma
    vie*), 218
History of Spanish Literature, 73, 185
Hobhouse, John Cam, 85
Hope of Macarena, Virgin of, 197
Hora de España, 212
Hotchner, A. E., 115–16
House of Bernarda Alba, The (*La casa
    de Bernarda Alba*), 146
Howell, James, 164
Howson, Gerald, 70–1
Huelva, 41–6, 50, 100

Alameda Sundheim, 43–4
Avenida Andalucía, 44
Avenida Martín Alonso Pinzón,
    45
Barrio Reina Victoria, 43
Museo de Huelva, 44
Hutchinson, Pearse, 110
Huxley, Aldous, 230–1
Huxley, Julian, 49

*Iberia: Spanish Travels and
    Reflections*, 46, 189
Images of Spain, 131
Imprenta Sur (publishers), 106
In Hiding: The Life of Manuel Cortes,
    120
In the Land of the Blessed Virgin, 18
In Spain and a Visit to Portugal,
    96–8
Inglis, Henry David, 97
Innocents Abroad, The, 84
Inquisition, The, 102, 182–3
Institución Libre de Enseñanza,
    206–7
Irving, Washington, 1, 4, 17, 37–8,
    52–3, 73, 151–3, 241
Irwin, Robert, 150
Isabella I of Castile (and Ferdinand
    II of Aragon) *see* Catholic
    Monarchs
Itálica, 34–7
Izquierdo, Leonor, 206

Jacobs, Michael, 42–4, 202–5,
    231–2, 242
Jaén, 194–9, 201, 203, 205
    Avenida de Madrid, 194, 196
    Paseo de la Estación, 194
    Plaza de la Constitución, 194–5
    Santa Catalina, Castle of, 194
    Santa Faz (St Veronica's
        handkerchief), 195–6
Janer Manila, Gabriel, 219–20
Jasmine and Lagarto, 110
Jeffs, Julian, 90

Jerez de la Frontera, 4, 43, 48–9, 89–95
  Alcázar, 91, 94
  Domecq, sherry bodega, 90, 92
  Fiesta de la Vendimia, 90
  González Byass, sherry bodega, 90–2
  Harveys, sherry bodega, 90
  Plaza de San Juan, 94
  San Salvador, Cathedral of, 91
  Sandeman, sherry bodega, 90
jinete polaco, El, 216
Journey through Spain, 219
Juan the Landless (Juan sin tierra), 232

Kazantzakis, Nikos, 190, 218
Kipling, Rudyard, 141
Koestler, Arthur, 116–18

La Alpujarra, 172
La Barraca (theatre troupe), 142, 193
La Chanca, 227, 232
La Línea, 83, 86–7
La Mancha, 26, 73, 132, 187, 195, 212, 217
La Rábida, 41, 50–2
  Muelle de la Reina, 51
  Muelle de las Carabelas, 52
Landscape with Yellow Birds, 230
Lange, Monique, 229
Last of the Abencerrajes, The (Les Aventures du dernier Abencérage), 156
Last Consolation, The, 74
Last Days of the Bus Club, The, 169
Last Temptation, 190
latifundia, 4, 199
'Leave-taking' ('Despedida'), 143
Lee, Laurie, 39, 60–1, 93–4, 170–1
Legends, The (Las leyendas), 27
Legends, Tales and Poems, 27
Leigh Fermor, Patrick, 19, 115, 130–1
Leo the African (Léon l'Africain), 158

Leone, Sergio, 236, 238
Lepe, 90
Libros de amor, 54
Life and Loves of Laurie Lee, The, 94
Life and Voyages of Christopher Columbus, The, 52
Linares, 202
Literature of the Spanish People, The, 165
Litoral, 106
Lorca, Federico García, 1, 3–4, 23, 66, 70, 77, 100, 106, 108, 110, 138–47, 149–50, 159–64, 185, 193, 209, 211, 233, 238, 242–3
Lorca's Granada, 139, 164
Lorca, poeta maldito, 146
'Los que quedamos', 69
'Lover's Rock, The', 134
Lucan (Roman poet), 187
lugar del poeta, El, 230
Luna Benamor, 86
Luque, Alejandro, 68–9
Lycett-Green, Candida, 214

Maalouf, Amin, 158
MacDonald, Ethel, 118
Machado, Antonio, 1, 206–9, 211–14
Madrid, 10, 16, 20, 29, 33, 54, 57, 63, 74, 76–8, 106, 112, 115, 142, 191, 206, 215, 222, 232
Maimonides (Moshe ben Maimon), 2, 180–2
Málaga, 3, 96–119, 122, 126, 134, 164, 168, 170
  Alameda, 99, 101, 109
  Alcazaba, 100
  Alcázar, 100–3
  Anglican Cemetery, 103–5
  Avenida Príes, 103–4
  Bar El Pimpi, 102
  Ben Gabirol Visitor Centre, 102
  bullring, 101, 108
  Café Chinitas, 108
  Calle Alcazabilla, 102

Málaga (*continued*)
Calle Granada, 103
Calle la Bolsa, 112
Calle San Lorenzo, 106
Calle Strachan, 112
Calle Tomás Heredia, 106
Calle Torremolinos, 113
Calle Zorrilla, 110
Casa Gerald Brenan, 113
Churriana, 104, 112–13, 115, 128, 164
La Cónsula, 115
Paseo del Parque, 99, 101
Plaza de la Constitución, 108
Plaza de la Marina, 99
Santa Iglesia Catedral Basílica de la Encarnación, 111
Teatro Cervantes, 110
Malaga Burning, 114
Malthus, Thomas, 219
Manhattan Transfer, 211
manifesto albertista, El, 145
Manilva, 119
Manresa, Josefina, 198
Manuscript of Ashes, A (*Beatus Ille*), 215–16
Manuscript Found in Saragossa (*Manuscrit trouvé à Saragosse*), 221
manuscrito carmesí, El, 187
Marbella, 119, 123, 126
Marcos: Wild Child of the Sierra Morena, 219
Mariana Pineda, 141
Marinero en tierra, 78
Mariscal Montes, Julio, 87
Martí, José, 71
Martínez Montañés, Juan, 11
Maugham, Somerset, 17–20, 129, 243
Mazagón, 50
Medina Azahara, 188–9, 191
Medina Sidonia (family), 47–8, 83
Mérimée, Prosper, 1, 16, 33, 148, 241
Michener, James A., 46, 190

Mijas, 120
Moguer, 53–8
Casa-Museo de Zenobia y Juan Ramón, 54–5
Mohammedan Dynasties in Spain, 189
Mojácar, 238–240
Mojácar Playa, 238
Mojácar Pueblo, 238–9
Molina, Jorge, 49
Molina, Tirso de, 16
Moment of War, A, 60
Montiel, Sara, 205
Moon and Sixpence, The, 18
Moor's Last Sigh, The, 157
Moorish Spain, 178
Moréas, Jean, 206
Morris, Jan, 71, 168
Morton, H. V., 155–6, 196–7, 199–200
Mule, The (*La mula*), 202, 204
mundo de Juan Lobón, El, 76
Muñoz Molina, Antonio, 214–17
Murciano, Antonio and Carlos, 87
Murillo, Bartolomé Esteban, 11

Napoleon Bonaparte, 14, 64, 80, 82
Nasrid Dynasty, 150, 153–4, 157
Boabdil (Muhammad XII), 154, 157–8, 187
Ismail I, 150
Muhammad III, 150
Yusuf I, 150
'National Episodes' ('Episodios Nacionales'), 63, 81
Nationalists (Spanish Civil War), 116, 160, 197, 202, 212
Naturalis Historia, 2
Nelson, Admiral, 80, 82
Nerja, 119, 124
Neruda, Pablo, 57, 78, 211
Nicholson, Max, 49
Nights in the Gardens of Spain, 149
Níjar, 231–5
barrio alfarero (potters' district), 233

Nobel Prize for Literature, 29, 57–8

O'Reilly, Karen, 121–2
Ocnos, 24–5
Odiel, River, 41, 50
Of Human Bondage, 18
Oh! Calcutta!, 240
ojos del tiempo, Los, 67
Olivares, Gerardo, 221
'Olive Pickers, The' ('Aceituneros'), 194, 198
Olive Tree, The, 200
'Olive Trees, The' ('Los olivos'), 208
Once Upon a Time in Italy: The Westerns of Sergio Leone, 236
'One Day's Poem' ('Poema de un día'), 212
Ora Maritima, 79
Ordóñez, Antonio, 115, 128
Orihuela, 197
Orlando, 168
Ortiz Nuevo, José Luis, 68
Orwell, George, 118
Ory, Carlos Edmundo de, 72
Ory, Eduardo de, 71, 242

Painted Veil, The, 18
País, El, 76, 239
Palabras mayores: Borges–Quiñones, 25 años de amistad, 68
Palos de la Frontera, 50, 53
Papa Hemingway, 115
'Pardoner's Tale', 90
Parque Minero de Riotinto, 45
Partridge, Ralph, 167
Pasan hombres oscuros, 87
'Paseo de los tristes', 145
Pedro I (the Cruel or the Just/Peter I of Castile), 12, 30
Pemán, José María, 87–9
Pepita, 48, 168
Perera, Victor, 101–2
Pérez Estrada, Rafael, 112
Pérez-Reverte, Arturo, 61–3, 81, 124
Personal Record, 166–7

Philip V (Felipe V, King of Spain), 79, 83
Picasso, Pablo, 106
Picture of Modern Spain: Music and Men, A, 149
Pillars of Hercules, 2, 83
Pinzón, Martín Alonso, 52–3
Planeta Prize, 188
Platero and I (Platero y yo), 53–5
Playa de Camposoto (Cádiz Bay), 75
Playa de la Casería (Cádiz Bay), 75
Pliny the Elder, 2, 239
Poema heróico de asalto y conquista de Antequera, 136
'Poems of Soledad con Biznagas', 100
Poet in Andalucía, 100–1
Poet in New York (Poeta en Nueva York), 100
Portbou, 212
Portrait of a Wilderness: The Story of the Coto Doñana Expeditions, 50
Potocki, Jan, 221–3
Prados, Emilio, 106–7, 110
Príncipe de Asturias Literary Prize, The, 216
Pueblo: A Mountain Village on the Costa del Sol, 120

Queen of the South, The (La Reina del Sur), 62, 124
Queipo de Llano, General, 161
Quiñones, Fernando, 67–9
Quzman, Ibn, 180

Rachel Papers, The, 129
Ramón Jiménez, Juan, 1, 53–7, 100, 106, 207
Read, Paul, 118–19
Relatos de Don Carnal, 67
Republicans (Spanish Civil War), 117–18, 197, 202, 216
Residencia de Estudiantes, Madrid, 142
'Rhyme 21', 28

Rhymes (Las rimas), 27
Richardson, Stanley, 24
Riga, 148
Rilke, Rainer Maria, 131–3
'Rinconete and Cortadillo', 20–1
Rio Tinto Company, 42, 44–5
Ríos, Fernando de los, 160
Rivero Taravillo, Antonio, 24–5, 30
Road from Ronda, The, 130
Roberts, Stephen G. H., 63
Rodríguez Pantoja, Marcos, 219–21
Ronda, 126–33, 135, 239
    bullring, 127–8, 131–2
    El Tajo, 126, 128
    Feria Goyesca, 128
    Hotel Reina Victoria, 131
    Palacio de Mondragón, 128–30
    Puente Nuevo, 126–8
Rosales, Luis, 161
Rose for Winter, A, 39, 60, 94, 170–1
Rosinante to the Road Again, 211
Rubenstein, Artur, 141
Rubio, Fanny, 207
Rushdie, Salman, 157–8
Russell, Bertrand, 114

Sackville-West, Vita, 168
Safar, Ibn, 224
'Sailor's Dream, The' ('Sueño del
    marinero'), 78
Salinas, Pedro, 23
San Fernando, 59, 75–7
San Roque, 83–4, 87
Sancti Petri, 63
Sanlúcar de Barrameda, 48, 89
Santiponce, 34, 36–7
Santo Custodio, 203–4
Scipio Africanus, General, 34–5
Sculpture in Spain, 11
Seagull, The (La gaviota), 74
Second Spanish Republic, 160
Segovia, 211
Seguiri, José, 112
Selected Poems (of Antonio
    Machado), 208

Semana Santa (Holy Week), 31–2
Seneca (Roman philosopher), 187
Servicio Español de Información,
    212
Seville, 3–37, 45, 55, 61, 65, 68,
    73–4, 90, 95–6, 100, 116, 131,
    151, 161, 180, 183, 186, 203,
    206, 243
    Alcázares Reales (Alcázar), 12, 17,
        25
    Anunciación, Church of the, 25
    Calle Acetres, 24
    Calle Aire, 25
    Calle de Agua, 17
    Calle Fabiola, 12
    Calle Francisco Bruna, 22
    Calle Guzmán el Bueno, 17
    Calle Judería, 25
    Calle Sierpes, 20, 22
    Calle Temprano, 17
    Calle Troya, 21
    Casa de Pilatos, 37
    Cathedral, 7–12, 17, 21, 34
    Expo 1929 (Ibero-American), 25
    Giralda, The, 7–8, 10, 30, 55
    Hospital de la Caridad, 16
    Hotel Alfonso XIII, 25
    Jardín de Crucero, 12
    Judería (Jewish Quarter), 12
    Monsalves, 25
    Museo de Bellas Artes, 34
    Parque de María Luisa, 25
    Patio de los Naranjos, 8
    Plaza de España, 25–6
    Plaza de Los Refinadores, 16
    Plaza del Pan, 24
    Plaza del Triunfo, 12
    Plaza El Salvador, 24
    Puente San Telmo, 21
    Royal Tobacco Factory, 32–4
    San Leandro, Convent of, 25
    San Salvador, Church of, 24
    Santa Cruz, district of, 12, 16
    Torre del Oro, 30
    Triana, 30–1

Shadows of the Pomegranate Tree, 158

Shakespeare, William, 79, 90, 107, 239

Sharpe's Trafalgar, 82

sherry, 4, 20, 48, 89–93, 95, 154

Sicily, 4, 31, 74, 83, 89, 158, 191

Siege, The (*El asedio*), 62

Sierra de Alhamilla, 232

Sierra Morena, 201, 217–22
   Despeñaperros Pass, 217
   La Carolina, 219

Sierra Nevada, 2, 138, 168, 243
   Mulhacén, 2

Singer Does Not Awaken, The (*No amanece el cantor*), 230

'Sixth Elegy', 132

Sketches of Spain (*Impresiones y paisajes*), 138–40, 210, 243

Solitudes (*Soledades*), 185

Songs (*Canciones*), 143

Soto de Rojas, Pedro, 148

South from Granada, 157, 164–5, 167, 224

Southey, Robert, 134

Spaghetti Westerns: Cowboys and Europeans from Karl May to Sergio Leone, 236

Spain, 190

Spain (*Spagna*), 7

Spain in 1830, 97

Spanish Civil War, 3, 23, 25, 39, 60, 76–7, 88, 108, 112, 115–16, 118, 120, 126–7, 145, 159, 161–3, 170, 190, 193, 201, 211–12, 215, 241

'Spanish Dancer, The', 132

'Spanish-English Lady, The' ('La española inglesa'), 21

Spanish Gypsy, The, 133

Spanish Labyrinth, The, 114, 165

Spanish Raggle-Taggle, 132

Spanish Testament (*Menschenopfer unerhört*), 116

Spanish Trilogy, 132

Spender, Stephen, 25

St John of the Cross, 215

Starkie, Walter, 132–3, 135

Stewart, Chris, 3, 42, 169–70, 243

'Stork in Jerez', 93

Strachey, Lytton, 167–8

Straits of Gibraltar, 62, 124

Stranger in Spain, A, 155, 196

Sultan in Palermo, A, 158

Swinburne, Henry, 8

Tabernas, 235–6

Tabernas Desert, 232, 235–8
   Fort Bravo, 236
   Mini Hollywood, 236

Tales of the Alhambra, 17, 37, 74, 151

Tartessos, 2

Tenison, Louisa, 109–11, 136

Tennyson, Alfred, 103

Thousand and One Stories of Pericón de Cádiz, A (*Mil y una historias de Pericón de Cádiz*), 68

Three-Cornered Hat, The (*El sombrero de tres picos*), 172

Through Spain to the Sahara, 176

'tiendas, Las', 24

'Time' ('El tiempo'), 24

Tinto, River, 41, 50–1

Tio Pepe sherry, 91–2

To the Lighthouse, 168

Todd, Jackie, 124–5

Toibín, Colm, 110–11

Toledo, 131, 201

Tongue without Hands, 111

Torremolinos, 115, 119

Torrox, 119

Townsend, Joseph, 219

Trafalgar, 64

Trafalgar, 80–2

Trafalgar, Battle of, 63

Trajan, Emperor, 35, 37

Travels through Spain, 1775 and 1776, 8

Travels with Virginia Woolf, 168

Treaty of Utrecht, 83

Tremlett, Giles, 95, 123

Trend, J. B., 149, 153
*Trickster of Seville and the Stone
   Guest, The* (*El burlador de
   Sevilla y convidado de piedra*), 16
Trueblood, Alan S., 208, 212
Turina, Joaquín, 28
Turner, J. M. W., 80
Twain, Mark, 83–5
*Two Middle-Aged Ladies in
   Andalusia*, 214
Tynan, Kenneth, 239–41

Úbeda, 214–17
   Palacio de las Cadenas, 214
   Parador, 214
   Plaza de Andalucía, 216
   Plaza San Lorenzo, 217
   Plaza San Pedro, 216
   Sacra Capilla del Salvador, 214
   Santa María de los Reales
      Alcázares, Church, 216
Uładówka, 223
último cuplé, El, 204
Umbral, Francisco, 146
Ummayad Dynasty, 178–80, 183
   Abd al-Rahman III, 176, 178,
      188–9
   al-Hakam II, 178
   Almanzor, 177
   Hisham II, 177
   Wallada, Princess, 179–80
Undiscovered Spain, 48
UNESCO (World Heritage), 7, 205,
   214

Valencia, 86, 115, 117, 231, 236
Valente, José Ángel, 229–30
Valéry, Paul, 105
Valladolid, 16, 105
Valverde, José Antonio, 50
Vandelvira, Andrés de, 194, 214, 216

Vega, Lope de, 16, 18, 186, 191–3,
   204
Vélez, 117
Verlaine, Paul, 206
'Very Mournful Ballad on the Siege
   and Conquest of Alhama, A', 107
viento de la luna, El (*The Wind of the
   Moon*), 216
Víznar, 161–2
   Barranco de Víznar, 161
*Voyages and Travels in the Years
   1809, 1810 and 1811*, 84

Waley, Arthur, 115
'Walking to the Alcázar', 100
Wanderings in Spain (*Un voyage en
   Espagne*), 10, 38
Webster, Jason, 162–3, 175, 225
Welles, Orson, 128
Wellesley, Arthur (Duke of
   Wellington), 14
Wells, H. G., 141
'When the Seagulls Take Flight', 112
Wild Spain, 41, 48–9
Wilkins, Juan Cobos, 55
Wilson, Robert, 31
Woods, Vincent, 110
Woolf, Virginia, 167–8
Woolsey, Gamel, 104, 112–14, 166
Words of Mercury, 131
Wordsworth, William, 15

Yañez Pinzón, Vicente, 53

Zamrak, Ibn, 151–2, 154
Zaragoza, 103, 221
Zaydun, Ibn, 179
*Zincali; or, An Account of the Gypsies
   of Spain*, 10, 30
Zorba the Greek, 190
Zorrilla, José, 16